MODERN HUMANITIES RESEARCH ASSOCIATION
CRITICAL TEXTS
VOLUME 70

EDITOR
STEFANO EVANGELISTA
(ENGLISH)

JEWELLED TORTOISE
VOLUME 6

EDITORS
STEFANO EVANGELISTA
CATHERINE MAXWELL

MATHILDE BLIND: SELECTED *FIN-DE-SIÈCLE* POETRY AND PROSE

EDITED WITH AN INTRODUCTION AND NOTES BY
JAMES DIEDRICK

Mathilde Blind:
Selected *Fin-de-Siècle* Poetry and Prose

Edited with an introduction and notes by
James Diedrick

Modern Humanities Research Association
2021

Published by

The Modern Humanities Research Association
Salisbury House
Station Road
Cambridge CB1 2LA
United Kingdom

© Modern Humanities Research Association 2021

James Diedrick has asserted his right under the Copyright, Designs and Patents Act 1988 to be identified as the author of this work. Parts of this work may be reproduced as permitted under legal provisions for fair dealing (or fair use) for the purposes of research, private study, criticism, or review, or when a relevant collective licensing agreement is in place. All other reproduction requires the written permission of the copyright holder who may be contacted at rights@mhra.org.uk.

First published 2021

ISBN 978-1-78188-962-6 (paperback)
ISBN 978-1-78188-963-3 (hardback)

Copies may be ordered from www.tortoise.mhra.org.uk

CONTENTS

	Acknowledgements	x
	Introduction	1
	A Note on the Texts	45
	Mathilde Blind: Chronology	46
1	Nocturne	49
2	*The Ascent of Man* (1889)	
	Prelude — Wings	55

Part I.
    Chaunts of Life   56
    A Symbol   81
    Time's Shadow   81

Part II.
    The Pilgrim Soul   83
    Saving Love   90
    Nirvana   90
    Motherhood   91

Part III.
    The Leading of Sorrow   92

Poems of the Open Air
    The Sower   104
    A Spring Song   105
    April Rain   105
    The Sleeping Beauty   106
    Apple-Blossom   106
    The Music-Lesson   107
    The Teamster   107
    A Highland Village   112
    On a Forsaken Lark's Nest   113
    Reapers   114
    Apple-Gathering   114

The Songs of Summer	115
Autumn Tints	116
Green Leaves and Sere	116
The Hunter's Moon	117
The Passing Year	117
The Robin Redbreast	118
The Red Sunsets, 1883	118
The Red Sunsets, 1883	119
On the Lighthouse at Antibes	119
On the Riviera	120
A Winter Landscape	121

Love in Exile

Songs

I. 'Thou walkest with me'	122
II. 'I was again beside my Love'	122
III. 'I am athirst, but not for wine'	123
IV. 'I would I were the glow-worm'	123
V. 'Dost thou remember?'	124
VI. 'O moon, large golden summer moon'	124
VII. 'Why will you haunt me unawares?'	125
VIII. 'When you wake from troubled slumbers'	125
IX. 'In a lonesome burial-place'	126
X. 'On life's long round'	127
XI. 'Ah, yesterday was dark and drear'	127
XII. 'Yea, the roses are still on fire'	127
XIII. 'We met as strangers'	127
XIV. 'You make the sunshine of my heart'	128
XV. 'Dear, when I look into your eyes'	128
XVI. 'Ah, if you knew'	129
XVII. 'Your looks have touched my soul'	129
XVIII. 'Oh, brown eyes with long black lashes'	130
XIX. 'Once on a golden day'	130
XX. 'What magic is there in thy mien?'	131

Heart's-Ease	131
Untimely Love	131
The After-Glow	132
L'Envoi	132

3 *Dramas in Miniature* (1891)

Dramas in Miniature

The Russian Student's Tale	137
The Mystic's Vision	141

The Message	143
A Mother's Dream	149
A Carnival Episode	157
The Battle of Flowers	161
The Song of the Willi	167
Scherzo	172

Lyrics

Love's Somnambulist	175
A Meeting	175
Your Face	176
Only a Smile	176
Sometimes I Wonder	176
Many Will Love You	177
A Dream	177
Rose d'Amour	178
Sonnet	178
A Parting	178
My Lady	179
On a Viola d'Amore	179
A Child's Fancy	180
Lassitude	181
Seeking	181

4 *Birds of Passage Songs of the Orient and Occident* (1895)

Prelude	184

Songs of the Orient

Welcome to Egypt	186
The Sphinx	186
Sphinx-Money	186
The Tombs of the Kings	187
Hymn to Horus	191
Nuit	193
Egyptian Theosophy	194
The Moon of Ramadân	195
The Beautiful Beeshareen Boy	197
The Dying Dragoman	201
A Fantasy	204
The Desert	206
Scarabæus Sisyphus	208
The Colossi of the Plain	209
Mourning Women	210
The Sâkiyeh	210
Internal Firesides	211

CONTENTS

On Reading the 'Rubáiyát' of Omar Khayyám in a Kentish Rose Garden — 211

Songs of the Occident

Roman Anemones — 212
Ave Maria in Rome — 212
The New Proserpine — 213
Soul-Drift — 213
On a Torso of Cupid — 214
The Mirror of Diana — 215
On Guido's Aurora — 217
Spring in the Alps — 217
The Agnostic — 218
A Bridal in the Bois de Boulogne — 219
A White Night — 220
The Forest Pool — 221
Noonday Rest — 222
Cross-Roads — 222
The Moat — 223

Shakespeare Sonnets

Anne Hathaway's Cottage — 224
Anne Hathaway — 224
Cleve Woods — 225
Lost Treasure — 226
The Avon — 226
Evensong (Holy Trinity Church) — 227
Shakespeare — 227
Cedars of Lebanon at Warwick Castle — 228

Miscellaneous Pieces

Pastiche — 229
Marriage — 229
Once We Played — 230
Affinities —
   I. — 230
   II. — 231
   III. — 231
To a Friend, With a Volume of Verses — 231
As Many Stars — 232
Love's Vision — 233
A Parable — 233
Between Sleep and Waking — 234
Rest — 234

	Contents	
	Mystery of Mysteries	235
5	Sea-Music	236
6	Selected Prose and Critical Responses	237
	Select Bibliography	275

ACKNOWLEDGEMENTS

I first need to thank Dennis Denisoff, editor of volume 4 in the MHRA Jewelled Tortoise series (*Arthur Machen: Decadent and Occult Works*), for suggesting that I propose an edition of Mathilde Blind's late poetry to the series editors. His superbly annotated edition also provided me guidance and inspiration as I spent the long quarantine summer of 2020 annotating Mathilde Blind's last three major volumes of verse. For many of these notes I drew on the rich manuscript holdings at four research libraries I have visited over the past two decades: the British Library; the Harry Ransom Center at the University of Texas at Austin; the Bodleian Library at Oxford University; and the University of British Columbia Library. I am grateful to the expert staff at these libraries for their assistance, and to travel grants from the British Academy and Agnes Scott College for extended stays at the British Library, the Bodleian, and the Ransom Center. My greatest debt is to the editors of the MHRA Jewelled Tortoise Series, Catherine Maxwell and Stefano Evangelista, for their careful reading and comments on earlier drafts and, more importantly, their belief in the value of this project.

This book is dedicated to my partner and fellow scholar LeeAnne M. Richardson.

INTRODUCTION

Mathilde Blind rose to prominence in the early 1870s, both as an expert on and proponent of the poetry of Percy Bysshe Shelley and as one of the few women writers published in the *Dark Blue* (1871–1873), a short-lived but influential journal that featured essays, tales, poems, and illustrations by Britain's leading Pre-Raphaelites and aesthetes. Her ballads 'The Song of the Willi' and 'Nocturne', which appeared in the journal, share with the poems of Algernon Charles Swinburne attitudes and literary strategies that would come to define and dominate Decadent poetry at the *fin de siècle*: a rejection of bourgeois values and norms; sexual nonconformity and transgression; a poetic style often characterized by 'sensational excess'.[1] Her career thus highlights the connections between mid-Victorian aestheticism and late-century Decadence.[2] It also serves as an important corrective to the male-focused narratives that long dominated accounts of these movements. In addition, and because Blind was born in Germany to Jewish parents, part of a community of European radicals who found refuge in England, her poetry and prose alike are characterized by a transnational, cosmopolitan outlook that ranges across national borders and consistently engages with Continental writers and ideas. This introduction will begin with a brief discussion of Blind's intellectual apprenticeship, and will then analyse some of her key works of the 1870s and early to mid-1880s, all of which inform the three volumes of poetry represented in this Jewelled Tortoise edition: *The Ascent of Man* (1889), *Dramas in Miniature* (1891), and *Birds of Passage: Songs of the Orient and Occident* (1895).[3]

Blind was born in 1841 in Mannheim, then part of the Grand Duchy of Baden in south-western Germany. (Germany would not become a unified nation for another thirty years.) She was the oldest child of a banker named Jacob Abraham Cohen and his second wife, born Friederike Ettlinger. Cohen died in

---

[1] Ana Parejo Vadillo, 'Poetries of Asceticism and Excess', in *The Cambridge Companion to Victorian Women's Poetry*, ed. by Linda K. Hughes (Cambridge: Cambridge University Press, 2015), pp. 230–46 (p. 241).
[2] Following John R. Reed, 'Decadent' and 'Decadence' are capitalized throughout this introduction (except in quotations by other scholars who use the lower-case form). This differentiates the literary movement that for writers like Swinburne, Wilde, Blind, and others signified dissent and a transvaluation of values from what Reed calls the 'concept of historical decline and associated anxieties' deemed 'decadent' by conservatives like Max Nordau and Lionel Johnson (John R. Reed, *Decadent Style* (Athens, Ohio: Ohio University Press, 1985), p. xiii).
[3] In 1893 Blind published *Songs and Sonnets*, but except for nine new poems this was an omnibus volume that republished verse from *The Prophecy of St. Oran*, *The Ascent of Man*, and *Dramas in Miniature*.

1848; the same year Blind's mother married Karl Blind, whom she met when both joined the struggle for a united and democratic Germany.[4] He became one of the leaders of the Baden Revolution, which led to his imprisonment and then to his exile from Germany. By 1849, he and his new family had also been exiled from France, and in 1851 they were expelled from Belgium. Granted asylum in England, along with fellow revolutionary Karl Marx, they settled in St John's Wood, just west of Regent's Park. Karl Blind and Marx, along with several other German expatriates, established the Committee of Support for German Political Refugees in London in September 1849, one year after Marx and Engels published *The Communist Manifesto*. For the next thirty years, the Blind household was both a haven for Europe's radical exiles and an important intellectual salon.

During her teenage years, Mathilde Blind attended schools in London and Zurich.[5] Her outlook was profoundly influenced by her parents' literary and political affiliations, their allies, and their various visitors. The latter included the exiled revolutionaries Giuseppe Mazzini and Marx, Swinburne, and the women's suffrage advocate Caroline Ashurst Stansfield. In his 1900 'Memoir', her lifelong friend and literary adviser Richard Garnett notes with telling ambivalence that 'the circumstances of Mathilde's girlhood' nurtured 'that 'independence which distinguished her for good and ill'. Within the society of political refugees that formed in St John's Wood, he continues, 'admiration must necessarily be reserved for audacity in enterprise, fortitude in adversity [...] anything breathing unconquerable defiance of the powers that were'. Garnett reports that by age twenty-five Mathilde's militancy regarding the Woman Question was fully developed: 'She was in favour of women following all callings, except the military and naval, and when invited by the present writer to consider the consequence of throwing a mass of cheap labour into occupations much overstocked, she rejoined, with decision, that the men might emigrate'.[6] By the time she began her writing career Blind was a committed freethinker, socialist, and feminist.

In 1866 Blind's beloved brother Ferdinand failed in an attempt to assassinate Otto von Bismarck, then chancellor of the North German Confederation, and

---

[4] According to Rudolf Muhs, the couple married in Paris because in Germany Friederike would have had to convert to Christiany (Rudolf Muhs, 'Karl Blind: Ein Talent in der Wichtigmacherei', in *Die 48-Er. Lebensbilder der Deutschen Revolution 1848/49*, ed. by Sabine Freitag (München: C. H. Beck, 1998), pp. 81–99).
[5] According to an unpublished autobiographical fragment in the British Library, she was expelled from London's St John's School for Girls because of her professed atheism (London, British Library, Add. MS 61930, fol. 18). Subsequent references to British Library manuscripts cite manuscript and folio numbers only.
[6] Richard Garnett, 'Memoir', in *The Poetical Works of Mathilde Blind*, ed. by Arthur Symons (London: T. Fisher Unwin, 1900), pp. 1–46 (p. 18).

committed suicide in prison.[7] He was motivated in part by London's radical refugees, who were outraged by the way Bismarck treated the German states like pawns in his empire-building strategy. The first, pseudonymous volume of poetry Blind published in the wake of Ferdinand's death (*Poems*, by Claude Lake, 1867) is dedicated to her early mentor, Mazzini, and many of the poems express a form of his revolutionary idealism. But they also obliquely register her grief at the loss of her brother.[8]

In 1870 Blind delivered two public lectures in London, the first on Shelley, stressing the poet's political radicalism, and the second on William Morris and Eiríkr Magnússon's translation of the Scandinavian epic *Volsunga Saga*. This was followed by a July 1870 *Westminster Review* essay on William Michael Rossetti's edition of *The Poetical Works of Percy Bysshe Shelley* that drew praise from Swinburne.[9] From 1871 to 1872 she published essays, poetry, and a short story in the *Dark Blue*, and when that journal ceased publication she began reviewing contemporary poetry and fiction for the *Athenæum* and the *Examiner*, where over the next fifteen years she passed judgment on a wide range of contemporary writers, from William Morris to Augusta Webster. In late 1872 she published *Selections from the Poems of Percy Bysshe Shelley*, containing an introductory 'Memoir' of Shelley's life, and in 1873 she brought out her translation of David Friedrich Strauss's 1872 work *Der Alte und der Neue Glaube: Ein Bekenntnis* (*The Old Faith and the New: A Confession*). In this book Strauss follows the demythologizing impulse first expressed in his 1835 *Das Leben Jesu* (*The Life of Jesus*, translated into English by George Eliot in 1846) to its logical conclusion, abandoning the Hegelian principles to which he had previously adhered and embracing an antitheist form of historical and scientific materialism.

The generic range of these early works (poetry, fiction, criticism, biography, translation), as well as their subject matter and themes (female autonomy and agency, antitheism, aestheticism, the interrelationship of literary and political radicalism) indicates the aesthetic principles and themes that would characterize the remainder of Blind's career. They also indicate the cosmopolitan nature of her sensibility and outlook. The same year she issued her Shelley edition,

---

[7] Mathilde and Ferdinand had been apart since 1864, when he left London in his eighteenth year to study in Germany.

[8] Contrary to some assertions that Ferdinand's action was widely condemned, and set back the republican cause in England, Bismarck was at this time unpopular throughout Europe and especially in England. As Erich Eyck notes, '[t]he sympathy of the population was with the assailant, not with Bismarck, so unpopular was Bismarck in spite of his proposals for reform' (*Bismarck and the German Empire* (New York: Norton, 1964), p. 120).

[9] Swinburne wrote that Blind's 'admirable essay' was 'full [...] of eloquent commentary and fervent thought', and 'was one of the earliest and most notable signs of the impulse given to the critical study of the poet' ('Notes on the Text of Shelley', in *Essays and Studies* (London: Chatto & Windus, 1875), pp. 184–237 (p. 235)).

another Anglo-Jewish writer, Benjamin Disraeli, delivered his Crystal Palace speech in which he castigated those who, like Blind, professed cosmopolitan views. Disraeli aligns the Conservatives with 'nationalism' and the Liberals (and their leader William Gladstone) with 'cosmopolitanism', which he equates with radicalism on the Continent.[10] Disraeli's dichotomies obscure a range of complex political positions. His opposition of 'nationalism' and 'cosmopolitanism', for example, leaves no room for Blind and her friend William Morris, socialists who also adhered to national principles in the sense that they supported national movements in Germany and Italy. Moreover, both were simultaneously cosmopolitans, socialists, and aesthetes, and their careers challenge views of the aesthetic movement as the apolitical precursor to the avant-garde. Borrowing a phrase from Friedrich Nietzsche, Regenia Gagnier describes late-Victorian cosmopolitans like Morris as 'citizens of the world' who 'perceived no conflict between individualism and the social state'.[11] Blind, like her countryman Nietzsche (whose books *Human, All Too Human: A Book for Free Spirits* and *Beyond Good and Evil: Prelude to a Philosophy of the Future* her friend Helen Zimmern would translate into English), writes from the perspective of those 'free spirits' or 'good Europeans' who in Nietzsche's words are characterized by 'a dangerous curiosity for an undiscovered world', one that 'flames and flickers up in all the senses'.[12] Blind uses a similar metaphor to express this same curiosity in the 'Songs of the Orient' section of *Birds of Passage*, her last volume of poetry. Implicitly rejecting Western exceptionalism, Blind invites her readers in one poem to honour the Egyptian god Horus: 'In manifold disguises, | And under many names, | Thrice-holy son of Isis, | We worship him who rises | A child-god fledged in flames' (see p. 192). For Blind, whom Garnett would describe as a 'traveller, continually on the move from land to land' who 'accumulated the impressions derived from many different regions, and many different societies',[13] this self-conception was part of her birthright and expatriate identity.

Blind's cosmopolitan identity is distinct from that of Morris, however, and not only because of her gender. In William Michael Rossetti's loaded words,

---

[10] Benjamin Disraeli, 'Conservative and Liberal Principles', *National Union*, 16 (1872), 9–11 (p. 10).
[11] Regenia Gagnier, *Individualism, Decadence, Globalization: On the Relationship of Part to Whole, 1859–1920* (New York and Basingstoke: Palgrave Macmillan, 2010), p. 137.
[12] Friedrich Nietzsche, *Human, All Too Human*, 2 vols, trans. by Helen Zimmern (Edinburgh: T. N. Foulis, 1909), I, p. 4. The German titles and original publication dates of these two volumes are *Menschliches, Allzumenschliches: Ein Buch für freie Geister* (1878) and *Jenseits von Gut und Böse: Vorspiel einer Philosophie der Zukunft* (1886).
[13] Richard Garnett, introduction to 'Mathilde Blind, 1841–1896', in *The Poets and Poetry of the Century, Vol. 7: Joanna Baillie to Mathilde Blind*, ed. by Alfred H. Miles (London: Hutchinson, 1893), pp. 609–10 (p. 609).

'she was of Jewish race'.¹⁴ Though thoroughly secular in her outlook (unlike her friend Amy Levy, she did not self-identify as Jewish), Blind was often identified as such in ways that cast her as an outsider. In addition, she identified and sympathized with those struggling for self-determination on the Continent as well as in Scotland and Ireland — a sympathy linked in part to her awareness of the Jews' history of being treated as aliens. As Disreaeli's rhetoric indicates, 'cosmopolitan' was often used as a pejorative term meaning stateless and not deserving of a state, as in the myth of the Wandering Jew. Though Blind was herself a self-confessed wanderer (a 'bird of passage', to cite the phrase she used in her profile of the painter Holman Hunt and in the title of her last book of poetry),¹⁵ frequently travelling throughout Britain and the Continent, she also thought of herself and described herself as English. After coming of age and establishing her writing career in London, she became, in the words of Kwame Anthony Appiah, a 'rooted cosmopolitan'.¹⁶ As her friend and fellow writer William Sharp observed, '[n]othing ever so disconcerted or even offended her as the imputation that she spoke or wrote English marvellously well for a German'.¹⁷ She would have been especially offended by the dismissive summary of her career in *The Times* (London), occasioned by the posthumous *Poetical Works of Mathilde Blind* (1900), which insisted on her outsider status, calling her a 'clever and vehement writer' who never attained the status of poet because 'she never learnt to use our speech with perfect freedom'.¹⁸

As a German-born child of the Enlightenment, Blind imbibed the ideas of Kant, Hegel, Feuerbach, Strauss, and Marx — and later Comte, Wollstonecraft, and J. S. Mill. And her own universalist ideals — concerning universal suffrage, equality of the sexes, the religion of humanity, and socialism — were shaped by them. Yet they were also productively complicated by her experiences of alienation — as a Jewish woman, a sexual nonconformist, a political radical, and an expatriate. And despite her support for the formation of independent national states governed by popular sovereignty (the goal of the European Revolutions of 1848) and later Irish Home Rule, Blind imagined a transnational future. In her translation of David Strauss's *The Old Faith and the New*, she

---

¹⁴ William Michael Rossetti, *Some Reminiscences of William Michael Rossetti*, 2 vols (New York: Scribner's, 1902), II, p. 388. Amy Levy includes Blind 'among distinguished women of today who are of Semitic origin', describing her as a 'graceful poet and writer of Belles Lettres', in 'Middle-Class Jewish Women of To-Day (by a Jewess)', *The Complete Novels and Selected Writings of Amy Levy, 1861–1899*, ed. by Melvyn New (Gainesville: University Press of Florida, 1993), pp. 525–27 (p. 527).
¹⁵ 'Mr. Holman Hunt: The Flight into Egypt, Portraits in Words — LVI', *The Whitehall Review* (21 April 1881), 509–10 (p. 510).
¹⁶ Kwame Anthony Appiah, 'Cosmopolitan Patriots', *Critical Inquiry*, 20 (1997), 617-39 (p. 618).
¹⁷ William Sharp, 'Mathilde Blind', *Academy* (5 December 1896), p. 498.
¹⁸ 'The Poetical Works of Mathilde Blind', *The Times* (London; 9 June 1900), p. 9.

wrote that those with a cosmopolitan, internationalist perspective 'would have the large consolidated states resolve themselves into groups of small confederated republics, organized on the socialistic principle, between which, thenceforth, differences of language and nationality could no longer act as barriers, or prove the cause of strife'.[19] As Nathan Sznaider has written, the Jewish experience 'straddles the interstices of universal identifications and particular attachments', adding that cosmopolitanism 'combines appreciation of difference and diversity with efforts to conceive of new democratic forms of political rule beyond the nation-state'.[20]

Blind's cosmopolitanism also helps explain, just as it served, her radicalism. Her four major works of prose, for instance — her translations of Strauss and Bashkirtseff, and her biographies of George Eliot and the French revolutionary Madame Roland — emerged from and reflect her pan-European perspective, and they demonstrate an 'audacity in enterprise' designed to challenge the status quo in Victorian Britain concerning faith, gender, and the political order. Stefano Evangelista has written that experiments 'with literary translation and transmission aided the internationalization of literature at the *fin de siècle* and offered deliberate or indirect counter-arguments to ideologies of nationalism', and that analysing these experiments can provide 'a broader theoretical understanding of the radical logic of entanglement that defines the aesthetic and political mission of literary decadence'.[21] Blind knew, for instance, that Strauss's *The Old Faith and the New* went even further in its antitheism than *The Life of Jesus*, incorporating as it did Charles Darwin's non-teleological view of natural selection, and that it would meet great resistance. But she was undaunted. Strauss was a fellow countryman, freethinker, and scientific materialist. He was also an associate of Ludwig Feuerbach, who was both a favourite and friend of Blind's mother. Both Strauss and Feuerbach were influential in developing and disseminating a form of historical materialism that bridged the ideas of Hegel and Marx and contributed to the political radicalism that characterized Blind's entire family.

Yet while her translation of Strauss was welcomed by her fellow freethinkers, it directly affronted the orthodox in Great Britain, and they attacked Strauss as a dangerous foreign influence. In a lengthy review essay in the August number of the *Edinburgh Review* that abandoned the urbane tone maintained by most

[19] David Friedrich Strauss, *The Old Faith and the New: A Confession*, with final preface and an original memoir of the author by Mathilde Blind, trans. by Mathilde Blind, 2 vols (London: Asher, 1874), II, p. 301.
[20] Nathan Sznaider, *Jewish Memory and the Cosmopolitan Order* (Cambridge: Polity Press, 2011), p. 5.
[21] Stefano Evangelista, 'Transnational Decadence', in *Decadence and Literature*, ed. by Jane Desmarais and David Weir (Cambridge: Cambridge University Press, 2019), pp. 316–31 (p. 330).

of its writers, the anonymous reviewer proclaimed that Strauss and 'his school […] have, in ludicrous fashion, entirely lost their heads [….] They cry out loudly and confidently, and with most damnable iteration, Great is the God Pan of the philosophers! […] they […] announce that Kant and Darwin have struck a death-blow at all the old systems, and preach that life is a piece of mechanism, religion a fable, immortality a dream founded upon a wish, and the resurrection of Christ — we refuse to pollute our English tongue with the blasphemy — "in Welt-historisches humbug".'.[22] Significantly, the title poem of the first volume of poetry Blind published under her own name, *The Prophecy of St. Oran and Other Poems* (1881), embodies the demythologizing spirit of Strauss's final work, envisioning a secular future for mankind,[23] and was withdrawn by her publisher within the year of its appearance because of its 'atheistic character'.[24]

Similarly, Blind was inspired to translate the *Journal de Marie Bashkirtseff* (*The Journal of Marie Bashkirtseff*), written by the Ukrainian-French painter who lived most of her short life in Paris, because of Bashkirtseff's radical view of gender: 'I have nothing of the woman about me but the envelope […] It is not I who say this, since it seems to me that all women are like myself'.[25] This is why Blind's 1889 translation became a sensation in Britain, ensuring that Bashkirtseff was celebrated as a proto-New Woman. In her introduction Blind invited her British audience to read the journal as 'an education in psychology', since Bashkirtseff 'has chosen to lay before us "the very pulse of the machine"'.[26]

---

[22] 'Dr. Strauss' Confession', *Edinburgh Review*, 138 (August 1873), p. 542.
[23] The title poem is a four-part, 148-stanza poem in which Blind retells the legend of the sixth-century monk who consented to be buried alive in order to appease certain demons of the earth who were preventing the Christian missionary St Columba from building a chapel on Iona, an island of the Inner Hebrides of Scotland. When Columba ordered the body to be dug up after three days, Oran arose from the dead to proclaim that there is no God, final judgment, or future state — which caused St Columba to order him buried once more. In Blind's revisions to the legend, Oran falls in love with the daughter of a native chieftain, Mona, whose proud paganism resists his attempts to convert her, and it is she who releases him from the grave before his reburial, not some supernatural intervention.
[24] Rossetti wrote about this in a letter to Ford Madox Brown, lamenting that Blind's publisher (Newman) 'had got frightened by somebody about the atheistic character of the book, and had determined to sell it no more' (*Selected Letters of William Michael Rossetti*, ed. by Roger Peattie (University Park: Pennsylvania State University Press, 1990), p. 400). In a historical irony that links the poetic and the political, Blind's fellow freethinker Charles Bradlaugh, who had been elected to Parliament in 1880, was prevented from taking his seat by a Conservative Party campaign that attacked him for his professed atheism. Disraeli had raised the spectre of atheism in the preface to his 1870 novel *Lothair*, writing that that an unholy trinity of scientific materialism, the 'powerful assault on the divinity of the Semitic literature of the Germans', and reaction to the power of the pope might turn England into an 'atheistical society' ('Preface' to *Lothair* (New York: Appleton, 1870), p. xvi).
[25] Marie Bashkirtseff, *The Journal of Marie Bashkirtseff*, trans. with an introduction by Mathilde Blind, 2 vols (London: Cassell, 1890), I, p. 371.
[26] Mathilde Blind, 'Introduction', *The Journal of Marie Bashkirtseff*, pp. vii–xxviii (p. vii).

but many reviewers diagnosed Bashkirtseff's racing pulse as a symptom of a thoroughly pathological form of decadence. In his review of Blind's translation, Lionel Johnson acknowledges that the journal will be embraced by everyone 'in the movement', but he mocks those who are moved by 'the spectacle of a young Russian lady suffering the *maladie de siècle*, and boldly exposing its symptoms to the world'.[27] Johnson's emphasis on Bashkirtseff's foreignness is a reminder that in Max Nordau's *Entartung* (*Degeneration*, 1892–1893), as Evangelista has noted, 'the real *bête noire* [...] was the accelerated internationalization of literary culture: as literary content passed from nation to nation, leading to a global or at least pan-European economy of transmission, decadent writers allegedly lost touch with their domestic readers and were no longer subjected to the restraining influence of national character'.[28]

Even in her 1883 biography of George Eliot, Blind invites her readers to step outside their nationalist framework to consider Eliot's views from a pan-European perspective.[29] To do so she resisted the advice of many to simply sing Eliot's praises and celebrate her Englishness. Writing to Blind while she was working on her manuscript, Garnett voiced concern about whether she felt 'sufficient enthusiasm for your heroine', reflecting his conception of Blind's project as a form of hagiography she did not share. 'The more you admire both her intellect, her genius, and her moral character', Garnett emphasized, 'the better you will write, and the more your reader will appreciate you'.[30] While Blind clearly admired Eliot as a supreme novelist, a fitful feminist, and (perhaps more important) a freethinker, her biography maintains a bracingly critical distance from its subject.

The first chapter, 'Introductory', begins on a decidedly feminist note by quoting from Eliot's 1854 essay 'Women in France: Madame de Sable' in a way that simultaneously establishes Eliot's own cosmopolitan credentials and subjects them to a mordant interrogation. In her essay, Blind writes, Eliot awards 'the palm of intellectual pre-eminence' to the women writers of France, who alone have 'had the courage of their sex', whereas the writings of English women are 'usually an absurd exaggeration of the masculine style, like the swaggering gait of a bad actress in male attire'. Blind then summarizes the reasons Eliot cites for this French pre-eminence, including the influence of literary salons as well as the 'physiological peculiarities of the Gallic race'.

---

[27] Lionel Johnson, 'Marie Bashkirtseff', *Anti-Jacobin* (10 October 1891), rpt. in *Post Liminium: Essays and Critical Papers*, ed. by Thomas Whittemore (New York: Mitchell Kennerley, 1912), pp. 245–50 (pp. 246, 250).
[28] 'Transnational Decadence', p. 329.
[29] Mathilde Blind and A. Mary F. Robinson inaugurated W. H. Allen's Eminent Women series of biographies, which continued until 1895 and ultimately numbered twenty-two volumes. Robinson's contribution was a biography of Emily Brontë.
[30] Richard Garnett ALS to Mathilde Blind, 13 August 1882, Add. MS 61928, fols 147–48.

And here Blind's own critical scepticism comes to the fore. While she admired Eliot in part because she embraced contemporary science, Blind clearly considers Eliot's physiological analysis a form of pseudo-science. After quoting Eliot's assertion that the 'small brain and vivacious temperament' of French women allow them to sustain 'the superlative activity requisite for intellectual creativeness', while 'the larger brain and slower temperament of the English and Germans are in the womanly organization dreamy and passive', Blind offers this deadpan observation: 'So knotty and subtle a problem must be left for the scientist of the future to decide'. She then suggests her own solution in the form of this rhetorical question: 'Was the author of *Adam Bede* not herself destined to be a triumphant refutation of her theory?'[31]

Blind's complaints about Eliot's treatment of Judaism in *Daniel Deronda* are worth noting, since they represent her own perspective as a secular Jew and rooted cosmopolitan. She notes that the Jewish characters in the novel are largely stereotypes, writes that the novel's endorsement of 'Jewish separateness' is 'repugnant to modern feelings', and condemns Eliot's sentimental celebration of the devout, passive Mirah Lapidoth and demonization of the Contessa Alcharisi, the novel's embodiment of rebellious Jewish womanhood and independence. After noting that the doctrine of separateness is presented as 'righteous, just, and praiseworthy', and alternatives as 'mischievous and reprehensible', Blind avers: 'This seems carrying the principle of nationality to an extreme, if not pernicious length. [...] This unwavering faithfulness to the traditions of the past may become a curse to the living'.[32] Blind's political radicalism and feminism also made her impatient with Eliot's treatment of these subjects in her fiction. Discussing Eliot's most political novel, *Felix Holt the Radical*, Blind dutifully but unenthusiastically notes that the novel's 'advice is mainly to the effect that genuine political and social improvements to be endurable must be the result of inward change rather than of outward legislation'. And she is dismayed that *Middlemarch* 'is the only work of George Eliot's, I believe, in which there is a distinct indication of her attitude towards the aspirations and clearly formulated demands of the women of the nineteenth century'.[33]

For her second biography, Blind turned to a woman whose politics were closer to her own. In *Madame Roland* (1886), she recounts the life of a revolutionary who died on the guillotine during the Reign of Terror after fighting for the principles of popular sovereignty and the rights of women. Blind's project was inspired in part by the research she conducted when writing her 1878 *New Quarterly Magazine* essay on the early feminist Mary Wollstonecraft, who spent

---

[31] Mathilde Blind, *George Eliot* (London: W. H. Allen, 1883), pp. 1–3.
[32] *George Eliot*, pp. 194–95.
[33] *George Eliot*, pp. 232, 185.

time in Paris during the early years of the Revolution and admired Roland.[34] Blind presented both these women to her late-Victorian readers as models of female agency and influence, even though in some respects they also fell short of her own more radical views. Analysing *A Vindication of the Rights of Woman*, for instance, Blind writes that Wollstonecraft 'never wearies of expressing her respect for family life "as the foundation of almost every social virtue"', adding tartly that *A Vindication* 'might perhaps with more justice be called the Duties instead of the Rights of Woman. For [...] it is in a great measure that they may properly fulfil their various duties as wives and mothers, sisters and daughters, that she claims for them certain rights'.[35] And in describing the period in Madame Roland's life when she became, along with her husband, a leader of the Girondists, Blind notes that her 'heroism did not consist in braving public opinion; on the contrary, she considered a certain conformity to it as part of the duty which the individual owed to the social compact, — duty to which was, from first to last, the motive spring of her actions'.[36] But Blind quotes Madame Roland's *Mémoires* to show that she voiced the same rebellion against gender constraints that Blind and many of her contemporaries were more openly expressing, in terms that would be echoed by Marie Bashkirtseff: '"In truth I am not a little annoyed at being a woman. I ought either to have had another sex, another soul, or another country. I ought to have been a Spartan or a Roman woman, or at least a Frenchman. As the latter I should have chosen the Republic of Letters for my country"'.[37]

Most importantly for an understanding of Blind's late poetry, and especially *The Ascent of Man*, is Blind's analysis of the Enlightenment philosophers whose ideas inspired Madame Roland and her fellow revolutionaries. Discussing the French *Encyclopédistes*, Blind calls them 'the light brigade of the Thought Militant of human progress. The very sound of the names of them — Voltaire, Diderot, D'Alembert, D'Holbach, Condillac, Helvetius — still rings upon our ears like so many battle-cries'. Their goal was to 'free men from the bondage of authority in religion and philosophy, to substitute for superstitious terror a faith in human reason and virtue, to transform regret for a lost Paradise to quenchless belief in the perfectibility of the race'. Blind credits these writers with enabling Marie-Jeanne Phlipon (Madame Roland's birth name) to transform

---

[34] Prior to Blind's essay, George Eliot was one of the few Victorian writers to discuss Mary Wollstonecraft in print (in her 1855 essay 'Margaret Fuller and Mary Wollstonecraft'). Most Victorian feminists remained silent about Wollstonecraft's importance as an ideological predecessor because they feared associating the struggle for women's equality with Wollstonecraft's own personal and sexual nonconformism.

[35] Mathilde Blind, 'Mary Wollstonecraft', *New Quarterly Magazine*, 10 (July 1878), 390–412 (p. 398).

[36] Mathilde Blind, *Madame Roland* (London: W. H. Allen, 1886), p. 81.

[37] *Madame Roland*, p. 75.

herself from an essentially conservative member of the petite bourgeoisie into an embodiment of the 'pure Republican ideal'. Describing the liberating effect of these ideas on Marie-Jeanne, Blind extends their implications to her contemporaries: 'Instead of a slavish following of custom, instead of trying to digest the old dough of superannuated ideas, which has spoiled the digestion of so many generations, let us dare to solve the problems of life in our own way and day; let us try and see for ourselves, not take it for granted that all our thinking has been done for us by our ancestors'. Quoting admiringly from a letter the twenty-year-old Marie-Jeanne wrote to a friend in 1774, when Louis XV was on his deathbed, Blind is describing her own cosmopolitanism as well as that of her subject: 'Nothing in the world is indifferent to me. I am something of a cosmopolitan, and a love of humanity unites me to everything that breathes. A Caribbean interests me; the fate of a Kaffir goes to my heart. Alexander wished for more worlds to conquer; I could wish for others to love'.[38]

Throughout her biography Blind sides with the revolutionaries of recent history — with Thomas Paine and against Edmund Burke, with Rousseau and against Thomas Carlyle. And her statements about these thinkers have specific relevance for *The Ascent of Man*. Rejecting Carlyle's 'strenuous teaching that Might is Right' while fully aware that 'we bred up in the Darwinian era [...] cannot help smiling at Rousseau's rose-coloured visions of a primitive state of nature', Blind insists that Rousseau's political idealism 'is nevertheless in harmony with the highest conception of justice, — justice which, like music, has its origin in the soul of man only; the most purely human of the virtues, and which is the goal towards which society is slowly and painfully working its way'. She concludes her biography by celebrating the Revolution for having 'modified the political and social life of Europe' and reminding her readers that 'there has never yet in the world's history been a fresh incarnation of the idea without violent convulsions'.[39]

The struggle for national self-determination is a central theme of Blind's narrative poem *The Heather on Fire: A Tale of the Highland Clearances* (1886), published in the midst of the Crofters War of the 1880s and infused with anticolonial indignation. Crofters were the Scottish peasant farmers and fisherman who had earned a subsistence living from the land for generations, and the conflict was rooted in the Highland Land Clearances that began in the eighteenth century and accelerated in the 1830s, the decade in which Blind's poem is set. One of the most infamous mass evictions of a class of people in British history, the clearances were part of the transformation of the west of Britain from a paternalistic society based on ties of kinship to a capitalist one based on commercial and exploitative landlordism. Crofters were brutally

---

[38] *Madame Roland*, pp. 100, 102, 130, 18, 25.
[39] *Madame Roland*, pp. 104, 254.

evicted from their homes and property by the English, who treated Scotland like a colonial possession, first to make way for sheep grazing, then to provide hunting grounds for wealthy British and American sportsmen. In the preface to her poem, Blind emphasizes that the atrocities rendered in her narrative are historical, not imaginative, and that 'the uprooting and transplantation of whole communities of Crofters from the straths and glens which they had tilled for so many generations must be regarded in the light of a national crime'.[40] In her introduction to her 1887 edition of Lord Byron's letters, Blind writes that '[a]ll his life Byron had felt a glowing sympathy with oppressed nations, and a hatred of oppressors', adding that '[n]othing proves more conclusively the genuine nature of his love of liberty than his staunch advocacy of Irish claims — a far more crucial test of true liberalism as applied to this English nobleman in 1820 than even his participation in Carbonari risings and revolutions in Greece'.[41] Blind's sympathies aligned with those of Byron — she too supported Irish Home Rule — and *The Heather on Fire* expresses a similar resistance to colonial oppression, in this case the appropriation of Scottish lands by the English.[42]

The Heather on Fire tells the story of a family destroyed by the actions of English landlords, one of whose agents boasts, 'of all these dirty huts the glen we'll sweep, | And clear it for the fatted lowland sheep'.[43] At the beginning of the poem the patriarch of this peasant family, Rory MacKinnon, is already crippled from injuries he suffered as a soldier fighting for the English king in the Peninsular War; as a result of this his son Michael had delayed marriage to his beloved Mary for nine years to provide for his parents. Their eventual union has produced four children, with another on the way, when the long-threatened evictions begin — at a time when Michael is away at one of his annual migrations to the herring fishery. The agents set the heather on fire, wreck the cottages, and smoke the villagers out of their homes. Rory's bedridden wife dies

---

[40] Mathilde Blind, *The Heather on Fire: A Tale of the Highland Clearances* (London: Walter Scott, 1886), p. 2.

[41] Mathilde Blind, *The Letters of Lord Byron [Selected]*, ed. with an introduction by Mathilde Blind (London: Walter Scott, 1887), p. xii.

[42] Blind was friends with the Irish nationalists and MPs Justin McCarthy and John Dillon; her presentation copy of *The Heather on Fire* (inscribed 'to Mrs. John Dillon with sincere esteem Mathilde Blind') is held by the Arizona State University Library <https://repository.asu.edu/items/43184> [accessed 11 January 2021]. Blind's support for the Scottish Crofters and for Irish Home rule coincided with William Gladstone's own political commitments in the 1880s; *The Heather on Fire* was published the same year that Parliament during Gladstone's third term as prime minister passed the Crofters Holdings Act that brought an end to the Highland Clearances. Blind sent Gladstone a copy of her book in May 1886, thus beginning a five-year correspondence (see James Diedrick, *Mathilde Blind: Late-Victorian Culture and the Woman of Letters* (Charlottesville: University of Virginia Press, 2016), pp. 201–02, 206–09).

[43] *The Heather on Fire*, p. 61.

in the flames; Mary is turned out with her youngest child, who dies of exposure. Michael returns just at this moment and flees with the remainder of his family to a ruined stronghold, where his wife gives birth to their fifth child, who also dies. The agents burst in, gather them together with the other villagers, and prepare to put them on a ship to be taken to a distant colony (Canada was the usual destination). The family's eldest daughter dies of grief and exhaustion at the churchyard where they gather to bury their dead, and Michael, along with his remaining twin boy and girl, is hurried onto the ship. Rory escapes his captors and remains ashore to witness the final catastrophe: soon after starting out, the ship is driven back to the rocky coast in a storm, and everyone aboard perishes.

As William Michael Rossetti wrote in his *Athenæum* review of the poem, '[t]his wholesale destruction is obviously a blemish on the invention'. Yet he went on to praise Blind for her 'boldness in choosing a subject of our own time, fertile in what is pathetic and awe-inspiring, and free from any taint of the vulgar or conventional'. Rossetti continues, 'Poetry of late years has tended too much towards motives of a merely abstruse and fanciful, sometimes a plainly artificial, character; and we have had much of lyrical energy or attraction with little of the real marrow of human life, the flesh and blood of man and woman. [...] we have them here'.[44] Representing one extreme of Blind's socially engaged aestheticism, *The Heather on Fire* embraces the poet's role as expressed in Book 5 of *Aurora Leigh*, where Elizabeth Barrett Browning criticizes the contemporary poet who seeks to escape the present, and 'trundles back his soul five hundred years, | Past moat and drawbridge, into a castle-court'.[45] She asserts that the poet's 'sole work' is to represent 'this live, throbbing age, | That brawls, cheats, maddens, calculates, aspires'.[46] Blind greatly admired Barrett Browning, whose poem 'A Drama of Exile' provides the epigraph for Part III of 'The Ascent of Man', and her late poetry performs the 'work' that Barrett Browning advocates here.

It is also worth noting that Blind's expatriate status gave her special leverage when attacking England's oppression of the Scots. Her close friend, the painter Ford Madox Brown, noted this in a letter to his friend Marion Harry Alexander Spielmann (the art critic for the *Pall Mall Gazette* and editor of the *Magazine of Art*) shortly before the poem appeared in print. Brown says that Blind's poem delves 'deeply into the matter' of the clearances, then calls it 'strange' that native-born Scots and reformers like Carlyle and Henry Brougham (who helped pass the Slavery Abolition Act of 1833 when he was Lord Chancellor) should

---

[44] [Unsigned], William Michael Rossetti, Review of *The Heather on Fire*, *Athenæum* (16 July 1886), 75–76.
[45] Elizabeth Barrett Browning, *Aurora Leigh* (London: Chapman & Hall, 1857), pp. 187–88.
[46] Browning, *Aurora Leigh*, p. 188.

'have been holding forth to spellbound listeners in Edinburgh and London and neither of them to have uttered (or shown that they knew) a word on the subject'. Brown suggests why: 'So clearly do the English nation screen their peccadillos from too ardent glare of publicity'.[47] Blind's anticolonial attitude is given further expression in many of her later poems, including 'The Ascent of Man', 'A Carnival Episode', and 'The Battle of Flowers' in *Dramas in Miniature*, and 'The Beautiful Beershareen Boy' in *Birds of Passage*.

By the time Blind published *The Ascent of Man* in 1889, the poetry and prose she had written up to this point — and the many friendships she had formed — had made her a central figure in London's literary and artistic community. She had emerged as a leader of the radical wing of the late-century aesthetic movement, sought out by young aspirants like Arthur Symons, lauded by fellow women writers like Mona Caird, and demonized by cultural conservatives like Hugh E. M. Stutfield. Stutfield's 1895 essay 'Tommyrotics' condemns 'the crazy and offensive drivel being poured forth over Europe — drivel which is not only written, but widely read and admired, and which the new woman and her male coadjutors are now trying to popularize in England'. Stutfield identifies a male writer as the founder of this co-conspiracy, but his claim that 'the new criticism, the new fiction, the new woman, are all merely creatures of Oscar Wilde's'[48] reveals his guiding and limiting assumptions about women. He is clearly ignorant, for instance, of Blind's contributions to the New Woman and Decadent movements, whose intersections and underground alliances her career underscores.[49] Oscar Wilde was after all four years away from the *succès de scandale* of *The Picture of Dorian Gray* when in 1887 he invited Blind to contribute an essay to *The Woman's World*, which led to her translation of *The Journal of Marie Bashkirtseff* and the intensification of late-century debates concerning gender and sexual identity.

The feminism and sexual nonconformism apparent in *The Ascent of Man*, *Dramas in Miniature*, and *Birds of Passage* owe in part to Blind's increasing contact with women writers who challenged the patriarchal order, especially Vernon Lee and Mona Caird. Vernon Lee's 1895 critique of Nordau's *Degeneration* argues for the necessity of what she calls 'the queer comradeship of outlawed thought',[50] a sense of difference based not just in sexual but also

---

[47] Ford Madox Brown ALS to Marion Harry Alexander Spielmann, 13 April 1866, John Rylands Library, University of Manchester, English MS 1290.
[48] Hugh E. M. Stutfield, 'Tommyrotics', *Blackwood's Edinburgh Magazine* (June 1895), 833–45 (p. 835).
[49] As Linda Dowling has noted, 'literary critics and reviewers persistently identified the New Woman with the Decadent, perceiving in the ambitions of both a profound threat to established culture' ('The Decadent and the New Woman in the 1890s', *Nineteenth-Century Fiction*, 33 (1979), 431–39 (p. 435)).
[50] Vernon Lee, 'Deterioration of Soul', *Fortnightly Review*, 59 (June 1896), 928–43 (p. 938). For a discussion of the late-Victorian connotations and implications of the terms 'queer' and

cultural nonconformism shared by Blind, Caird, and Lee. In September 1893, Blind and Caird spent the first half of the month together in the English countryside, renting a small cottage in Wendover, in the Chiltern Hills in Buckinghamshire. The two women took many walks together through the countryside, where the landscape becomes feminized and eroticized in Blind's imagination, as she recorded in her Commonplace Book: 'Walk to the twilight wood on the hill-side with the silvery broken light on the barley field. We were struck by the singular outline of a hornbeam with the trunk + branches half thrown back curiously resembling a woman's body. It might have been some female struggling passionately to escape pursuit [...] Daphne herself changing into a shrub.' Blind's descriptions of Caird also carry an erotic charge. Recounting a sunny afternoon on a hillside field when Caird began caressing a horse that approached them, Blind writes, 'I shall long remember the picture. [...] She wore a blue serge gown with a shirt dotted with little blue + red spots. The delicate lines of her slim form were on the green background [...] she reminded me of Titania when she begs Bottom to be quiet "while I thy amiable cheeks do coy"'.[51] As readers of this volume will note, several of the lyrics in *Dramas in Miniature* and *Birds of Passage* accommodate lesbian or bisexual readings; their ambiguously gendered speakers and/or addressees indicate a willingness to explore and express same-sex desire ('Scherzo', My Lady', 'A White Night', and 'The Forest Pool'; see pp. 172, 179, 220, 221).

Organization of this Volume

The poems presented in this Jewelled Tortoise volume are organized chronologically. Three full volumes of Blind's late poetry are included, and they are bookended by two individual poems published nearly 25 years apart: 'Nocturne', published in the *Dark Blue* in 1872, and the sonnet 'Sea-Music', which appeared in the inaugural issue of *The Savoy* in 1896. The ballad 'Nocturne' embodies and illustrates Blind's affiliations with the aesthetic movement of the 1870s, just as the last, 'Sea-Music', registers her willing association with the Decadent movement. Two sections follow the poetry: selected prose by Blind, including her 1886 lecture *Shelley's View of Nature Contrasted with Darwin's* and three of her reviews of poetry by fellow poets; and seven critical responses to Blind's poetry by her contemporaries. The remainder of this introduction provides a general overview of Blind's versification, followed by contextual and critical analyses of the poetry included in the volume, as well as a brief

'comradeship', see Richard Dellamora, 'Productive Decadence: "The Queer Comradeship of Outlawed Thought": Vernon Lee, Max Nordau, and Oscar Wilde', *New Literary History*, 35 (2004), 529–46.
[51] 'The Commonplace Book of Mathilde Blind', Oxford, Bodleian Library, MS Walpole e.1., pp. 15, 24–25.

discussion of Blind's lectures and reviews, and selected reviews of her poetry.

* * * * *

Blind had a wide knowledge of verse forms (English but also Greek, German, and French), and even before the three volumes featured here, she adopted a variety of specific forms appropriate to her subject matter. These include the medieval ballad form used in 'Nocturne'; the Venus and Adonis stanza of 'The Prophecy of St. Oran' (whose two lovers' stories parallel those of the mythic pair); and the octave stanzas comprised of heroic couplets (the first seven lines in iambic pentameter couplets and the final in iambic hexameter) of *The Heather on Fire*. She also published over thirty sonnets in her career, many of them represented in this volume, and as early as 1882, when T. Hall Caine published his collection *Sonnets of Three Centuries*, he included two of hers alongside examples by D. G. and Christina Rossetti, Swinburne, and Matthew Arnold.[52]

Blind's experiments with verse form only accelerated in the late 1880s and 1890s: readers of this volume will encounter line lengths ranging from dimeter to octometer, and stanza forms that include couplets, tercets, septets, and sonnets, as well as elaborate forms with intricate rhyme schemes and mixed line lengths. The annotations to individual poems throughout the volume will alert readers to notable formal features, but one metrical pattern that Blind makes repeated use of is worth noting here. While most English poetry follows an iambic pattern, with the first syllable unstressed and the second stressed, Blind often favours the trochaic — a type of metrical foot in which this pattern is reversed. The octometer lines of the 'Prelude' to *Birds of Passage* exemplify this, as its first line illustrates:

Where at **night** the **an**cient **heavens bend** above the **ancient earth**, ...

As noted by Theodore Watts-Dunton, the lead poetry critic of the *Athenæum* during Blind's most productive years, the 'trochaic measure' is 'where Miss Bind is metrically most at home'.[53] This metrical pattern is one source of what Watts-Dunton calls the 'weight of thought and fervour' of her 'best work'.[54] But

---

[52] They were 'Time's Shadow' and 'The Dead'. Blind reprinted the former as the last of two sonnets in Part I of 'The Ascent of Man' (see p. 81), and the latter, which originally appeared in the 2 April 1881 issue of the *Athenæum*, reappeared in *The Prophecy of St. Oran*.

[53] Citing the witches' chant in *Macbeth* ('double, double toil and trouble'), Annie Finch notes that '[f]or almost as long as iambic meter has been the meter of logic, reason, power and civilization, trochaic meter has tended to be associated with the uncanny and subversive' (Annie Finch, *A Poet's Ear: A Handbook of Meter and Form* (Ann Arbor: University of Michigan Press, 2013), p. 121).

[54] [Unsigned], Theodore Watts-Dunton, Review of *Birds of Passage: Songs of the Orient and Occident*, *Athenæum* (24 August 1895), p. 242.

he also identified weaknesses in Blind's reliance on this pattern, exacerbated by a rhetorical tendency apparent in much of her verse. The result, he wrote in a memorial essay published a month after her death, was that 'the verbal substance, lacking both exactitude and idiomatic spring, hung like a coloured curtain between the writer's conception and the reader's eyes'.[55]

Blind avoids this tendency in 'Nocturne', the earliest of her poems included here, whose very title evokes the aestheticist belief in the interrelationship among music, painting, and poetry she shared with Pater, Swinburne, and the painter James McNeill Whistler. (A musical 'nocturne' is a composition evocative of night-time and dream-states, whose melody is repeated with embellishments.) In his essay 'Notes on Some Pictures of 1868' Swinburne discusses the 'melody of ineffable colour' in Whistler's paintings, and in his 1871 *Dark Blue* essay on the painter Simeon Solomon he describes some of Solomon's designs as 'music made visible'.[56] A year before Blind published 'Nocturne' Whistler exhibited two paintings at the Dudley Gallery titled 'Harmony in Blue Green — Moonlight', which in 1872 he renamed 'Nocturne in Blue and Silver — Chelsea'. Blind knew Whistler, and her own 'Nocturne', like Whistler's paintings, is an impressionistic dreamscape (see p. 49). The voices of fellow poets echo throughout the poem as well; its subject matter and musical effects evoke Swinburne's sexual and stylistic preoccupations, and two passages explicitly evoke Keats and Robert Browning, guiding spirits of the Pre-Raphaelites and aesthetes.[57] So too does the voice of Walter Pater, whose 1868 *Westminster Review* essay on Morris's poetry informs Blind's ballad.[58]

---

[55] Theodore Watts-Dunton, 'Miss Blind', *Athenæum* (5 December 1896), p. 796.

[56] 'Notes on Some Pictures of 1868', in William Michael Rossetti and A. C. Swinburne, *Notes on the Royal Academy Exhibition* (London: John Camden Hotten, 1868), rpt. in *Essays and Studies*, 358–80 (p. 373); and 'Simeon Solomon: Notes on his "Vision of Love" and Other Studies', *Dark Blue* (July 1871), p. 574. For analysis of the importance of Whistler to Swinburne's aesthetic theory, specifically the synaesthetic relation between music and painting, see Catherine Maxwell, *The Female Sublime from Milton to Swinburne: Bearing Blindness* (Manchester: Manchester University Press, 2001), pp. 180, 195–99, 253; *Swinburne* (Tavistock: Northcote House, 2006), pp. 22, 89; and 'Whistlerian Impressionism and the Venetian Variations of Vernon Lee, John Addington Symonds, and Arthur Symons', *The Yearbook of English Studies*, 40 (2010), 217–45 (pp. 218–22).

[57] 'Nocturne' exists in a suggestively dialogic relationship to two poems that appeared in *Dark Blue* a year before: Swinburne's 'The End of a Month' (April 1871) and D. G. Rossetti's 'Down Stream' (October 1871). All three explore the relationship between Eros and death; all three feature couples locked in destructive embraces; all three employ nature imagery to represent sexual experience (Swinburne's poem was reprinted as 'At a Month's End' in *Poems and Ballads, Second Series* (London: Chatto & Windus, 1878), pp. 37–45). For more on these three poems, see James Diedrick, 'A Pioneering Female Aesthete: Mathilde Blind in *The Dark Blue*', *Victorian Periodicals Review*, 36 (2003), 210–41.

[58] Pater used the final section of this essay as the conclusion to his *Studies in the History of the Renaissance* (1873), which became an unofficial, and controversial, manifesto of aestheticism. It is likely that Blind read Pater's essay when preparing her lecture on Morris.

One of Pater's themes is especially relevant to the freethinking Blind and to 'Nocturne': the neo-paganism that characterizes much aesthetic poetry. Pater says that the 'writings of the romantic school', which for him range from Shelley to Morris, 'mark a transition not so much from the pagan to the medieval ideal, as from a lower to a higher degree of passion in literature', adding that 'a return to true Hellenism was as much a part of this reaction as the sudden preoccupation with things medieval'. Writing of the kind of love represented in Morris's 'Galahad: A Mystery' from *The Defence of Guinevere*, Pater might also be describing 'Nocturne': a passion that 'begets a tension of nerve, in which the sensible world comes to one with a reinforced brilliance and relief — all redness is turned into blood, all water into tears. Hence a wild, convulsed sensuousness [...] in which the things of nature begin to play a strange delirious part'.[59]

As for 'Sea-Music', it is ironic that for literary historians this single poem guaranteed Blind's association with the Decadent movement: it lacks the transgressive themes and stylistic extremes of many poems in her last three volumes. For Garnett, however, to whom she submitted this poem in manuscript asking his opinion about publishing it with Symons in *The Savoy*, Blind was courting scandal by association. Symons had recently become notorious as the author of *London Nights* (1895), one of the key *fin-de-siècle* texts, published amid the Oscar Wilde trials, and Garnett worried about the effect on Blind of publishing with him. 'Under the circumstances you do right to let Symonds [sic] have your poem', Garnett begins his response; 'Even if there is a scandal you will hardly be made responsible'. He warns her, however, to 'watch the course of his periodical very narrowly. I detest his last volume, and all the more because there is real poetical power in it. The erotic poetry of the ancients and the great moderns I can tolerate and even admire, but I cannot stand the nauseous effeminacy of our "decadents"'.[60] Notably, much of Blind's late poetry implicitly challenges the heteronormativity that Garnett's condemnation so anxiously asserts.

The Ascent of Man

'From Chaos to Kosmos, from the "indefinite incoherent homogeneity" to the "definite coherent heterogeneity", she *hurries* her reader along, breathless and perspiring perhaps, but never anxious to stop'.[61] This unsigned *Athenæum*

She mentions reading Pater in an 1895 letter to Garnett: 'I am reading Pater's "Appreciations" which I had long wished to see' (Mathilde Blind ALS to Richard Garnett, 15 October 1885, Add. MS 6129, fols 145–47).
[59] Walter Pater, 'Poems by William Morris', *Westminster Review*, 34 (October 1868), 300–12 (pp. 308–10).
[60] Richard Garnett ALS to Mathilde Blind, 8 November 1895, Add. MS 61929, fols 151–52.
[61] [Unsigned], H. F. Wilson, Review of 'The Ascent of Man: and other Poems', *Athenæum*

review of the title poem in Mathilde Blind's 1889 volume *The Ascent of Man* conveys both the enthusiasm that greeted its initial appearance and the sense of temporal dilation and dislocation it elicited in readers.[62] After hearing Blind read the first section of the poem aloud at one of her literary salons before its publication, Mona Caird reported that, as she read, 'it seemed as if she had carried us all back to the beginnings of the world's existence, and made us travel, in that short evening, through untold aeons of time'.[63] Caird is here describing Part I of the title poem, which narrates the entire history of life on earth, employing dozens of stanza forms and abrupt shifts of tone that mimic the fecundity, profligacy, and unruliness that Charles Darwin identifies with nature itself, most notably during his discussion of sexual selection in *The Descent of Man, and Selection in Relation to Sex* (1871). Moreover, as Monique Morgan has observed, her '*sequence* of stanza types' in Part I 'evokes the passage of time: dactylic hexameter, the meter of classical epics; iambic tetrameter, which is close to the rhythms of medieval ballads; heroic couplets, popular in the eighteenth century; and elaborate stanza forms with intricate rhyme schemes and mixed line lengths, similar to Romantic poets' metrical experiments'.[64]

The thematic reach of 'The Ascent of Man' is equally sweeping. It represents the culmination of Blind's quest to weave a new, humanist (and feminist) mythology from the resistant threads of Darwinian theory, a quest that began

---

(20 July 1889), p. 87. This excerpt reveals Wilson's familiarity with the writers who influenced, and whose work is echoed in, the poem. At the beginning of this passage he quotes from Alfred Lord Tennyson's 'Locksley Hall Sixty Years After': 'Chaos, Cosmos! Cosmos, Chaos! who can tell how all will end! | Read the wide world's annals, you, and take their wisdom for your friend'. He also cites Herbert Spencer, the philosopher and biologist who used the terms 'indefinite incoherent homogeneity' and 'definite coherent heterogeneity' on numerous occasions in his work *First Principles* (1860), including this example: 'The more specific idea of Evolution now reached is — a change from an indefinite, incoherent homogeneity, to a definite coherent heterogeneity, accompanying the dissipation of motion and integration of matter'; *First Principles* (New York: Caldwell, 1880), p. 320. The *Athenæum* review mis-states the title of the volume as *The Ascent of Man: and other Poems*, likely because some advertisements used this title.

[62] *The Ascent of Man* (London: Chatto & Windus, 1889). This volume marked the beginning of Blind's relationship with Chatto & Windus, who published all four of the subsequent volumes of poetry that appeared in her lifetime. Blind wrote a series of letters to the publisher between March and August 1889, negotiating everything from the design and colour of the cover to the price of the volume to advertising strategies to which magazines and newspapers should receive review copies. In a letter (6 May) she asked the firm to list the title as 'The Ascent of Man and Other Poems' in subsequent advertisements, noting that their earlier advertisements describing the book as 'a Poem' 'gives the wrong idea'. Los Angeles, Chatto & Windus Records UCLA Library Special Collections, Charles E. Young Research Library, Collection 426.

[63] 'Mathilde Blind', *South Place Magazine* (February 1897), p. 65.

[64] Monique Morgan, 'Genres', in *The Cambridge Companion to Victorian Women's Poetry*, ed. by Hughes, pp. 13–27 (p. 14).

during her own intellectual 'beginnings', when she was in her late teenage years and following a curriculum suggested by Mazzini, which emphasized the study of the sciences, including geology: 'The idea possibly first took root in my mind when, as a mere girl, I used to go to Mazzini's little room in Brompton, and with my whole soul on tip toe with eagerness, heard him dwell on the progressive stages of man's development as the central fact in history'.[65] Parts 2 and 3, titled 'The Pilgrim Soul' and 'The Leading of Sorrow', enact this vision, though, in Blind's telling, it is woman who is the agent of progress. These two sections are quasi-allegorical narratives imagining how, through ethical struggle, the 'elemental forces of nature' are transformed 'into the nimblest of servants', as she wrote in her 1886 lecture *Shelley's View of Nature Contrasted with Darwin's* (see p. 245). In many ways this vision is in accord with the Victorian ethical naturalisms espoused by Herbert Spencer, Darwin, and Alfred Russel Wallace. But like Thomas H. Huxley, she rejected analogical naturalism, the idea that evolutionary processes provided a model for human social progress, and denied that evolutionary principles could in themselves be taken as ethical principles.[66]

In addition to the title poem, *The Ascent of Man* volume consists of two other sections: 'Poems of the Open Air' and 'Love in Exile'. The poems in both sections exist in an implicitly dialogical relationship to the title poem. Most of the verses in 'Poems of the Open Air', for instance, hearken back to (and elicit nostalgia for) a pre-Darwinian conception of nature (as the epigraph from Coleridge that heads the section suggests). In so doing they invite the reader to confront the epistemic shifts that occurred in the long nineteenth century when pantheistic visions of nature gave way to scientific perspectives. As Blind put it in *Shelley's View of Nature Contrasted with Darwin's*, she and her late-century contemporaries were forced to acknowledge 'the oppression, strife, and cruelty, which seem to pervade all organic beings according to that dread law formulated by Darwin: "Let the strongest live and the weakest die"' (see p. 243). The sequence of poems in the 'Love in Exile' section, which includes twenty numbered poems subtitled 'Songs' followed by four individually titled lyrics, registers this seismic cultural shift through intimate expressions of personal loss. This section begins with an epigraph from Tennyson's *In Memoriam A. H. H.* (1850), whose famous phrase 'Nature, red in tooth and claw' anticipated the

[65] Anon., 'Interview. Miss Mathilde Blind', *Women's Penny Paper* (14 June 1890), p. 397. Mazzini especially encouraged Blind to read astronomy and geology since these would help her become familiar 'with the laws unfolded by that astonishing science [astronomy], and when you have grasped its elements, dive down, through geology, to the forces that have elaborated our globe' (Mathilde Blind, 'Personal Recollections of Mazzini', *Fortnightly Review* (May 1891), p. 707).

[66] See James Paradis, '"*Evolution and Ethics*" in its Victorian Context', in *Evolution and Ethics: T. H. Huxley's 'Evolution and Ethics' With New Essays on its Victorian and Sociobiological Context*, ed. by James Paradis and George C. Williams (Princeton: Princeton University Press, 1989), pp. 3–55.

troubling implications of Darwin's theory. Tennyson's poem grieves both the loss of a loved one and of faith in a benign universe, and thus Blind's allusion to Tennyson in the final section of *The Ascent of Man* is doubly appropriate. The lyrics in 'Love in Exile' give voice to feelings of isolation, exile, and unrequited love that echo those of Tennyson's lyric speaker.[67] They also implicitly link these personal griefs to broader cultural dislocations engendered by an increasingly naturalistic world view.

The following overview of *The Ascent of Man* will proceed by discussing significant details of the volume's history, including its composition, the original publication of some of its individual poems, the production of the original volume, its republication (in part and whole), and its posthumous reputation. It will then move on to analyse the historical and cultural contexts, ethical implications, and formal heterogeneity of the title poem, the most ambitious poetic work of Blind's career and a distinctively *fin-de-siècle* text.

Darwin engaged Blind's interest from the start of her career. In a letter to Blind (8 March 1871), Garnett alerts her to the latest 'uncommonly interesting' issue of the *Saturday Review*,[68] containing a review of *The Descent of Man, and Selection in Relation to Sex*, and two years later she began translating David Friedrich Strauss's last book, *The Old Faith and the New: A Confession*, which posits a 'Conception of the Universe' ruled by natural law adapted from Darwin's *On the Origin of Species by Means of Natural Selection, or the Preservation of Favoured Races in the Struggle for Life* (1859).[69] She later told an interviewer that in the summer of 1874 *Origin of Species* was 'almost my sole companion' during an extended stay in the Scottish Highlands.[70] Darwin's evolutionary theory would preoccupy her for much of her creative life, and in poems ranging from 'The Song of the Willi' (1871) to *Birds of Passage: Songs of the Orient and Occident* (1895) she would envision alternatives to Darwin's view of the female of the species summarized in volume II of *Descent*: 'Man is more powerful in body and mind than woman, and in the savage state he keeps her in a far more abject state of bondage than does the male of any other animal'.[71] She attended lectures on science throughout her life, including an 1876 talk by John Tyndall, at the time professor of physics at the Royal Institution of Great Britain in London and a vocal supporter of Darwin's theory of evolution.

---

[67] For Blind, an expatriate and atheist, the word 'exile' has special resonance. An entry in the commonplace book she kept between 1892 and 1896 expresses this succinctly: 'I have been an exile in this world. Without a God, without a country, without a family' ('The Commonplace Book of Mathilde Blind', Oxford, Bodleian Library, MS Walpole e.1., p. 23).
[68] Richard Garnett ALS to Mathilde Blind, Add. MS 61927, fols 113–16.
[69] Strauss, *The Old Faith and the New*, II, p. 42.
[70] Anon., 'Interview. Miss Mathilde Blind', *Women's Penny Paper* (14 June 1890), 397.
[71] Charles Darwin, *The Descent of Man, and Selection in Relation to Sex*, 2 vols (London: John Murray, 1871), II, p. 371.

By 1887, Blind had already written many of the poems that would constitute *The Ascent of Man*, including, as noted earlier, the sonnet 'Time's Shadow'. The two 'Red Sunsets, 1883' sonnets in the 'Poems of the Open Air' section, inspired by the atmospheric changes wrought by the eruption of the Krakatoa volcano in 1883, were composed around the time of the eruption. And in 1887, three more poems that became a part of *The Ascent of Man* appeared in Elizabeth Sharp's *Women's Voices. An Anthology of the most Characteristic Poems by English, Scotch, and Irish Women*: 'Wings', the prelude to the title poem; 'Nirvana', the penultimate sonnet of Part II of the title poem; and 'The Sower', from 'Poems of the Open Air'. On 27 April 1887 Blind read a draft of the title poem aloud to her close friend William Michael Rossetti (which he called 'a fine impressive thing'),[72] and the next year Symons read a manuscript version of the poem, writing to Katharine Bradley (who, with Edith Cooper, wrote poetry as Michael Field) that 'some of the city scenes' possess 'an agonizing vividness', adding that 'if it is all up to the level of what I have seen, the book *must* be noted when it is published'.[73]

The Ascent of Man arrived in London bookstores in early May 1889. It was widely and favourably reviewed in Britain and the United States, and Blind was the subject of two profiles (in *Woman* and *Women's Penny Paper*) that emphasized the impact of the book on the public and on Blind's increasing reputation.[74] Sections and editions of the volume continued to appear both during her lifetime and after her death in 1896. She included an expanded version of the 'Love in Exile' section in her 1893 volume *Songs and Sonnets*, which reappeared (with the order revised by Symons) in the first of Symons's two edited volumes of Blind's poetry, *Selection from the Poetry of Mathilde Blind* (1897). And the title poem appeared in the second, *The Poetical Works of Mathilde Blind* (1900). In 1899, T. Fisher Unwin brought out a new edition of *The Ascent of Man* with an introduction by the naturalist and biologist Alfred R. Wallace. Wallace, who conceived the theory of evolution through natural selection independently of Darwin (both read papers laying out their versions of the theory at the Linnean Society on 1 July 1858), had corresponded with Blind in the late 1880s. (Blind cited his work on evolution in her lecture *Shelley's View of Nature Contrasted with Darwin's*.) In his introduction Wallace writes that Tennyson was the first poet to take up the subject of evolution, but notes that Blind has made it the central theme of 'an important and lengthy poem,

---

[72] William Michael Rossetti, Diary, 26 April 1887, Vancouver, B.C., Angeli-Dennis Collection, University of British Columbia Library, Rare Books and Special Collections, Box 15, File 2.
[73] Arthur Symons, ALS to Katharine Bradley, 1888, Add. MS 46867, fol. 8. The letter does not include a month or day.
[74] Anon., 'Interview. Miss Mathilde Blind', *Women's Penny Paper* (14 June 1890), 397-98; Anon., 'A Chat with Mathilde Blind', *Woman* (3 July 1890), 1.

devoted more especially to Man — physical, intellectual, and spiritual — in his relation to the Cosmos, to the lower forms of life, and to the Deity'.[75]

By her choice of title alone, Blind announces that *The Ascent of Man* is in direct dialogue with the evolutionary theory of Charles Darwin, specifically *The Descent of Man*. But Darwin's earlier, epoch-making *Origin of Species* was in fact a more proximate influence. Two years after 'The Ascent of Man' appeared Blind, in an interview with *Hearth and Home*, described the effect *Origin* had on her when she first read it in 1874: 'the birds, the beasts, the sweet flowers even, seemed all engines of destruction, the universe appeared void, and death the only reality. It was then I thought out "The Ascent of Man", in which I dealt with the evolution of humanity, and the gradual development of love, pity, and justice which impart value to life'.[76] All three sections of the title poem register dismay at the universal struggle for existence that Darwin describes in the third chapter of *Origin of Species*:

> Nothing is easier than to admit in words the truth of the universal struggle for life, or more difficult — at least I have found it so — than constantly to bear this conclusion in mind. Yet unless it be thoroughly engrained in the mind, I am convinced that the whole economy of nature, with every fact on distribution, rarity, abundance, extinction, and variation, will be dimly seen or quite misunderstood. We behold the face of nature bright with gladness, we often see superabundance of food; we do not see, or we forget, that the birds which are idly singing round us mostly live on insects or seeds, and are thus constantly destroying life; or we forget how largely these songsters, or their eggs, or their nestlings, are destroyed by birds and beasts of prey.[77]

Echoes of this passage can be heard throughout the poem, as in this passage from Part I: 'The thickets scream with bird and beast | The love of life burns in their veins, | And from the mightiest to the least | Each preys upon the other's life | In inextinguishable strife' (see p. 59).[78]

In terms of its claims concerning gender, however, *The Descent of Man* was the work that most provoked Blind and other late-century women writers. 'The Ascent of Man' is a thoroughgoing rejection of Darwin's claim that women

---

[75] Alfred Russel Wallace, 'Introductory Note', *The Ascent of Man* (London: T. Fisher Unwin, 1899), p. v.
[76] Anon., 'Chats with Celebrities', *Hearth and Home* (24 December 1891), p. 165.
[77] Darwin, *On the Origin of Species by Means of Natural Selection, or the Preservation of Favoured Races in the Struggle for Life* (London: John Murray, 1859), p. 62.
[78] Blind had read and greatly admired John Stuart Mill's 1874 essay 'Nature', in which Mill argues that 'nature impales man, breaks him as on the wheel' (John Stuart Mill, *Three Essays on Religion* (New York: Henry Holt, 1874), pp. 3–68 (p. 29)). In a letter to Garnett (1 December 1874), Blind said of this essay 'how profoundly true are all the author's remarks about the relentlessness and inhumanity of nature — her aloofness, so it seems, from our morality' (Add. MS 61928, fols 40–41).

share the faculties and characteristics of 'the lower races, and therefore of a past and lower state of civilization', and that the 'general struggle for life' has rendered men superior to women not only in physical strength but also in all intellectual endeavours, 'whether requiring deep thought, or reason, or imagination'.[79] Linda K. Hughes has noted that if Darwin could be employed by conservatives to refute works like Mill's *On the Subjection of Women* 'by arguing that women's subordinate position was the fit outcome of natural selection, evolution could also suggest to feminists that women were evolving into a new and higher form'.[80] Female creative power — biological, moral, poetic — is central to 'The Ascent of Man' and its vision of ethical progress. In Part I, Blind audaciously links the violence of tectonic creation to childbirth, comparing the process whereby 'the rocky | Heights of confederate mountains' are 'upheaved in volcanic convulsion' from 'the womb of the waters' (see p. 56) to the physical upheaval of childbirth as well as other forms of redemptive female struggle. Part II ends with the sonnet 'Motherhood', which begins with this description of birth: 'From out the font of being, undefiled, | A life hath been upheaved with struggle and pain; | Safe in her arms a mother holds again | That dearest miracle — a new-born child' (see p. 91). As Isobel Armstrong has written of this passage, Blind 'may have been the first nineteenth-century woman poet to describe the birth of a child, where for a moment violence is productive'.[81] The phrase 'font of being' refers to the mother's womb, but the placement of the modifier 'undefiled' is intentionally ambiguous; Kathleen Hickok has noted that 'undefiled' can refer either to the mother or the child. 'If the former', Hickok writes, 'then this mother is the Virgin Mary herself; if the latter, then the poem stands in defiance of the doctrine of original sin.' Given the demythologizing emphasis of Blind's other poetry, it makes sense to read this sonnet, following Hickok, as 'an attempt to translate the myth of the Madonna into the experience of the ordinary woman', one that asserts that every mother's womb, and every new life, is 'undefiled'.[82]

In 'The Ascent of Man', Blind set out to write a feminist epic, an ambition announced in the opening lines of the poem, addressed to the poet herself: 'Ascend! take wing on the thoughts of the Dead, my Soul, | Breathing in colour and stone, flashing through epic and song: | Thoughts that like avalanche snows gather force as they roll, | Mighty to fashion and knead the phenomenal throng | Of generations of men as they thunder along' (see p. 51). Barbara Barrow notes that Blind 'uses the device of the bardic speaker to write the woman poet back

---

[79] Darwin, *The Descent of Man*, pp. 326-27, 858.
[80] Linda K. Hughes, '1870', in *A Companion to Victorian Literature and Culture*, ed. by Herbert Tucker (Oxford: Blackwell, 1999), pp. 35-50 (pp. 42-43).
[81] Isobel Armstrong, *Victorian Poetry: Poetry, Poetics and Politics* (New York: Routledge, 1993), p. 376.
[82] Kathleen Hickok, *Representations of Women: Nineteenth-Century British Women's Poetry* (Westport, CT: Greenwood Press, 1984), pp. 78-79.

into the male literary tradition and into geological prehistory' in order to 'revise the destructive process of species change which will be transformed by the feminized creator, or the "healing love of woman"'.[83] In place of a single epic hero, there are several individual heroines in the poem (ranging from a tree-dwelling 'hairy quadruped' to the pregnant Titan Latona, mother of Apollo and Diana), but the ur-heroine is the female poet, who in Part III is called upon by the 'Voice' of an evolving world-spirit (reminiscent of Swinburne's 'Hertha') to bring forth a new era of transformative poetics. This Voice, which has 'crystallized in granite rocks' for 'ages rolled o'er ages', briefly describes the earth before the speaker arose from 'the Ocean slime', and then issues this command to 'my heir and hope of my tomorrow': 'Oh, redeem me from my tiger rages, | Reptile greed, and foul hyæna lust; [...] | Till there break from passion of the Human | Morning-glory of transfigured life' (see p. 103). In Barrow's words, this 'feminized creator will usher in an epoch of transcendent poetics, working from "formless Chaos" and learning to "translate gross earth to luminous heaven"'.[84]

In addition to the feminist affirmation that characterizes 'The Ascent of Man', the poem also voices a form of neo-pagan aestheticism that Blind shared with many late-century writers, from Pater and the philosopher and mathematician W. K. Clifford[85] to three poets she counted as friends: Swinburne, Symons, and Rosamund Marriott Watson.[86] She imagines that poetry after Darwin can intimate an equally inspiring, if godless, form of transcendence. Symons was especially responsive to this aspect of the poem, however overheated his rhetoric in describing it: 'The Ascent of Man is a hymn to religious ecstasy; for

---

[83] Barbara Barrow, 'Deep Time and Epic Time in Alfred Tennyson's *In Memoriam* (1850), Matthew Arnold's *Empedocles on Etna* (1852), and Mathilde Blind's *The Ascent of Man* (1889)', *Nineteenth-Century Contexts*, 40 (2018), 115-31 (p. 125). Other readings of 'The Ascent of Man' as an epic include Katy Birch, '"Carrying Her Coyness to a Dangerous Pitch": Mathilde Blind and Darwinian Sexual Selection', *Women*, 24 (Spring 2013), 71-89; Helen Groth, 'Victorian Women Poets and Scientific Narratives', in *Women's Poetry, Late Romantic to Late Victorian*, ed. by Isobel Armstrong and Virginia Blain (Basingstoke: Macmillan, 1999), pp. 61-82; Lindsay Wilhelm, 'The Utopian Evolutionary Aestheticism of W. K. Clifford, Walter Pater, and Mathilde Blind', *Victorian Studies*, 59 (2016), 9-34; and Sara Lyons, 'Secularism and Secularisation at the Fin de Siècle', in *The Edinburgh Companion to Fin de Siècle Literature, Culture, and the Arts*, ed. by Josephine M. Guy (Edinburgh: Edinburgh University Press, 2017), pp. 124-45.
[84] 'Deep Time and Epic Time', p. 128.
[85] Clifford, and his wife Lucy (who became a best-selling novelist), were close friends with Blind. From his position on the faculty at University College London Clifford articulated a form of materialist idealism that informs all of Blind's writing, His lectures and writings argue that modern science is a liberating force, freeing individuals from stultifying social conventions and from the brute reality of nature. For more on the relationship between Clifford's ideas and Blind's poetry, see Wilhelm, 'The Utopian Evolutionary Aestheticism of W. K. Clifford'.
[86] Sara Lyons explores the pagan aestheticism of these poets in 'Secularism and Secularisation', pp. 138-40.

the scientific teaching of Darwin, to most people a very negative sort of gospel, inflamed her with the ardour of a worshipper; she believed it, by an act of faith, as the devout Christian believes in the mysteries of his church'.[87] Blind marries evolution and poetic form in 'The Ascent of Man' in such a way that life on earth aspires to the condition of metre, from 'A pulse stirred in the plastic slime' to 'Harmonies of confluent sound' that 'Lift you at one rhythmic bound | From the thraldom of the ground' (see p. 79). In Blind's evolutionary model, as Jason Rudy has written, humankind achieves 'a flaming world embrace' by accessing the metrical uniformity of a 'universal heart', a rhythmic beating with which every human being might sympathize.[88]

This is not to say that Blind's account of evolution ignores either the brutality of nature or humanity's repeated failure to transcend violence. These are recurrent themes in the poem. Rather, she asserts that the 'ascent of man', which for her combines faith in moral progress with a quasi-religious sublimity achievable through poetry, can survive in a post-Darwinian world. The opening of Part I, with its echo of Genesis, envisions evolutionary forces themselves as sources of the sublime: 'Struck out of dim fluctuant forces and shock of electrical vapour | Repelled and attracted the atoms flashed mingling in union primeval | And over the face of the waters far heaving in limitless twilight | Auroral pulsations thrilled faintly' (see p. 56). The violence of these natural forces is answered by the force of the human imagination, a 'fiery furnace' which chastens and subdues: 'The balm of Thought's divine control | And rapt absorption in the whole: | Delivery in the realm of art | Of the world-racked human heart — Forms and hues and sounds that make | Life grow lovelier for their sake' (see p. 78).

Blind's characterization of human thought as 'divine' is typical of her secularism, and it has deep intellectual roots. In her late teens and early twenties Blind read the work of Benedict Spinoza, a pioneer of demythologizing hermeneutics; Ludwig Feuerbach, whose *Essence of Christianity* George Eliot

---

[87] Arthur Symons, 'Introduction', *A Selection from the Poems of Mathilde Blind*, ed. by Arthur Symons (London: T. Fisher Unwin, 1897), p. v. Since 'The Ascent of Man' implicitly rebuts certain of Darwin's assumptions and claims, especially his generalizations about gender in *The Descent of Man*, Symons's claim here is misleadingly reductive.

[88] Jason Rudy, 'Rapturous Forms: Mathilde Blind's Darwinian Poetics', *Victorian Literature and Culture*, 34 (2006), 443–29 (p. 444). As Rudy notes, Blind's identification of poetry with the rhythms of the natural world derives in part from *The Descent of Man*, especially those sections of chapters 13 and 19 that deal with specific secondary sexual characteristics of birds and humans — voice and musical ability. See also Gregory Tate, 'Mathilde Blind: Rhythm, Energy, and Revolution', in *Nineteenth-Century Poetry and the Physical Sciences: Poetical Matter* (New York and Basingstoke: Palgrave Macmillan, 2020), pp. 185–222, who argues that Blind 'uses her knowledge of the physical sciences to postulate a kind of rhythmic communication that connects living organisms and non-living things across the universe' (p. 185).

translated in 1854; and David Friedrich Strauss. Like these thinkers, her appropriation of Christian language and tropes throughout her career is used to express and emphasize humanist ideals. When Blind concludes 'The Ascent of Man' with a 'Voice' proclaiming from the 'peaks of time' that 'From Man's martyrdom in slow convulsion | Will be born the infinite goodness — God' (see p. 103), 'God' in this context represents those human aspirations and ideals which the concept of a divine being personifies. Additionally, this godlike voice is a distinctly feminine creative principle, one that 'bore' and nurtured humanity, and it asserts that the 'healing love of woman' will ultimately 'transfigure' the horrors of nature and civilization.

Blind's secularism, though not her feminism, derives in part from *The Old Faith and the New*, in which Strauss abandons spiritual philosophy and fully embraces historical materialism. Strauss's book begins by answering the question 'Are We Still Christians?' in the negative, moves on to denying the supernaturalism that all faiths assert, then posits a 'Conception of the Universe' ruled by natural law. It concludes that our 'Rule of Life', to be guided by great art and artists, should be an ethical commitment to social improvement, guided by the 'cardinal virtues' of courage, justice, perseverance, and prudence.[89] In the 'Memoir' of Strauss Blind wrote for the second edition of *The Old Faith and the New* (1874) she traces Strauss's progress from piety to pantheism and then to his critical questioning of the Bible, noting the successive influence of Novalis, Schleiermacher, Kant, and Hegel on his developing ideas. Tellingly, Blind likens Strauss to a chemist, whose 'keen decomposing action of criticism acted as a solvent which reduced the apparently solidly-constructed and coherent story of the miraculous birth, actions, and resurrection of Jesus into the luminous but intangible fabric of the mythopoeic tendency of a people's collective imagination'.[90]

While 'The Ascent of Man' honours this mythopoeic impulse, it is unsparing in its critique of organized religion, and purposely parallels the violence of nature and the 'violent feud of clashing creeds' and 'lurid universal night' Christianity brought to the world. Its 'flame of mystical desires' embodies rather than transcending the predatory violence of nature, engendering 'fury fiercer than a leopard's' (see p. 71). So too does industrial capitalism, as is made abundantly clear in Part III of the poem. This section begins with the speaker repeating her journey at the beginning of the poem through 'forest glooms primeval', but now emerging into a modern city divided by poverty and class divisions. The speaker then tells the story of a woman driven to prostitution, declaring that contemporary life has in fact descended rather than ascended

---

[89] Strauss, *The Old Faith and the New*, I, p. 2, 42.
[90] Mathilde Blind, 'Memoir of David Friedrich Strauss', in Strauss, *The Old Faith and the New*, I, i–liii (pp. xxvi–xxvii).

from a state of nature, since the 'masquerade of culture' merely conceals what 'The frank ravening of the raw-necked vulture' makes nakedly manifest. Desponding, she calls on nature to 'let earth be split and cloven asunder | With man's still accumulating curse', declaring that 'Life is but a momentary blunder | In the cycle of the Universe' (see p. 101). She is saved from this despair by an immemorial 'Voice' who shapes rather than transcends nature, and who elevates the role of the poet in an ever-changing universe, 'Whose mighty potencies of verse | Move through the plastic Universe, | And fashion to their strenuous will | The world that is creating still' (see p. 79).[91]

This concluding emphasis on a world in constant flux, which echoes and brings to full circle the poem's opening account of planetary evolution, serves as a reminder that 'The Ascent of Man' is a poem in which Decadent elements exist alongside epic designs. In its preoccupation with violent upheaval and change — in nature and culture — as well as the dizzying array of stanza forms used to represent them, it resists closure. In his 'Memoir' of Blind, Garnett asserts that in writing 'The Ascent of Man' Blind 'produced [...] not indeed the desiderated epic, but a dithyramb'. There is more than a whiff of condescension in Garnett's characterization here, especially since he goes on to claim that the poem is 'here and there marred by grandiloquence and want of artistic form'.[92] But it is possible to see in his characterization a way of describing the poem's distinctively Decadent qualities.

A dithyramb is a Greek choric hymn, sung in honour of Dionysus, 'vehement and wild in character'.[93] This quality is especially evident in Part I of 'The Ascent of Man', where Blind envisions a natural world in which a libidinal fever flows in the veins of all creatures, 'beasts and birds, [...] floating fish and fleet-foot herds', without distinguishing between species or sexes. 'The lust of

---

[91] W. K. Clifford saw this same principle of flux operating in human beings: 'Human nature is fluent, it is constantly, though slowly changing, and the universe of human action is changing also' ('Cosmic Emotion', *Nineteenth Century*, 1 (1877), 411–29 (p. 420)). Three years after the publication of *The Ascent of Man*, Thomas H. Huxley presented his celebrated lecture 'Evolution and Ethics', which expresses a similar sense of the world in flux: 'The more we learn of the nature of things, the more evidence is it that what we call rest is only unperceived activity; that seeming peace is silent but strenuous battle. In every part, at every moment, the state of the cosmos is the expression of a transitory adjustment of contending forces' (Thomas H. Huxley, 'Evolution and Ethics', *The Second Romane Lecture* (London: Macmillan, 1893), p. 49).
[92] Garnett, 'Memoir', p. 35. Garnett may have had in mind C. C. Fauriel's characterization of Bertrand de Born's poetry, which Fauriel describes as 'martial dithyrambs, full of ardor, of high-mindedness and of a certain savage impetuosity' (*History of Provencal Poetry*, trans. by G. J. Adler (New York: Debry and Jackson, 1860), p.8). Blind read this work in preparing her 1873 *Examiner* review of John Rutherford's *The Troubadours: Their Loves and their Lyrics, Examiner* (15 November 1873), 1145–46.
[93] 'Dithyramb, n.', OED Online, Oxford University Press, March 2020 <www.oed.com/view/Entry/55957> [accessed 11 January 2021].

life's delirious fires | Burned like fever in their blood', Blind writes, adding that 'voluptuously the leopard lies', and 'stirs with intoxicating stress | The pulses of the leopardess' (see p. 58). Vadillo's description of *fin-de-siècle* poetic style as 'sensational excess' is particularly apt here.[94] It is also telling that the imagery Blind employs throughout the poem to represent sexual relations — in both the animal and human realms — often combines pain, predation, and strange beauty. In a letter to her friend and fellow poet John Todhunter, Blind describes her shock at confronting the pervasiveness and coexistence of these elements in all of nature, and uses Decadent imagery to do so:

> Blake asks very justly whether He who made the Lamb made the Tiger likewise. But why should we look upon the tiger as a symbol of especial cruelty? Those exquisite, flowerlike, half animate sea anemones are not a whit less merciless. To see them suddenly close like a tightly drawn sack upon a lot of little living creatures, to see these wildly struggling through the semi diaphanous substance in which they are entombed, is a shock to one's moral being.[95]

Swinburne was the English poet who had the earliest influence on Blind's verse, and her description of the leopard's 'intoxicating stress' stirring 'the pulses of the leopardess' calls to mind Swinburne's 1871 poem 'The End of a Month', whose speaker, obsessing over a failed affair, says that his beloved's 'savage stamp and savour hangs' onto his soul, 'The print and perfume of old passion, | The wild-beast mark of panther's fangs'.[96] Blind's Decadent style throughout the poem problematizes rather than supports the meliorism of the visionary 'Voice' in Part III, calling to mind David Weir's claim that 'Decadence is transition, a drama of unsettled aesthetics, [...] less a period of transition than a dynamics of transition'.[97] Moreover, when 'The Ascent of Man' is considered in relation to the other two sections in the volume, which as suggested earlier exist in a productive interpretive tension with the title poem, *The Ascent of Man* itself can be viewed as drama of unsettled aesthetics *and* ethics.

Dramas in Miniature

Dramas in Miniature appeared on bookstore shelves in October 1891. One year earlier, Blind had published her English translation of *The Journal of Marie Bashkirtseff*, which was widely discussed in the British press and placed both

---

[94] Parejo Vadillo, 'Poetries of Asceticism and Excess', p. 241.
[95] Mathilde Blind ALS to John Todhunter, 1 September 1880, Reading, University of Reading Library Special Collections, fols 230–32.
[96] 'The End of a Month', with an illustration by Simeon Solomon, *Dark Blue* (April 1871), p. 220. Blind's 'The Song of the Willi' appeared in the August issue.
[97] David Weir, *Decadence and the Making of Modernism* (Amherst: University of Massachusetts Press, 1995), pp. 14–15, 20.

women at the centre of debates about both Decadence and the New Woman.[98] In her introduction, and in language that anticipates the eight 'Dramas' given pride of place in her verse volume, Blind calls Bashkirtseff's story 'the drama of a woman's soul; at odds with destiny, as such a soul must needs be, when endowed with great powers and possibilities, under the present social conditions; where the wish to live, of letting whatever energies you possess have their full play in action, is continually thwarted by the impediments and restrictions of sex'. In recommending Bashkirtseff's journal to her English audience, Blind describes it in terms that could describe some of Robert Browning's dramatic monologues: 'To read it is an education in psychology. For in this startling record a human being has chosen to lay before us "the very pulse of the machine", to show us the momentary feelings and impulses, the uninvited back-stair thoughts passing like a breath across our consciousness, which we ignore for the most part when presenting our mental harvest to the public'.[99] Near the end of her journal, Bashkirtseff records an observation that also relates to Blind's 'Dramas'. Bashkirtseff has been writing about what happens when human nature is observed 'through the microscope', which she then turns on herself: 'I am neither painter, nor sculptor, nor musician; neither woman, nor daughter, nor friend. Everything reduces itself with me into subjects of observation, reflection, and analysis'.[100]

'Observation, reflection, and analysis', especially in relation to gender and

---

[98] One indication of the *Journal*'s wide reach is the spell it cast on William Gladstone. His 1889 essay on the original French edition, which he describes as 'a book without parallel', also recommends to his readers Mathilde Blind's 'vivid and striking' 1888 essay on the painter in *The Woman's World*, noting that it 'furnishes much needful information for such as may desire to obtain it' (W. E. Gladstone, 'Journal de Marie Bashkirtseff', *Nineteenth Century*, 126 (October 1889), 602–07 (p. 602)). He subsequently read Blind's English translation, which she presented to him in May 1890. Gladstone's interest in Bashkirtseff's autobiographical musings is extensively documented in the Gladstone Library in Hawarden, Flintshire, Wales, which contains his extensive annotations on the original French edition as well as Blind's presentation copy of her translation, inscribed to 'the Rt. Hon. W. E. Gladstone, M.P. with Mathilde Blind's Compliments May 1st 1890'.
[99] Blind, 'Introduction', *The Journal of Marie Bashkirtseff*, I, vii–xxxiv (p. vii).
[100] Bashkirtseff, *The Journal of Marie Bashkirtseff*, II, p. 451. Quoting this statement in her introduction, Blind makes it clear that she sees Bashkirtseff as a kindred poetic spirit. She asks rhetorically '[w]hat is this but saying in other words that she is a poet, a painter, a psychologist, and that her brain, in its enormous activity, draws to itself and consumes all the other elements of her being'. Blind then likens Bashkirtseff's self-description to Elizabeth Barrett Browning's poem 'A Musical Instrument' with its metaphor of 'the reed that has had the pith taken out of it, and henceforth gives forth the sweetest sounds at Pan's bidding, but will never grow again "as a reed with the reeds in the river"' (p. xv). In Part 2 of her essay on Bashkirtseff for *The Woman's World*, Blind quotes a passage from Bashkirtseff's diary that expresses another aspect of the painter's sensibility that appealed to Victorian aesthetes — her Paterian impulse to 'burn with a hard, gem-like flame': 'Even from my decease, I shall manage to extract some exquisite and delightful sensations' (Mathilde Blind, 'Marie Bashkirtseff, the Russian Painter', *Woman* (August 1888), p. 456).

INTRODUCTION 31

sexuality, are all at play in the eight poems in the first half of *Dramas in Miniature*. Six of these 'Dramas' are spoken by women. They include a nun whose midnight prayers both mask and channel her erotic desire ('The Mystic's Vision'); a dying prostitute who bitterly assails the sexual double standard ('The Message'); a seduced and abandoned mother who gives her illegitimate child up for adoption ('A Mother's Dream'); a proud courtesan who flaunts her sexual availability in public ('The Battle of Flowers'); and the ghost of a bride-to-be whose unconsummated desire for her lover not even death can quell ('The Song of the Willi').[101] 'Scherzo', the last of the 'Dramas' in this section of the volume, is spoken by a woman who has defiantly thrown off 'the impediments and restrictions of sex': she inverts conventional gender roles, appropriates the male gaze, and inhabits an 'unclouded sphere' of female sexual agency and choice (see p. 172). While the remaining two 'Dramas' feature male speakers ('The Russian Student's Tale' and 'A Carnival Episode'), their monologues lay bare the will to power underlying their fantasies of seduction. All of these poems (five are dramatic monologues, two are what James Phelan calls 'portraiture', and the last is a monodrama), invite the reader to observe, reflect on, and analyse the social conditions that condition (and corrupt) gender relations.[102] And all eight adopt the attitude toward their subjects that Robert Langbaum identifies with the perspective of the dramatic monologue generally: 'the literary equivalent of the scientific attitude [...], where men and women are the subject of investigation, the historicizing and psychologizing of judgment'.[103] Glennis Byron supplements Langbaum's broad definition in ways that apply particularly to Blind's 'Dramas', noting that in some cases Victorian women poets 'use the dramatic monologue as an instrument of criticism by giving a voice to

[101] 'The Song of the Willi' is the only poem in this section that was previously published — nearly twenty years earlier, in the *Dark Blue* (August 1871), pp. 741–45.
[102] 'Portraiture' in James Phelan's formulation occupies '[t]he space between narrativity and lyricality', and is 'a rhetorical design inviting the authorial audience to apprehend the revelation of character. [...] In portraiture, events typically are present, but not because they are essential to the progression of a story of change but because they are an effective means to reveal character. Change is not present, because portraiture is focused on depicting a character at a particular moment or a particular phase of life that we understand as ongoing' (*Experiencing Fiction: Judgments, Progressions, and the Rhetorical Theory of Narrative* (Columbus: The Ohio State University Press, 2007), p. 153). Phelan's concept of 'portraiture' describes two of Blind's 'Dramas': 'A Mother's Dream' and 'A Battle of Flowers'. Patricia Rigg argues for the use of 'monodrama' when describing poetry by women that makes use of a speaker distinct from the poet. She writes that in contrast to Robert Browning's dramatic monologues, 'dramatic poetry by women tends to be less specific in defining the speaker, thereby retaining an important attribute of lyric poetry and delineating a rather transparent dramatic "mask"' (Patricia Rigg, 'Augusta Webster: The Social Politics of Monodrama', *Victorian Review*, 29 (2000), 75–107, (p. 75)). 'Scherzo' is the only dramatic monologue in *Dramas in Miniature* that fits this description.
[103] Robert Langbaum, *The Poetry of Experience* (Chicago: Chicago University Press, 1957), p. 95.

marginalized figures'. In others the speaker's account of her or his situation 'is simultaneously offered for objective analysis, demonstrating and critiquing the cultural conditions which produce it'.[104]

Dramas in Miniature is divided into two sections, the first labelled 'Dramas in Miniature' and the second 'Lyrics'. By subsuming both her 'dramatic' and 'lyric' poems in a volume titled *Dramas in Miniature*, Blind is intentionally blurring the distinction between these two poetic genres. In effect, she is inviting her readers to think of all these poems as what Monique Morgan calls 'lyric narrative hybrids'.[105] Isobel Armstrong's concept of the 'double poem' is also relevant here — a poem in which the speaker's utterance is always also 'the *object* of analysis and critique. It is, as it were, reclassified as drama in the act of being literal lyric expression'.[106] In this regard it is worth noting that its position as the last 'drama' of the first section allows 'Scherzo' to function as a kind of bridge to the 'lyrics' that make up the second. A monodrama of female erotic desire, 'Scherzo' in one sense fully embraces the Romantic tradition of direct subjective expression. It begins with a direct expression of the speaker's desire for the presence of a lover: 'Oh, beloved, come and bring | All the flowery wealth of spring!' (see p. 172). But in the second half of the poem, this speaker relates the story of Diana's love for Endymion as a way of validating this desire. Blind thus makes use of narrative and dramatic elements that serve to 'objectify' the speaker's lyric effusion.

As Carol Christ notes, Victorian (and Modernist) poets reacted against the subjectivity they associated with Romanticism 'by attempting to objectify the materials of poetry', often turning to 'structures of myth and history which provide a narrative that contains and gives significance to personalities'.[107] Of the fifteen 'lyrics' in the volume three are narratives or include narrative elements; one ('A Child's Fancy') contains dialogue; and many rely on metaphorical indirection to express the speaker's feelings, from the use of vividly detailed landscape tableaux, to comparisons of the speakers to sleepwalkers, Tantalus, even a viola d'amore. Furthermore, the lyrics in this section employ a wide array of metrical patterns and verse forms, including iambic and trochaic dimeter, trimeter, tetrameter, and pentameter; quatrains, quintets,

---

[104] Glennis Byron, *Dramatic Monologue* (New York: Routledge, 2003), pp. 54, 64–65. For more on dramatic monologues written by women, see Dorothy Mermin, *The Audience in the Poem* (New Brunswick: Rutgers University Press, 1983); Cynthia Scheinberg, 'Recasting "sympathy and judgment": Amy Levy, Women Poets, and the Victorian Dramatic Monologue', *Victorian Poetry*, 35 (1997), 173–91; and Monique Morgan, 'Lyric Narrative Hybrids in Victorian Poetry', *Literature Compass*, 4 (2007), 917–34 <https://doi.org/10.1111/j.1741-4113.2007.00457> [accessed 11 January 2021].
[105] Morgan, 'Lyric Narrative Hybrids', p. 917.
[106] Armstrong, *Victorian Poetry*, p. 12.
[107] Carol T. Christ, *Victorian and Modern Poetics* (Chicago: University of Chicago Press, 1984), pp. 2–3, 3.

sexains, octets, and Spenserian stanzas, which foreground the formal qualities of each poem. Indeed, one of these lyrics, a sonnet, is titled 'Sonnet', verbally objectifying its form.

This 'Sonnet' alludes to Shakespeare's sonnet 18, whose speaker assures his beloved that 'thy eternal summer shall not fade' thanks to his immortalizing verse, which will live 'So long as men can breathe or eyes can see'. The speaker in Blind's sonnet, seeking to 'shield' her lover 'from time's fraying wear and tear', asks 'How save you, fairest, but to set you where | Mortality kills death in deathless art?' (see p. 178). Like many of the 'lyrics' in this section, this poem registers Blind's acute awareness of the tradition of English lyric poetry in which she is writing. Some ten months before she published *Dramas in Miniature*, Blind's friend and fellow poet Edmund Gosse published the essay 'Is Verse in Danger?'. Gosse writes that contemporary poets are so haunted by the poets of the past that the 'activity of the dead is paramount and threatens to paralyse original writing altogether', adding that many 'suggest that poetry has had its reign, its fascinating and imperial tyranny, and that it must now make way for the democracy of prose'. But Gosse goes on to assert the vitality of verse, and speculates that the 'poetry of the future' will represent more successfully than fiction the nature of human consciousness, those 'ephemeral shades of emotion which prose scarcely ventures to describe', those 'divisions and revulsions of sensation, ill-defined desires, gleams of intuition and the whole gamut of spiritual notes descending from exultation to despair'. Because 'untroubled by the necessity of formulating a creed, a theory, or a story', this poetry 'will describe with delicate accuracy, and under a veil of artistic beauty, the amazing, the unfamiliar, and even the portentous phenomena which it encounters'.[108] Gosse could here be describing the poems in *Dramas in Miniature*.

In fact, it was Blind's 'negative capability' in this volume, and especially the poems in its first section, that generated most interest in the contemporary press — and interpretive anxiety among male reviewers. Eric Robertson begins his review in *The Academy* by confessing his confusion over the title. 'Does it promise us real condensed drama — brief stories containing plots that a more diffuse writer might be glad to expand into a novel? Does it rather suggest a kind of toy-drama — stories of which the plots may be sharply articulated, while yet their interests are mock-heroic? Or, again, is it intended to denote nothing more than dramatic episodes?' As he confronts the poems themselves, it becomes clear that Robertson's unease stems more from their startling subject matter (pre-marital intercourse, eroticized religious reverie, prostitution, adultery, sexual violence, female sexual aggression) than from their generic affiliations.

---

[108] Edmund Gosse, 'Is Verse in Danger?', *Forum* (January 1891), 517–26 (pp. 517, 520, 524). For more on the friendship between Blind and Gosse, see Diedrick, *Mathilde Blind*, pp. 68, 122, 128, 144, 187.

Robertson is especially struck by the frankness of 'The Battle of Flowers', which he writes 'gives us a contrasting picture of the courtesan triumphant, as she drives along the Quai Anglais at Nice'. Sensing that Blind's own fearlessness in these 'Dramas' — her disinclination to moralize, her willingness to explore the desires of the flesh — will unsettle a wider audience, Robertson avers that 'most of her readers, will, indeed, continue to think that Miss Blind is at her highest in the earlier study of that "Ascent of Man", whose noble strenuousness is missing from the less profound "dramas" now published'.[109]

Symons attempts to impose a 'noble strenuousness' on *Dramas in Miniature* itself in his *Athenæum* review (see p. 266. Falsely asserting that all but one of the 'dramas' are rightly labelled 'tragedies', he adds 'they are tragedies of the kind which many people are apt to sum up, and, as they imagine, to condemn, in the one word "painful"'. Later in the review he comes much nearer the mark when he calls them 'flowers of evil', suggesting the ways in which many of these verses, like those of Baudelaire, provocatively commingle aestheticism and naturalism.[110] Symons ends his review by retreating to a generalization equating female creativity with artlessness — a generalization designed to reassure many male writers during the gender troubles of the 1890s. 'Miss Blind is pre-eminently successful as a writer of lyrics. In her lyrics she is "simple, sensuous, and passionate": she catches at times the heart's own rhythm in its troubled exquisite moments.'[111] While a few of the fifteen lyrics in the second section of the volume might be characterized this way, the variety of verse forms, personae, and themes they represent belie this generalization.

Although Symons's review questions the efficacy of her strategy, 'objectifying' many of the poems in *Dramas in Miniature* in the ways she did allowed Blind to explore transgressive ideas without being directly identified with them. The need for such a strategy becomes clear when reading Symons's December 1891 letter to Katherine Willard, who had written him to ask about Blind. Symons tells Willard that he has just sent her a copy of *Dramas in Miniature*, noting that it 'may interest you for other than its poetic quality when I tell you that

---

[109] Eric Robertson, Review of *Dramas in Miniature*, *The Academy*, 40 (12 December 1891), p. 531.
[110] In his 1862 review of Baudelaire's *Les Fleurs du Mal*, Swinburne identifies Baudelaire's focus as 'sad and strange things — the weariness of pain and the bitterness of pleasure — the perverse happiness and wayward sorrows of exceptional people' (Algernon Charles Swinburne, 'Charles Baudelaire: Les Fleurs du Mal', *Spectator* (6 September 1862), p. 999). This characterization also applies to the focus of many of Blind's 'dramas', although few of her speakers are 'exceptional'.
[111] [Unsigned], Arthur Symons, Review of *Dramas in Miniature*, *Athenæum* (21 May 1892), 659–60.

"The perfume of the breath of May
Had passed into her soul." p. 25.

Ford Madox Brown's frontispiece to *Dramas in Miniature* (Chatto & Windus, 1891)

the later poems, from "Scherzo" onwards some twenty pages are written about my humble self. [...] I would tell no one but you, for I confess it seems to me rather ridiculous to be sentimentalized over by a middle-aged woman, whom I appreciate as a friend, whom I admire as a writer, but whose demonstrations of affection are a little uncomfortable to me'.[112] As an unmarried woman holding radical views of sexual politics, Blind knew that some of her contemporaries viewed her as a threat to bourgeois sexual morality and would equate her with the speaker of poems like 'Scherzo'. If 'Scherzo' were included with the poems in section headed 'Lyrics', it would have been read as a direct expression of erotic desire — Blind's own. Her placement emphasizes its status as a monodrama representing and validating women as desiring subjects.

Since Symons's *Athenæum* review was anonymous, Blind was likely unaware that he was its author. Certainly, she continued to trust his friendship and advice, which began in 1888, when she was the established writer who helped Symons gain entry into London's most exclusive literary circles. They read and admired each other's poetry, and in 1892, the year Symons published *Silhouettes*, Blind reportedly announced to an older critic attending one of Ford Madox Brown's salons that Symons was 'the coming poet, the Poet of the New Time, for whom we were all looking'.[113] Along with Garnett, Symons became one of Blind's most trusted literary advisers, and in late August 1891, when she was reading proofs of the *Dramas in Miniature* manuscript, she wrote to Garnett from the Swiss Alps to report that the proofs were arriving 'much faster than I could wish as I should much have liked you or Arthur Symons to go over them in case of my overlooking misprints', adding 'I will send proofs to you and you could send me corrections which I can then make in the revise'.[114]

Another friend who aided Blind in the publication of *Dramas in Miniature* was Ford Madox Brown. Their friendship began in the 1860s, when Blind was a regular attendee at his famous Fitzroy Square salons, and it deepened in the subsequent two decades. They spent a great deal of time together, and Blind often lived with or near Brown and his wife Emma, both in Manchester and London. From 1889 to early 1891 she lived with them at their St Edmund's Terrace home in London while she was writing *Dramas in Miniature*.[115] Brown

---

[112] *Arthur Symons: Selected Letters, 1880–1935*, ed. by Karl Beckson and John M. Munro (Basingstoke and London: Macmillan, 1989), p. 91. Symons later regretted his treatment of Blind, writing to his future wife Rhoda Bowser in 1900 that 'she was very good to me and very fond of me, and I, as usual, very ungrateful. It horrifies me sometimes to think how badly, in one way or another, I have treated the people who have cared for me most' (qtd in Karl Beckson, *Arthur Symons: A Life* (Oxford: Clarendon Press, 1987), p. 186).

[113] Qtd in Ernest Rhys, *Everyman Remembers* (London: J. M. Dent and Sons, 1933), p. 111.

[114] Mathilde Blind ALS to Richard Garnett, 23 August 1890, Add. MS 61929, fols 70–71.

[115] Based on Blind's knowledge of Brown's paintings, the poet Rosamund Marriott Watson, who co-edited the short-lived *Art Weekly* in 1890, commissioned Blind to review one of Brown's exhibitions in London. See Mathilde Blind, 'Mr. Ford Madox Brown's Pictures at

was a fervent admirer of and proselytizer for Blind's poetry, and for *Dramas in Miniature* he drew a rendering of the deathbed scene of the prostitute Nellie from 'The Message' that became the frontispiece for the volume.[116]

Birds of Passage: Songs of the Orient and Occident

Birds of Passage: Songs of the Orient and Occident was published in May 1895 by Chatto & Windus, which had also published Blind's three previous volumes of verse. Before contracting with Chatto, however, Blind offered the manuscript to John Lane and Elkin Mathews. In an undated letter to Lane likely written in early 1895, Blind says that she stopped by his offices 'this afternoon to see what decision you had come to about my ms. "Echoe [sic], from the Nile"', adding, 'You will much oblige by an early answer'.[117] Lane and Mathews had published John Davidson's *Fleet Street Eclogues* and George Egerton's short story collection *Keynotes* in 1893,[118] and in 1894 began publishing the *Yellow Book*, where the work of many of Blind's friends and fellow poets was published — Symons, Davidson, Garnett, Gosse, Dollie Radford, Edith Nesbit, and Charlotte Mew. The content of *Birds of Passage* demonstrates why she thought it would have kept good company with the aesthetes, Decadents, and New Woman writers Lane and Mathews were publishing at this time. Symons himself recognized this, writing in his review that 'more than most women Miss Blind has lived her own life, has followed the dictates of her own individuality; now singing of the "Ascent of Man", now of the crofters, becoming a biographer for the sake of Madame Roland, a translator for the sake of Marie Bashkirtseff, a novelist in order to invent a new form for experiences and emotions which could scarcely have been rendered in any other way' (see p. 269).

Dowdeswell's', *Art Weekly* (19 April 1890), 70–71. The review focuses on the tenth of the twelve large murals Brown painted for Manchester City Hall, on display at this exhibition.

[116] Emma died in October of 1890, after which Brown and Blind were often together. In an eerie instance of visual doubling, Brown's drawing of Nellie (now lost) is based on two nearly identical colored chalk drawings of Emma he had made during her recovery from a serious illness in 1872, both titled 'Convalescent'. One of the two drawings is now held by the Birmingham Museum and Art Gallery, UK, the other at Metropolitan Museum of Art, New York. For more on the relationship between Blind and Brown, see Diedrick, *Mathilde Blind*.

[117] Mathilde Blind, ALS to John Lane, n.d., Harry Ransom Center, University of Texas at Austin.

[118] George Egerton was born Mary Chavelita Dunne Bright. The stories in *Keynotes* all assail the cult of female purity as a patriarchal construct designed to deny women autonomy and sexual freedom. The unexpected success of Egerton's book led Lane and Mathews to issue a series of novels as part of a 'Keynote' series, featuring such New Woman-themed novels and short story collections as Egerton's *Discords* (1894); Grant Allen's *The Woman Who Did* (1895); Victoria Cross's *The Woman Who Didn't* (1895); Ella D'Arcy's *Monochromes* (1895); and Edith Nesbit's *In Homespun* (1896).

The volume is divided into five sections: 'Prelude', 'Songs of the Orient', 'Songs of the Occident', 'Shakespeare Sonnets', and 'Miscellaneous Pieces'. Because of its musical connotations, 'Prelude' may seem to apply only to the second and third sections. In fact, it frames the entire volume, both in its imagery and themes. Most importantly, the literal avian migration that is the controlling imagery in the poem — the 'passage' from one region to another, followed by a return — becomes a metaphor for a cosmopolitan vision and a transnational impulse which the entire volume embraces. So too does the poem's celebration of the 'undaunted wing' of the birds' journeys as they 'face the fluctuant storm-winds and the elemental night' express the volume's embrace of both imaginative risk-taking and acceptance of fate. The final stanza of the 'Prelude', with its reminder of personal mortality, anticipates the final two poems in the volume's final section. The 'Prelude', along with the poems 'Rest' and 'Mystery of Mysteries', are fittingly valedictory expressions of Blind's antitheism and aestheticism, and a reminder that, like her friend Helen Zimmern, she was a close reader of Nietzsche. Nietzsche expressed his conception of *amor fati* (love of fate) in terms that describe the sensibility everywhere apparent in *Birds of Passage*: 'I want to learn more and more to see as beautiful what is necessary in things; then I shall be one of those who make things beautiful. *Amor fati*: let that be my love henceforth! I do not want to wage war against what is ugly. I do not want to accuse; I do not even want to accuse those who accuse. *Looking away* shall be my only negation. And all in all and on the whole: some day I wish to be only a Yes-sayer'.[119]

The poems in the 'Songs of the Orient' section of the volume were inspired and informed by two three-month visits Blind made to Egypt, the first in the spring of 1892 and the second in early 1894. She wrote to Garnett on 24 January 1894 that she had just reached Aswan and planned eventually to continue down the Nile to Luxor, which she visited on her 1892 trip, 'and go once more to those tombs and temples that surpass everything one sees elsewhere in grandeur and mystery'.[120] Blind's accounts of this second trip, and several of the poems in 'Songs of the Orient', express the perspective of what Ali Behdad has called a 'belated traveler', someone whose experience of the Orient is always already mediated by tourism and colonialism.[121] This is registered in multiple ways: Blind travelled in Egypt via Thomas Cook's steamers; she stayed at modern tourist hotels; she took with her volumes of poetry by her friends who had either

---

[119] Friedrich Nietzsche, *The Gay Science*, in *Basic Writings of Nietzsche*, ed. and trans. by Walter Kaufmann (New York: Modern Library, 1966), p. 714. Originally published in 1887 as *Die fröhliche Wissenschaft*, and sometimes translated as *The Joyful Wisdom* or *The Joyous Science*.
[120] Mathilde Blind ALS to Richard Garnett, Add. MS 61929, fols 104–06.
[121] Ali Behdad, *Belated Travelers: Orientalism in the Age of Colonial Dissolution* (Durham, NC: Duke University Press, 1994), pp. 41–43.

literally or imaginatively been there before her — from Garnett's *Io in Egypt* (which she first read in 1873 and praises anew in her letter to him) to James ('B. V.') Thomson's 'A Voice from the Nile' (1881), which Garnett recommended she read as inspiration for her own poetry.[122] Her letter to her friend Lily Wolfsohn during her second trip also expresses a sense of disappointment, while acknowledging the emotional tonic provided by the change of geography and climate in the wake of Ford Madox Brown's death in 1893: 'Perhaps the sunshine and brightness of Egypt were the best antidote to the grief caused me by Madox Brown's death. But, perhaps owing to mental as well as physical causes, Egypt has not quite realized my expectations'.[123]

While some of the poems in *Birds of Passage*, most notably 'The Beautiful Beeshareen Boy', express Blind's anticolonial perspective, the volume as a whole is not primarily a volume of anticolonial verse — at least not in the mode of *The Heather on Fire*.[124] (As Robert Fletcher rightly notes, at times Blind 'participates in ideologies of imperialism', demonstrating 'how the subjectivity of an independent woman in the Victorian period — or at least the subjectivity constructed in a book of her verse — may be reliant nevertheless on binaries of "East" and "West" fundamental to imperialist ideology'.[125]) Instead, New Woman and Decadent tropes and themes dominate the volume, and Blind employs a wide variety of verse forms to express her unique synthesis of these intertwined discourses. Of the twenty 'Songs of the Orient', 'Nuit' represents her most radical appropriation of Decadent conventions, and it embodies the revisionist spirit that characterizes many of the poems in the volume. Blind explains in a note that the title refers to 'one of the names for the primeval night of Egyptian mythology', and then quotes an inscription 'cut on the floor of the mummy-case of Mykerinos, the builder of the third great Pyramid: "Thy Mother Nuit has spread herself out over thee in her name of Mystery of the Heavens"' (see p. 193). Blind places this mother at the centre of a radical cosmology in the poem. While on her second trip to Egypt, Blind wrote to Garnett asking him to send her a copy of Max Müller's *Comparative Mythology* (1856). 'It would be extremely interesting to read it here with the old gods of Egypt confronting me everywhere'.[126] 'Nuit' inverts (and subverts) Müller's account of primeval Night — a Christianized narrative in which a pious male

---

[122] Richard Garnett ALS to Mathilde Blind, 23 December 1894, Add. MS 61929, fol. 130.
[123] Qtd in Garnett, 'Memoir', *The Poetical Works of Mathilde Blind*, p. 38.
[124] See Katherine E. Ostdiek, 'Mathilde Blind, the Highland Clearances, and the "Trappings of Nationality" in the British Isles', *Journal of the Midwest Modern Language Association*, 51.2 (2018), 137–68.
[125] Robert Fletcher, '"Heir of all the Universe": Evolutionary Epistemology in Mathilde Blind's Birds of Passage: Songs of the Orient and Occident', *Victorian Poetry*, 43.4 (2005), 435–53 (p. 436).
[126] Mathilde Blind ALS to Richard Garnett, 24 January 1894, Add. MS 61929, fols 104–06.

worshipper watches 'the dark heaving night' as she brings forth her 'bright son, the sun of the day'.[127]

The same revisionist spirit is present in 'The New Proserpine', from 'Songs of the Occident'. As Margot K. Louis has written, this poem 'challenges the whole tradition of male poetry on goddess figures', most significantly Swinburne's 'The Garden of Proserpine', which Blind knew well. As Louis also notes, it is no accident that the very title of this poem alludes to 'the "New Woman" of the era'. The final stanza of the poem imagines the consciousness of a human woman who 'might'st have been that Queen of Sighs, | Love-bound by Hades' dreadful spell; | For veiled within thy heaven-blue eyes, | There lay the Memory of Hell' (see p. 213). In contrast to poems about Proserpine by Tennyson, Arnold, and Swinburne, Blind here restores subjectivity to a goddess who in their poems simply symbolizes beauty and harmony or their opposites. In so doing she emphasizes, as Louis notes, 'how women have been mis-seen and misinterpreted'.[128] 'The New Proserpine' functions as a kind of echoing counterpart to 'Nuit', as do many of the implicitly paired poems in the volume's first two sections. The sympathy the speaker expresses for 'Mourning Women' in 'Songs of the Orient', for instance, 'whom your prophet dooms | To take love's penalties without its prize!' (see p. 210) is echoed in 'Noonday Rest' from 'Songs of the Occident', about a seduced and abandoned woman and her infant on Hampstead Heath. Fletcher emphasizes that Blind's sympathy with the Muslim women in the former poem reflects not only her demythologizing impulse but also her tendency 'to assign Egyptian culture the status of ancient, static, pre-modern Other',[129] but it is worth noting that Blind also scorns the Judeo-Christian God who has 'no pity' on the 'nameless castaway' of the latter poem (see p. 222).

Birds of Passage also embodies and expresses Blind's 'rooted cosmopolitanism', as is clear from the eight 'Shakespeare Sonnets' in its penultimate section. Among other things, these poems constitute the expatriate Blind's assertion of her self-conception as an English writer. Her interest in Shakespeare can be traced to the beginning of her career: she began her correspondence with Garnett in 1869 by asking questions about the chronology of Shakespeare's plays, and read an edition of Coleridge's *Notes and Lectures Upon Shakespeare* (1849) at his suggestion. During her visit to Stratford-upon-Avon in 1894, she wrote to him imagining the area in Shakespeare's time: 'how plentiful wood

---

[127] Max Müller, 'Comparative Mythology', in *Selected Essays on Language, Mythology and Religion* (London: Longmans, Green, 1881), pp. 299–424 (p. 401).
[128] Margot K. Louis, *Persephone Rises, 1860–1927: Mythography, Gender, and the Creation of a New Spirituality* (Burlington, VT: Ashgate, 2009), pp. 72–73.
[129] Fletcher, '"Heir of all the Universe"', p. 452. As Fletcher notes, Blind 'participates in the Orientalist historiography of Islamic women', adopting the 'spurious' idea that Islamic doctrine asserts that women have no souls (p. 453).

must have been [...] when all these villages and hamlets were still emblossomed in the green recesses of the Forest of Arden. One seems to come upon Shakespeare's tracks here and to get in closer touch with him and such plays as "As You Like It," "Midsummer Night's Dream," etc. etc.'.[130]

Blind brings her own distinctive sensibility to these sonnets, immediately apparent in the first two, which focus not on Shakespeare himself but on his wife, Anne Hathaway. In Blind's original version of the octave in the second sonnet, 'Anne Hathaway', Anne is the desiring subject: 'She leaped into his arms, with arms all bare, | Flung round him in a perfect lover's knot' (see p. 224 n. 2). Following Garnett's dubious literary advice, Blind revised the octave, diminishing both the status of Anne and the erotic charge of the poem itself. Anne is reduced to his subordinate rather than his equal, and her agency is reduced to passivity as she 'Clung round him in a perfect lover's knot' (see p. 225). In the last sonnet in this sequence, 'Cedars of Lebanon at Warwick Castle', about the landscape surrounding this medieval castle (originally built by William the Conqueror in 1068), Blind brings a transnational, obliquely personal perspective to bear on what might seem like a simple landscape poem. The trees of the poem's title, for instance, signal the sonnet's rejection of the religious and nationalist binaries that sustain imperial discourse.[131] The trees' provenance in the eastern Mediterranean might remind a reader that William's eldest son Robert was one of the leaders of the first crusade; Blind's use of the verbs 'fired', 'rushed', and 'poured' in describing England's participation in the crusades implies a frenzied, irrational response to Rome's call for a holy war on Muslims in the Middle East (see p. 228). Moreover, as part of a sonnet sequence about Shakespeare, Blind may assume readers are aware that in *Henry IV Part 1*, King Henry's announced desire for another crusade to Jerusalem is revealed as a ploy to distract his subjects from domestic civil war. On an autobiographical level, the cedars themselves are a foreign species that have nonetheless come to thrive in this landscape. Not unlike such cosmopolitans as Blind herself, they have found a new home even while missing their lost homeland (see p. 228, n. 13).

Blind died a year and a half after *Birds of Passage* was published, and she was clearly aware of her own mortality as she arranged the poems in her final volume.[132] The last two poems in the 'Miscellaneous Pieces' section — 'Rest'

---

[130] Mathilde Blind ALS to Richard Garnett, 21 September 1894, Add. MS 61929, fols 122–24.
[131] Cedars of Lebanon are native to the mountains of the eastern Mediterranean basin and can grow to be over thirty metres tall and twenty-four metres wide. They were introduced to England in 1638, and the Warwick Castle grounds boast several of the finest specimens in Great Britain.
[132] The certificate recording Blind's death indicates 'uterine cancer 10 months' as the cause of death, and notes that her step-sister Ottilie was present at her deathbed (General Register Office, London, 30 November 1896, no. 109).

and 'Mystery of Mysteries' — are valedictory verses. The last line of the first poem appropriates a religious term to express a humanist wish as the speaker genuflects before death to seek 'the absolution of the grave' (see p. 235). The second begins by echoing the last line of the first, this time referring to the 'unanswering grave'. But it ends by wondering if some kind of 'life' will 'from Life's disguises break' as it is 'Called to that vast confederacy of minds | Which casts all flesh as chaff to all the winds' (see p. 235). The rhyme is imperfect, but this closing poem of the volume perfectly expresses the antitheistic idealism that characterizes Blind's entire poetic career.

Shelley's View of Nature Contrasted with Darwin's

On 10 November 1886 Blind took the stage in a University College London lecture hall to deliver 'Shelley's View of Nature Contrasted with Darwin's' to members of the Shelley Society.[133] The Society, whose membership included Garnett, George Bernard Shaw, William Michael Rossetti, John Todhunter, and Eleanor Marx, was formed in 1885, and by 1887 it had 400 members.[134] Blind's lecture, subsequently published in the Shelley Society Papers, illuminates her aims in 'The Ascent of Man'; it is also important in demonstrating the intersecting lines connecting science and aestheticism in late-Victorian culture. The first poems Blind published under her own name, 'Nocturne' and 'The Song of the Willi' (see pp. 49, 167), are steeped in the aesthetic theory of Pater and the aesthetic practice of Morris, and Pater's theory was in part his way of responding to the same sense of flux and impermanence revealed by science that Blind confronts in this lecture and in 'The Ascent of Man'. 'To regard all things and principles of things as inconstant modes or fashions has more and more become the tendency of modern thought', Pater writes in his 1868 essay 'Poems by William Morris'. He calls our physical life 'a perpetual motion' of 'natural elements' and adds: 'Far out on every side of us these elements are broadcast, driven by many forces; and birth and gesture and death and the

---

[133] William Michael Rosetti noted the event in his diary: 'Mathilde Blind read her paper on Shelley and Darwin: I liked it well, + she declaimed the poetic quotations with feeling and effect. I was in the chair, and made a couple of speeches — also Furnivall, Garnett, Forman, and Todhunter, spoke' (William Michael Rossetti, Diary, 10 November 1886, Angeli-Dennis Collection, Box 15, File 2.) F. J. Furnivall was a lawyer and philologist who founded the society; Buxton Forman was a bibliographer (of Keats and Shelley) and bookseller who was later discovered to have perpetrated a number of literary forgeries.

[134] Angela Dunstan, 'The Shelley Society, Literary Lectures, and the Global Circulation of English Literature and Scholarly Practice', *MLQ*, 75 (2014), 279-96 (p. 282). The Society was most active during the decade of the 1880s, and caused something of a scandal six months before Blind delivered her lecture by staging a production of Shelley's *The Cenci*, a play about incestuous rape and patricide, which Oscar Wilde attended and praised (Oscar Wilde, 'The Cenci', *Dramatic Review* (15 May 1886), 66-69).

springing of violets from the grave are but a few out of ten thousand resulting combinations'. While acknowledging that '[s]uch thoughts seem desolate at first', Pater affirms the 'splendour of our experience' in the face of 'its awful brevity'.[135]

Both Pater and Blind see art and artists as providing a way of valorizing individual experience and faith despite what Blind in her lecture calls 'the dread law formulated by Darwin: "Let the strongest live and the weakest die"' (see p. 243). The aim of 'The Ascent of Man', as noted earlier, is emancipation from this desolate Darwinian vision — 'delivery in the realm of art' (see p. 78). Her allied purpose in her lecture is twofold. The first is to recognize that 'Shelley [...] never quite looked Nature in the face', meaning that his Rousseauian idealism located the source of human depravity in social structures that alienate individuals from a benign nature. By contrast, her lecture and poem acknowledge that nature itself is a site of competition and predation, that 'the original bias of humanity' spawned infanticide, slavery, and oppression of women, while maintaining that social and moral evolution will enable humanity to counteract this 'bias'. Secondly, she presents Shelley as an embodiment of the post-Darwinian poet's role precisely because of what she calls his 'beautiful idealisms, [...] his glowing anticipation of a better future in store for humanity'. She ultimately aligns Shelley and Darwin, asserting a 'junction of their views in the glorious vistas they disclose of ever higher types of life replacing those that had gone before' (see p. 246). In doing so, she is also aligning Shelley with her own project in 'The Ascent of Man'.

Reviews

In addition to this and her earlier lectures, Blind was active as a reviewer and essayist throughout her career.[136] The acclaim that greeted her 1871 *Westminster Review* essay on Rossetti's edition of Shelley's poetry brought her to the attention of several London journal editors, and in 1872 she began a fifteen-year stint as

---

[135] Walter Pater, 'Poems by William Morris', p. 312. Kate Hext relates Pater's later work to late-century Decadence; the same year Blind delivered her lecture, Pater published *Imaginary Portraits*, where his depictions of nature, in Hext's words, encourage the reader 'to envisage evolution with the perverse pleasure of a decadent' (*Walter Pater: Individualism and Aesthetic Philosophy* (Edinburgh: Edinburgh University Press, 2013), p. 137).

[136] Blind also published a novel, *Tarantella*, in 1885, and two short stories: 'A Month at the Achensee', *Dark Blue* (October 1872), 227–38, and 'At Cross Purposes', *Black and White* (14 May 1892), 641–45. The latter is a New Woman-themed short story about an aspiring landscape painter who achieves fame when one of her paintings is selected for exhibition at the Royal Academy in London. See James Diedrick, 'Mathilde Blind's (Proto-) New Women', *The Latchkey: Journal of New Woman Studies*, 9 (2017/18) <http://www.thelatchkey.org/Latchkey9/essay/Diedrick.htm> [accessed 11 January 2021].

a regular staff reviewer for the *Athenæum*.[137] Her first review was a scathing notice of Denis Florence MacCarthy's *Shelley's Early Life, from Original Sources* (1872), the first of four reviews of editions or biographies of Shelley. More often she reviewed volumes of poetry for the journal — by William Morris (see p. 249), Frances Anne Kemble, Richard Watson Dixon, Thomas Woolner, and many minor poets.[138] Blind also wrote five signed reviews for *The Examiner* in 1873 and 1874, which included Arthur O'Shaughnessy's *Music and Moonlight: Poems and Songs* (1874) and Augusta Webster's *Yu-Pe-La's Lute: A Chinese Tale in English Verse* (1874) (see pp. 254, 257).[139] The three poetry reviews included in this volume have been chosen to illustrate her aestheticism, her knowledge of poetic form, her abiding interest in the lyric, and her cosmopolitan sensibility. Beyond these critical appraisals, Blind wrote essays on a wide variety of subjects (the maxims of Goethe, Mary Wollstonecraft, John Trelawny, Holman Hunt, the Celtic legend of Tristram and Iseult, Mazzini, Marie Bashkirtseff) for *Fraser's Magazine*, *New Quarterly Magazine*, *Whitehall Review*, *National Review*, *The Woman's World*, *Art Weekly*, *Fortnightly Review*, and *Black and White*. Her 1878 *New Quarterly Magazine* essay on Wollstonecraft was an important contribution to the late-Victorian rehabilitation of Mary Wollstonecraft's reputation, which continued with Elizabeth Robbins Pennell's 1884 biography (reviewed by Blind for the *Athenæum*) and an 1891 republication of Wollstonecraft's *A Vindication of the Rights of Woman* (1792) with an introduction by the suffragist Millicent Fawcett.

---

[137] In 1871 Charles Dilke, the radical MP and *Athenæum* publisher, appointed Norman MacColl as editor, himself a political, social, and literary progressive. MacColl opened the *Athenæum* to new ideas, choosing reviewers open to such movements as Darwinism and Pre-Raphaelitism. Under MacColl the journal, founded in 1823, experienced a renaissance in quality, becoming noted for its scholarship, even-handedness, and cosmopolitan outlook. MacColl recruited reviewers for their expertise and their willingness to criticize rather than simply promote books. Most importantly for Blind, he appointed many women as reviewers, who in addition to Blind included Augusta Webster, Millicent Garrett Fawcett, Rosamund Marriott Watson, Vernon Lee, and A. Mary F. Robinson.

[138] In keeping with the journal's editorial policy, all these reviews were unsigned, but Blind's authorship is noted in the editor's 'marked file' of the journal, held by the library of the City University of London.

[139] For unknown reasons, Blind was unceremoniously dismissed from the journal when William Minto took over as editor in 1874. In a 22 November 1875 letter to Swinburne, William Michael Rossetti criticized Minto's action: 'I wish he had not, on taking possession of the Examiner forthwith ousted our good friend and really capable critic Miss Blind from her post of contributor of poetical critiques. He undertook, I believe, to do most of these himself — to which of course no outsider can start the least objection: but I do think it seemed harsh — and ill-judged as well — never to give Mathilde the least further employment of any kind' (*Selected Letters of William Michael Rossetti*, p. 331).

Critical Responses

Blind's poetry was widely reviewed by her contemporaries, increasingly so in the 1880s and 1890s. Six of the seven reviews included here illustrate the range of responses generated by the three volumes of poetry in this volume. The seventh — a review by Edith Nesbit of Symons's *A Selection from the Poems of Mathilde Blind* (1897) — is featured in part because it is one of the few by one of Blind's fellow New Woman writers. The other review by a woman in this section — Louise Chandler Moulton's notice of *The Ascent of Man* in the *Boston Herald* — indicates that Blind's poetry reached across the Atlantic. Among the male reviewers gathered here, Symons's *Athenæum* reviews of *Dramas in Miniature* and *Birds of Passage* are significant because of his role in shaping her literary legacy both during her lifetime and beyond. Blind named him her literary executor a year or so before she died, and he edited both *A Selection from the Poems of Mathilde Blind* (1897) and *The Poetical Works of Mathilde Blind* (1900). Because all *Athenæum* reviews were anonymous, Blind was likely unaware of Symons's decidedly mixed reviews there (by contrast, his signed review of her translation of *The Journal of Marie Bashkirtseff* in *The Academy* is fulsome in its praise).[140] Certainly she would have been pained by his complaint when reviewing *Birds of Passage* that her poetry is often 'careless and unfinished' (see p. 269). She would likely have taken even more offence at his exclusion of all of her dramatic monologues and monodramas from his 1897 edition, an editorial decision that made it easier for him to condescendingly claim in his introduction that Blind was 'a poet, almost in spite of herself [...] it was direct, and not directed, emotion which gave her verse its share of that rapture without which poetry cannot exist'.[141] Readers who consult the full range of poems and verse forms in this volume have a wider range of Blind's poetic forms on which to base their own judgments.

A Note on the Texts

This edition reproduces in full the last three volumes of original verse Mathilde Blind published in her lifetime: *The Ascent of Man* (London: Chatto & Windus, 1889), *Dramas in Miniature* (London: Chatto & Windus, 1891), and *Birds of Passage: Songs of the Orient and Occident* (London: Chatto & Windus, 1895). It also reprints two poems originally published in magazines: 'Nocturne' (*Dark Blue* (March 1872), pp. 25–26) and 'Sea-Music' (*The Savoy* (January 1896), p. 111, reprinted in *The Poetical Works of Mathilde Blind*, edited by Arthur Symons

---

[140] In the lead review of the issue, Symons calls Blind's translation a 'genuine triumph [...] almost as living as the original', adding that it 'reads like a book originally written in English' (*The Academy* (5 July 1890), p. 5).
[141] Symons, 'Introduction', p. vi.

(London: T. Fisher Unwin, 1900), p. 438). And it includes her 1886 lecture *Shelley's View of Nature Contrasted with Darwin's*, published the same year by the Shelley Society, along with three of her reviews.

These texts have been lightly modernized, specifically in relation to typographical presentation and punctuation. Titles and first words of poems capitalized in the original texts have been converted to lower-case forms; I have also removed full stops from poem and section titles. All double quotation marks have been converted to single marks, and book titles enclosed by double quotation marks have been converted to italics. I have retained Blind's spellings ('engulphs', 'seamstress', for example); her conversion of nouns into verbs ('impearled'); her tendency to separate words like 'for ever'; and her irregular use of hyphenation, wherein she hyphenates 'water-side' but not 'to day').

When individual poems were published before appearing in the volumes, footnotes indicate the place and date of the original publication.

The section titled 'Selected Prose and Critical Responses' includes an annotated selection of Blind's prose: her reviews of poetry by William Morris, Arthur O'Shaughnessy, and Augusta Webster, and her lecture *Shelley's View of Nature Contrasted with Darwin's*. This is followed by seven reviews of Blind's poetry by her contemporaries. Because these reviews often include lengthy quotations from her poetry, the longer quotations have been replaced with parenthetical notes indicating where these passages appear in this volume.

Mathilde Blind: Chronology

1841	Birth of Mathilda Cohen, 21 March — daughter of Jacob Abraham and Friederike Cohen.
1847	Travels to Bavaria with her mother, brother Ferdinand (born 1834), and the revolutionary Karl Blind.
1848	Father dies in October. Karl Blind becomes a leader of the Baden Uprising; he and Friederike marry. Friederike moves to Belgium with Mathilde and Ferdinand. In August, Karl Blind is expelled from Germany, France, and Belgium for revolutionary activities. He is granted political asylum in England.
1849	Takes the last name of her stepfather.
1851	Attends boarding school in Brussels.
1852	Writes the first of her surviving poems, a birthday ode to her mother in German, and the first document she signs 'Mathilde'. The family joins Karl Blind in London in the fall, settling in St John's Wood.
1855	Attends The Ladies' Institute, a day school on Adelaide Road.
1857	Travels to Zurich, studies with philosopher and Sanskrit scholar Kuno Fischer.

1860	Back in London, begins programme of self-education and becomes acquainted with radical exiles including Giuseppe Mazzini, who frequented her parents' house.
1866	Goes into mourning after her brother Ferdinand commits suicide in prison following a failed attempt to assassinate Otto von Bismarck, Minister-President of Prussia.
1867	Publishes *Poems* under the pseudonym 'Claude Lake'.
1868	Becomes friends with a group of artists and writers, including Algernon Charles Swinburne, William Michael Rossetti, and Catherine, Lucy, Emma, and Ford Madox Brown; regularly attends salons hosted by Brown.
1870	Delivers lecture on Shelley, 9 January, and on the *Volsunga Saga*, translated by William Morris and Eiríkr Magnússon, 25 May. Publishes a review of *The Poetical Works of Percy Bysshe Shelley*, with notes and a memoir by W. M. Rossetti, in the *Westminster Review* in July.
1871	Contributes signed essays, poems, and a short story to the magazine *Dark Blue*.
1872	Edits and writes the introduction for *A Selection from the Poems of Percy Bysshe Shelley*. Begins publishing reviews and poems in the *Athenæum*.
1873	Publishes translation of *Der Alte und der Neue Glaube: Ein Bekenntnis* (*The Old Faith and the New: A Confession*) by David Friedrich Strauss. For third edition in 1874, adds a biographical essay on Strauss.
1878	Publishes 'Mary Wollstonecraft', *New Quarterly Magazine*.
1881	Publishes *The Prophecy of St. Oran and Other Poems*.
1883	Publishes *George Eliot*, the first biography of the novelist.
1885	Publishes *Tarantella: A Romance*, her only novel.
1886	Publishes narrative poem *The Heather on Fire: A Tale of the Highland Clearances*, and *Madame Roland*, her biography of the influential member of the Girondist faction during the French Revolution. Edits and writes the introduction to a two-volume edition of *The Poetical Works of Lord Byron* for the Canterbury Poets series. Delivers the lecture *Shelley's View of Nature Contrasted with Darwin's* at University College London.
1887	Edits and writes the introduction for a selection of *The Letters of Lord Byron*.
1888	Publishes profile 'Marie Bashkirtseff, The Russian Painter' in *The Woman's World*, the magazine edited by Oscar Wilde.
1889	Publishes *The Ascent of Man*.

1890	Publishes translation of *Journal de Marie Bashkirtseff* (*The Journal of Marie Bashkirtseff*).
1891	Publishes *Dramas in Miniature*.
1893	Publishes *Songs and Sonnets*. Elected president of the Women Writers' Dinner.
1895	Publishes *Birds of Passage: Songs of the Orient and Occident*.
1896	Publishes the sonnet 'Sea-Music' in the inaugural issue of *The Savoy*, edited by Arthur Symons. Dies in London, 26 November.
1897	Publication of *A Selection from the Poems of Mathilde Blind*, edited by Symons.
1898	Unveiling of Mathilde Blind monument in St Pancras and Islington Cemetery, designed by French sculptor Edouard Lanteri.
1899	Publication of new edition of *The Ascent of Man*, with introduction by the evolutionary biologist Alfred R. Wallace.
1900	Publication of *The Poetical Works of Mathilde Blind*, edited by Symons, with a memoir by Richard Garnett.
1902	Publication of *Shakespeare Sonnets*, originally published in *Birds of Passage*.

Nocturne[1]

The sweet breeze freshened, the moon shone bright;
We pushed out to sea at the dead of night,
At the dead of night, when the heart beats free,
My Love and I we pushed out to sea.

And wood and valley and hill and stream
As the waning forms of a broken dream,
Or the dying fall of a mournful lay,
Afar in the moonlight faded away.

And speeding swift from the haunts of men,
Our light boat bore our light hearts then,
Swanlike sailing, with wings outspread,
Under the arch of the stars overhead.

The moon, and the small stars caught in her rays,
Struggling pale through the luminous haze,
Saw how fair was my Love, and came
Wandering round her in high-bleached flame.

The sea, and the waves in their fall and rise,
Bosomlike heaving with languid sighs,
Lifted, and tumbled, and broke with desire,
Licked, and fawned on her with tongues of fire.

For what on the earth, the sea, or the air,
Could with my beautiful Love compare?
So delicate subtle pure and intense;
The rich world's honey and quintessence.

Her eyes, where love like a great light shone,
Thrilled to their depths as they met my own —
Thrilled, and kindled, and flashed in mine,
Luminous tremors of love divine.

---

[1] *Dark Blue* (March 1872), 24–26. 'Nocturne' was not reprinted in either *A Selection from the Poems of Mathilde Blind* (1897) or *The Poetical Works of Mathilde Blind* (1900). The poem appeared in the same issue of the *Dark Blue* as G. A. Henty's 'A Pipe of Opium' and chapter six of Sheridan Le Fanu's *Carmilla*. While adopting the medieval ballad form, Blind eschews the familiar abab ballad meter in favour of an aabb rhyming couplet pattern that mirrors the structure of parallelism and antithesis on which the entire poem is based. For more on the relationship of this poem to the poetry to the aesthetic movement see Introduction, pp. 17–18.

As the fierce hot shock of cloud on cloud,
When the lightning leaps through its sultry shroud
Till the whole sky reddens — thus, frame to frame
Flung convulsive, and mixed in flame.

Yea, her whole life swooned into mine, as swoons
The sunset into the broad lagoons;
Ruddy red radiance of sunset that flows
To the sea, till the sea blossoms like a rose.

Low lisped the light wind, low laughed the wave;
The sleek sea rocked us, meek as a slave,
In silver linen the moon us laid,
And sleep o'erlapped us with curtaining shade.

* * * * *

Is it the night-wind sighs in a dream?
Shrills thus through my slumber the sea-gull's scream,
Wailing afar with a homeless cry?
Dank on my bosom the nigh-dews lie.

Blurred is the moonlight, the starlight is quenched,
The sun-bright locks of my Love are drenched
With a limber mist, that has stealthily crept
Over her limbs while she lay and slept.

Her fervid limbs, and her flower-like face,
They feel so chill in my fond embrace;
And yet she slumbers as deep and mild
In her ocean nest as a cradled child.

Awake, though Dearest! See, yonder the white
Bright moon, the radiant Queen Lily of night,
Strains through wan drifts to gaze down on the sea;
Thus break through thy dream, Love and stream, Love, o'er me.

Lo, the moon bursts forth in warm splendour and might,
The fiery small stars swarming after her light,
All at once, all together, shine straight from above —
Awfully clear — on the face of my Love.

The face of my Love! My faint body quakes
Like a rattling leaf which the winter-wind shakes;
A curdling horror thickens my breath.
O God! in my Love's face I meet that of Death!

Icily beautiful! terribly fair!
Her eyes with a wide, blank, lustreless stare
Are fixed upon mine, and the strangling gold
Of her hair coils over me fold upon fold.

Her snow-soft arms freeze round me, like chains
Whose strange cold eats through my burning veins
Till the sick heart rears, and its pulses moan
'Gainst a heart that is as a heart of stone.

Hide, hide thy light, garish moon, lest I see
The dull, froze, passionless eyes upon me.
Come Darkness engulph us; black Storms come and hide
The glittering marble that once was a bride!

Rage round us, old Ocean, with primal pain;
Roll over, confounding the forms of the brain;
Roar round with large roarings, trample my head;
Bury the quick that is chained to the dead!

Bury the dead and the quick in one gloom —
One ebbing, and flowing, and earth-girdling tomb —
Ever, for ever quench Light, that is shed
As in derision, on sweet Love dead!

The Ascent of Man (1889)

Prelude

Wings[1]

Ascend, oh my Soul, with the wings of the lark ascend![2]
  Soaring away and away far into the blue.
Or with the shrill seagull to the breakers bend,
Or with the bee, where the grasses and field-flowers blend,
  Drink out of golden cups of the honey-dew.

Ascend, oh my Soul, on the wings of the wind as it blows,
  Striking wild organ-blasts from the forest trees,
Or on the zephyr bear love of the rose to the rose,
Or with the hurricane sower cast seed as he goes
  Limitless ploughing the leagues of the sibilant seas.

Ascend, oh my Soul, on the wings of the choral strain,
  Invisible tier above tier upbuilding sublime;
Note as it scales after note in a rhythmical chain
Reaching from chaos and welter of struggle and pain,
  Far into vistas empyreal receding from time.

Ascend! take wing on the thoughts of the Dead, my Soul,
  Breathing in colour and stone, flashing through epic and song:
Thoughts that like avalanche snows gather force as they roll,
Mighty to fashion and knead the phenomenal throng
  Of generations of men as they thunder along.[3]

---

[1] This poem, which here serves as a prelude to 'The Ascent of Man', originally appeared independently in Elizabeth Sharp's volume *Women's Voices: An Anthology of the Most Characteristic Poems by English, Scotch, and Irish Women, Selected, Arranged and Edited by Mrs. William Sharp* (London: Walter Scott, 1887), p. 315.

[2] The spirit of Percy Bysshe Shelley presides over these verses. Blind echoes several of his poems here, including 'To a Skylark', 'Ode to the West Wind', and 'Mont Blanc', though her use of the cinquain stanza evokes earlier, metaphysical poets like John Donne and George Herbert.

[3] This stanza is dense with allusions, beginning in the first line with an evocation of Blind's most famous sonnet, 'The Dead', a hymn to godless transcendence and a favourite among late-Victorian freethinkers, agnostics, and atheists. The stanza as a whole asserts the power of the poetic imagination to mould the entire world of sense experience into patterns that give shape, meaning, and a unifying voice to all individuals. 'Phenomenal' as used here alludes to the Kantian meaning of the term, emphasizing the human mind's ability to shape perception of the external world in a way that evokes the opening of Shelley's 'Mont Blanc'.

The Ascent of Man

Part 1.

As compressed within the bounded shell
Boundless Ocean seems to surge and swell,
Haunting echoes of an infinite whole
Moan and murmur through Man's finite soul.[4]

Chaunts of Life[5]

1.

Struck out of dim fluctuant forces and shock of electrical vapour,
Repelled and attracted the atoms[6] flashed mingling in union primeval,
And over the face of the waters far heaving in limitless twilight
Auroral pulsations thrilled faintly, and, striking the blank heaving surface,
The measureless speed of their motion now leaped into light on the waters.
And lo, from the womb of the waters, upheaved in volcanic convulsion,
Ribbed and ravaged and rent there rose bald peaks and the rocky
Heights of confederate mountains compelling the fugitive vapours
To take a form as they passed them and float as clouds through the azure.[7]
Mountains, the broad-bosomed mothers of torrents and rivers perennial,
Feeding the rivers and plains with patient persistence, till slowly,
In the swift passage of æons recorded in stone by Time's graver,
There germ grey films of the lichen and mosses and palm-ferns gigantic,
And jungle of tropical forest fantastical branches entwining,
And limitless deserts of sand and wildernesses primeval.[8]

---

[4] This poetic epigraph to Part 1, one of many antitheistic assertions threaded throughout the poem, serves to alert readers that the invocation to the poet's 'Soul' in 'Wings' is a secular one. Poetry itself may be immortal, but not the individual — or the individual poet.
[5] This long section, an overview of the creation of the earth and human history, encompasses the animal world before the emergence of homo sapiens, the organization of tribal society (including gender divisions), the establishment of early religions, towns, and cities, and progress toward the social structures of modern society. In the first stanza Blind employs the dactylic hexameter of Greek epic poetry: lines of six metrical feet in which five dactyls (long and short syllables) are followed by a spondee (two long syllables).
[6] While the Greek philosopher Democritus introduced the idea of the atom around 450 BC, it wasn't until 1802 that the English chemist, physicist, and meteorologist John Dalton provided evidence for the existence of atoms and developed atomic theory ('Dalton's Law').
[7] Plate tectonic theory was not formulated until Alfred Wegener's *The Origin of Continents and Oceans* (1915), but Alfred Russel Wallace, who wrote the preface for the 1900 edition of *The Ascent of Man*, anticipated modern plate tectonics by asserting that paleogeographic factors control the differences in fauna between some islands. See D. G. Howell, *Tectonics of Suspect Terranes: Mountain Building and Continental Growth* (London: Chapman & Hall, 1989). pp. 22–79.
[8] Alfred Russel Wallace, *The Geographical Distribution of Animals*, 2 vols (New York: Harper & Brothers, 1876). Part I explains why different regions possess distinct and

II.[9]

Lo, moving o'er chaotic waters,
  Love dawned upon the seething waste,
Transformed in ever new avatars[10]
  It moved without or pause or haste:
Like sap that moulds the leaves of May
It wrought within the ductile clay.[11]

And vaguely in the pregnant deep,
  Clasped by the glowing arms of light
From an eternity of sleep
  Within unfathomed gulfs of night
A pulse stirred in the plastic slime
Responsive to the rhythm of Time.

Enkindled in the mystic dark
  Life built herself a myriad forms,
And, flashing its electric spark
  Through films and cells and pulps and worms,
Flew shuttlewise above, beneath,
Weaving the web of life and death.

And multiplying in the ocean,
  Amorphous, rude, colossal things

---

characteristic fauna.

[9] Blind shifts here to sestain stanzas that follow an ababcc rhyme scheme.
[10] In Hindu mythology, an avatar is a deity that descends to earth in an incarnate form; here, Blind is referring to the various forms Love assumes in the organic world.
[11] In these lines, Blind conflates an evolutionary view of the creation of Earth with Christian, Hindu, and pantheist conceptions of earth's origins. In doing so she is offering a universal origin story which transcends time and culture, but one which is also amenable to subsequent scientific discoveries. The early influence of Mazzini on Blind's thinking can be seen here, especially his account of the universal deity: 'He is not the Christian God. He is not the arbitrary dispenser of grace. He has made laws; He has given you powers and liberty; He has put before you evil, so that you fight it' (Blind, 'Personal Recollections of Mazzini', p. 709). The roots of Blind's secularism pre-date her encounter with Mazzini: in 1859, when she was eighteen, she travelled throughout Germany and Switzerland and spent time studying with one of the leading intellectual lights in Europe, Kuno Fischer (Garnett, 'Memoir', p. 10). In 1854 Fischer had begun work on his *History of Modern Philosophy: Descartes and His School*, completed in 1865, which among other things had a direct influence on Friedrich Nietzsche. In Fischer's account of Spinoza and his ideas, Nietzsche recognized a kindred philosophical spirit. The two philosophers share a radical philosophy of immanence and the negation of all transcendence, a philosophical outlook also shared by David Strauss, in *The Old Faith and the New: A Confession*. All four thinkers, and the adult Blind, reject teleology — the idea that there is an end goal or ultimate purpose to things. For them the immanent world, devoid of inherent purpose, constitutes the horizon of being and the sole possible source of value. As Spinoza writes, '[t]here will now be no need of many words to show that nature has set no end before herself, and that all final causes are nothing but human fictions' (*Ethics*, trans. by W. H. White (Herefordshire, England: Wordsworth Editions, 2001), p. 37).

Lolled on the ooze in lazy motion,
  Armed with grim jaws or uncouth wings;
Helpless to lift their cumbering bulk
They lurch like some dismasted hulk.

And virgin forest, verdant plain,
  The briny sea, the balmy air,
Each blade of grass and globe of rain,
  And glimmering cave and gloomy lair
Began to swarm with beasts and birds,
With floating fish and fleet-foot herds.

The lust of life's delirious fires
  Burned like a fever in their blood,
Now pricked them on with fierce desires,
  Now drove them famishing for food,
To seize coy females in the fray,
Or hotly hunted for prey.

And amorously urged them on
  In wood or wild to court their mate,
Proudly displaying in the sun
  With antics strange and looks elate,
The vigour of their mighty thews
Or charm of million-coloured hues.

There crouching 'mid the scarlet bloom,
  Voluptuously the leopard lies,
And through the tropic forest gloom
  The flaming of his feline eyes
Stirs with intoxicating stress
The pulses of the leopardess.

Or two swart bulls of self-same age
  Meet furiously with thunderous roar,
And lash together, blind with rage,
  And clanging horns that fain would gore
Their rival, and so win the prize
Of those impassive female eyes.

Or in the nuptial days of spring,
  When April kindles bush and brier,
Like rainbows that have taken wing,
  Or palpitating gems of fire,
Bright butterflies in one brief day
Live but to love and pass away.

And herds of horses scour the plains,
  The thickets scream with bird and beast
The love of life burns in their veins,

And from the mightiest to the least
Each preys upon the other's life
In inextinguishable strife.

War rages on the teeming earth;
  The hot and sanguinary fight
Begins with each new creature's birth:
  A dreadful war where might is right;
Where still the strongest slay and win,
Where weakness is the only sin.

There is no truce to this drawn battle,
  Which ends but to begin again;
The drip of blood, the hoarse death-rattle,
  The roar of rage, the shriek of pain,
Are rife in fairest grove and dell,
Turning earth's flowery haunts to hell.

A hell of hunger, hatred, lust,
  Which goads all creatures here below,
Or blindworm wriggling in the dust,
  Or penguin in the Polar snow:
A hell where there is none to save,
Where life is life's insatiate grave.

And in the long portentous strife,
  Where types are tried even as by fire,
Where life is whetted upon life
  And step by panting step mounts higher,
Apes lifting hairy arms now stand
And free the wonder-working hand.

They raise a light aërial house
  On shafts of widely branching trees,
Where, harboured warily, each spouse
  May feed her little ape in peace,
Green cradled in his heaven-roofed bed,
Leaves rustling lullabies o'erhead.[12]

And lo, 'mid reeking swarms of earth
  Grim struggling in the primal wood,
A new strange creature hath its birth:
  Wild — stammering — nameless — shameless — nude;
Spurred on by want, held in by fear,

---

[12] Compare this description of the female ape, who effortlessly ascends to the tree branches where she is able to 'feed her little ape in peace', to the 'cumbered wife' of a hunter-gatherer family, bent double in the field, 'whose multifarious toil | Seems never done' (see pp. 60–61). Given the fact that marriage was the site of increasing contention in the intertwined debates on evolution and the Woman Question in the 1880s, it is significant that nowhere in 'The Ascent of Man' does Blind propose marriage as a model of redemptive social relations.

He hides his head in caverns drear.

Most unprotected of earth's kin,
  His fight for life that seems so vain
Sharpens his senses, till within
  The twilight mazes of his brain,
Like embryos within the womb,
Thought pushes feelers through the gloom.

And slowly in the fateful race
  It grows unconscious, till at length
The helpless savage dares to face
  The cave-bear in his grisly strength;
For stronger than its bulky thews
He feels a force that grows with use.

From age to dumb unnumbered age,
  By dim gradations long and slow,
He reaches on from stage to stage,
  Through fear and famine, weal and woe
And, compassed round with danger, still
Prolongs his life by craft and skill.

With cunning hand he shapes the flint,
  He carves the horn with strange device,
He splits the rebel block by dint
  Of effort — till one day there flies
A spark of fire from out the stone:
Fire which shall make the world his own.

III.[13]

And from the clash of warring Nature's strife
Man day by day wins his imperilled life;
For goaded on by want, he hunts the roe,
Chases the deer, and lays the wild boar low.
In his rude boat made of the hollow trees
He drifts adventurous on the unoared seas,
And, as he tilts upon the rocking tide,
Catches the glistening fish that flash and glide
Innumerably through the waters wide.
He'll fire the bush whose flames shall help him fel[14]
The trunks to prop his roof, where he may dwell
Beside the bubbling of a crystal well,
Sheltered from drenching rains or noxious glare
When the sun holds the zenith. Delving there,
His cumbered wife, whose multifarious toil

---

[13] Blind now marks the emergence of mankind by employing heroic couplets.
[14] Variant of 'fell'.

Seems never done, breaks the rich virgin soil,
And in the ashes casts the casual seeds
Of feathered grass and efflorescent weeds;
When, as with thanks, the bounteous earth one morn
Returns lush blades of life-sustaining corn.
And while the woman digs and plants, and twines
To precious use long reeds and pliant bines,
He — having hit the brown bird on the wing,
And slain the roe[15] — returns at evening,
And gives his spoil unto her, to prepare
The succulent, wildwood scented, simmering fare,
While with impatient sniffs and eager-eyed
His bronze-limbed children gather to his side.
And, when the feast is done, all take their ease,
Lulled by the sing-song of the evening breeze
And murmuring undertones of many-foliaged trees;
While here and there through rifts of green the sky
Casts its blue glance like an all-seeing eye.
But though by stress of want and poignant need
Man tames the wolf-sprung hound and rearing steed,
Pens up the ram, and yokes the deep-horned ox,
And through wide pastures shepherds woolly flocks;
Though age by age, through discipline of toil,
Man wring a richer harvest from the soil,
And in the grim and still renewing fight
Slays loathly worms and beasts of gruesome might
By the close-knitted bondage of the clan,
Which adding up the puny strength of man
Makes thousands move with one electric thrill
Of simultaneous, energetic will;
Yet still behind the narrow borderland
Where in security he seems to stand,
His apprehensive life is compassed round
By baffling mysteries he cannot sound,
Where, big with terrors and calamities,
The future like a foe in ambush lies:
A muffled foe, that seems to watch and wait
With the Medusa eyes of stony fate.[16] —

---

[15] A small, tailless Eurasian deer.

[16] Given the feminist emphasis of the poem, it is worth noting that according to Ovid's *Metamorphoses*, Medusa was once a beautiful young maiden, the only mortal of three sisters known as the Gorgons. Her beauty caught the eye of the sea god Neptune, who raped her in the sacred temple of Minerva. Furious at the desecration of her temple, Minerva transformed Medusa into a winged monster with snakes in the place of hair and the deadly capacity to turn whoever looked upon her face to stone. Patricia B. Salzman-Mitchell, in *A Web of Fantasies: Gaze, Image, and Gender in Ovid's Metamorphoses* (Columbus: Ohio State

Great floods o'erwhelm and ruin his ripening grain,
His boat is shattered by the hurricane,
From the rent cloud the tameless lightning springs —
Heaven's flame-mouthed dragon with a roar of wings —
And fires his hut and simple household things;
Until before his horror-stricken eyes
The stored-up produce of long labour lies,
A heap of ashes smoking 'neath the skies. —
Or now the pastures where his flocks did graze,
Parched, withered, shrivelled by the imminent blaze
Of the great ball of fire that glares above,
Glow dry like iron heated in a stove;
Turning upon themselves, the tortured sheep,
With blackening tongues, drop heap on gasping heap,
Their rotting flesh sickens the wind that moans
And whistles poisoned through their chattering bones;
While the thin shepherd, staring sick and gaunt,
Will search the thorns for berries, or yet haunt
The stony channels of some river-bed
Where filtering fresh perchance a liquid thread
Of water may run clear. — Now dark o'erhead,
Thickening with storm, the wintry clouds will loom,
And wrap the land in weeks of mournful gloom;
Shrouding the sun and every lesser light
Till earth with all her aging woods grows white,
And hurrying streams stop fettered in their flight.
Then famished beasts freeze by the frozen lakes,
And thick as leaves dead birds bestrew the brakes;
And, cowering blankly by the flickering flame,
Man feels a presence without a form or name,
When by the bodies of his speechless dead
In barbarous woe he bows his stricken head.
Then in the hunger of his piteous love
He sends his thought, winged like a carrier dove —
Through the unanswering silence void and vast,
Whence from dim hollows blows an icy blast —
To bring some sign, some little sign at last,
From his lost chiefs — the beautiful, the brave —
Vanished like bubbles on a breaking wave,
Lost in the unfathomed darkness of the grave.
When, lo, behold beside him in the night, —
Softly beside him, like the noiseless light
Of moonbeams moving o'er the glimmering floor

University Press, 2005), notes that Ovid's text 'stresses that Medusa the girl was an object of amazement and visual enchantment', and that once transformed, '[t]he petrifying power of Medusa's eyes' became 'a hyperbolic metaphor for any woman who wishes to see and to affect the world with her eyes' (p. 83).

That come unbidden through the bolted door, —
The lonely sleeper sees the lost one stand
Like one returned from some dim, distant land,
Bending towards him with his outstretched hand.
But when he fain would grasp it in his own,
He melts into thin moonshine and is gone —
A spirit now, who on the other shore
Of death hunts happily evermore.[17] —
A Son of Life, but dogged, while he draws breath,
By her inseparable shadow — death,
Man, feeble Man, whom unknown Fates appal,
With prayer and praise seeks to propitiate all
The spirits, who, for good or evil plight,
Bless him in victory or in sickness smite.
Those are his Dead who, wrapped in grisly shrouds,
Now ride phantasmal on the rushing clouds,
Souls of departed chiefs whose livid forms
He sees careering on the reinless storms,
Wild, spectral huntsmen who tumultuously,
With loud halloo and shrilly echoing cry,
Follow the furious chase, with the whole pack
Of shadowy hounds fierce yelping in the track
Of wolves and bears as shadowy as the hosts
Who lead once more as unsubstantial ghosts
Their lives of old as restlessly they fly
Across the wildernesses of the sky.
When the wild hunt is done, shall they not rest
Their heads upon some swan-white maiden's breast,
And quaff their honeyed mead with godlike zest
In golden-gated Halls whence they may see
The earth and marvellous secrets of the Sea
Whereon the clouds will lie with grey wings furled,
And in whose depths, voluminously curled,
The serpent looms whose girth engirds the world?
Far, far above now in supernal power
Those spirits rule the sunshine and the shower!
How shall he win their favour; yea, how move
To pity the unpitying gods above,
The Dæmon[18] rulers of life's fitful dream,

---

[17] In this description of primitive humanity coming to terms with death, the departed return via memory, not an afterlife — which Blind emphasizes in the next line by describing the survivor as 'Son of Life', not of God. Throughout this section, Blind is describing animism, which the German-born philologist and Orientalist Friedrich Max Müller (1823–1900) defined as 'the belief and worship of ancestral spirits' in *Anthropological Religion* (London: Longmans, Green and Co., 1892), p. 160. Blind read Müller's earlier work *Comparative Mythology* (1856) and was familiar with his theories of natural religion.

[18] Variant of demon, here personifying the seeming capriciousness and malevolence of

Who sway men's destinies, and still would seem
To treat them lightly as a game of chance,
The sport of whim and blindfold circumstance —
The irresponsible, capricious gods,
So quick to please or anger; whose sharp rods
Are storms and lightnings launched from cloven skies;
Who feast upon the shuddering victim's cries,
The smell of blood, and human sacrifice.
But ever as Man grows they grow with him;
Terrific, cruel, gentle, bright, or dim,
With eyes of dove-like mercy, hands of wrath,
Procession-like, they hover o'er his path
And, changing with the gazer, borrow light
From their rapt devotee's adoring sight.
And Ormuzd, Ashtaroth, Osiris, Baal[19] —
Love spending gods and gods of blood and wail —
Look down upon their suppliant from the skies
With his own magnified, responsive eyes.
For Man, from want and pressing hunger freed,
Begins to feel another kind of need,
And in his shaping brain and through his eyes
Nature, awakening, sees her blue-arched skies;
The Sun, his life-begetter, isled in space;
The Moon, the Measurer of his span of days;
The immemorial stars who pierce his night
With inklings of things vast and infinite.
All shows of heaven and earth that move and pass
Take form within his brain as in a glass.
The tidal thunder of the sea now roars
And breaks symphonious on a hundred shores;
The fitful flutings of the vagrant breeze
Strike gusts of sound from virgin forest trees;
White leaping waters of wild cataracts fall
From crag and jag in lapses musical,
And streams meandering amid daisied leas
Throb with the pulses of tumultuous seas.
From hills and valleys smoking mists arise,
Steeped in pale gold and amethystine dyes.
The land takes colour from him, and the flowers
Laugh in his path like sun-dyed April showers.
The moving clouds in calm or thunderstorm,

those natural forces that bring suffering to humans.
[19] Ormuzd is the chief deity of Zoroastrianism, a source of light and embodiment of good; Ashtaroth, named after the Mesopotamian goddess Ishtar, is part of the evil trinity along with Beelzebub and Lucifer; Osiris is the Egyptian Lord of the Underworld and Judge of the Dead; Baal is a Canaanite god often portrayed as the primary enemy of the Hebrew God Yahweh.

All shows of things in colour, sound, or form
Moulded mysteriously, are freshly wrought
Within the fiery furnace of his thought.[20]

IV.[21]

    No longer Nature's thrall,
    Man builds the city wall
That shall withstand her league of levelling storms;
    He builds tremendous tombs
    Where, hid in hoarded glooms,
His dead defy corruption with her worms:
High towers he rears and bulks of glowing stone,
Where the king rules upon a golden throne.

    Creature of hopes and fears,
    Of mirth and many tears,
He makes himself a thousand costly altars,
    Whence smoke of sacrifice,
    Fragrant with myrrh and spice,
Ascends to heaven as the flame leaps and falters;
Where, like a king above the Cloud control,
God sits enthroned and rules Man's subject soul.

    Yet grievous here below
    And manifold Man's woe;
Though he can stay the flood and bind the waters,
    His hand he shall not stay
    That bids him sack and slay
And turn the waving fields to fields of slaughters;
And, as he reaps War's harvest grim and gory,
Commits a thousand crimes and calls it glory.

    Vast empires fall and rise,
    As when in sunset skies
The monumental clouds lift flashing towers
    With turrets, spires, and bars
    Lit by confederate stars
Till the bright rack dissolves in flying showers:
Kingdoms on kingdoms have their fleeting day,
Dazzle the conquered world, and pass away.

---

[20] This Pantheist conception of humanity's relationship to nature is also an example of Blind's own neo-pagan aestheticism.

[21] Here Blind complicates her rhyme scheme to mirror the increasing complexity of human civilization, shifting from iambic pentameter couplets to octet stanzas that combine trimeter and pentameter lines, rhyming aabccbdd. Given the ways in which 'The Ascent of Man' extends the evolutionary themes of Tennyson's *In Memoriam*, it is noteworthy that the middle four lines of each of these stanzas echo the abba rhyme scheme of what has come to be known as the *In Memoriam* stanza.

   In golden Morning lands
   The blazing crowns change hands,
From mystic Ind to fleshly Babylon,
    Assyria, Palestine
    Armed with her book divine,
Dread Persia whose fleet chariots charged and won
Pale Continents where prostrate monarchs kneel
Before the flash of her resistless steel.[22]

   As one by one they start
   With proudly beating heart
Fast in the furious, fierce-contested race,
    Where neck to neck they strain
    Deliriously to gain
The winning post of power; the meed of praise;
Some drop behind, fall, or are trampled down
While the proud victor grasps the laurel crown.

   Not only great campaigns
   Shall glorify their reigns,
But high-towered cities wondrous to behold,
    With gardens poised in air
    Like bowers of Eden fair,
With brazen gates and shrines of beaten gold,
And Palace courts whose constellated lights
Shine on black slaves and cringing satellites.

   Eclipsing with her fate
   Each power and rival state
With her unnumbered stretch of generations,
    A sand-surrounded isle
    Fed by the bounteous Nile,
Egypt confronts Sahara — sphinx of nations;
Taught by the floods that make or mar her shore,
She scans the stars and hoards mysterious lore.[23]

   Hers are imperial halls
   With strangely scriptured walls

---

[22] Ancient empires that rose, flourished, and fell, from the Bronze Age Indus Valley civilization, which along with Egypt and Mesopotamia was one of the three early civilizations of the Near East and South Asia, to Palestine, occupied and controlled by various independent kingdoms and powers (including Rome), to the Persian Achaemenid Empire, invaded and conquered by Alexander the Great in 334 BC.

[23] Egypt reached the height of its power in the late Bronze Age, and ruled much of Nubia and a sizable portion of the Near East. Its capital city, Thebes, was built along the left and right banks of the Nile with steep embankments to contain the river's seasonal floods. The sphinx is a mythical creature with the head of a human, a falcon, a cat, or a sheep, and the body of a lion with the wings of an eagle. Nine hundred sphinxes with ram's heads, representing the Egyptian god Amon-Ra, were built in Thebes, where his cult was strongest.

And long perspectives of memorial places,
    Where the hushed daylight glows
      On mute colossal rows
Of clawed wild beasts featured with female faces,
And realmless kings inane whose stony eyes
Have watched the hour-glass of the centuries.

    There in the rainless sands
    The toil of captive hands,
That aye must do as their taskmaster bids,
    Through years of dusty days
    Brick by slow brick shall raise
The incarnate pride of kings — the Pyramids —
Linked with some name synonymous with slaughter
Time has effaced like a name writ in water.[24]

    For ever with fateful shocks,
    Roar as of hurtling rocks,
Start fresh embattled hosts with flags unfurled,
    To meet on battle-fields
    With clash of spears and shields,
Widowing the world of men to win the world:
The hissing air grows dark with iron rain,
And groans the earth beneath her sheaves of slain.[25]

    Triumphant o'er them all,
    See crowns and sceptres fall
Before the arms of iron-soldered legions;
    As Capitolian Rome
    Across the salt sea foam
Orders her Cæsars to remotest regions:
From silver Spain and Albion's[26] clouded seas
To the fair shrines and marble mines of Greece.[27]

---

[24] This last line contains a dual allusion: to the fallen Egyptian pharaoh in Shelley's sonnet 'Ozymandias', whose crumbling statue symbolizes the ephemeral nature of political power; and to the words written on John Keats' tombstone in the Protestant Cemetery in Rome: 'Here lies One Whose Name was writ in Water'.
[25] The Romans conquered Egypt in 30 BC and ruled there for 700 years. This was three years after the Roman Republic became the Roman Empire, under the autocratic rule of Augustus Caesar.
[26] 'Albion' is the Ancient Gallo-Latin name for Britain.
[27] This and the next four stanzas recount the rise and ascendancy of the Roman Empire (27 BC to 286 AD), which invaded and occupied most of Europe and portions of northern Africa and western Asia. They also describe the empire's rapaciousness in gathering the spoils of war, as well as the cruelty of gladiatorial combat in the Colosseum. Blind's anti-imperialism is evident in her language in this section, which links the barbarity of the ancient Romans to that of early humans in Part I of the 'The Ascent of Man'.

>   Pallas[28] unmatched in war,
>   To her triumphal car
> Rome chains fallen despots and discrownèd queens
>   With many a rampant beast,
>   Birds from the gorgeous East,
> And wool-haired Nubians torn from tropic scenes;[29]
> There huge barbarians from Druidic woods[30]
> Tower ominous o'er the humming multitudes;
>
>   For still untamed and free
>   In loathed captivity,
> Their spirits bend not to the conqueror's yoke,
>   Though for a Roman sight
>   They must in mimic fight
> Give wounds in play and deal Death's mortal stroke,
> While round the arena rings the fierce applause
> Voluptuous, as their bubbling life-blood flows
>
>   In streams of purple rain
>   From hecatombs of slain
> Saluting Cæsar still with failing breath,
>   But in their dying souls
>   Undying hate, which rolls
> From land to land the avalanche of Death,
> That, gathering volume as it sweeps along,
> Pours down the Alps throng on unnumbered throng.
>
>   From northern hills and plains
>   Storm-lashed by driving rains,
> From moorland wastes and depths of desolate wood,
>   From many an icebound shore,
>   The human torrents pour,
> Horde following upon horde as flood on flood,
> Avengers of the slain they come, they come,
> And break in thunder on the walls of Rome.

---

[28] In Homer's *Iliad*, Pallas Athene is represented as the goddess of wisdom and skill, and she plays a major role in working to protect the Achaean warriors fighting against the Trojans. In contrast to Ares, the wild war-god, she is the patroness and teacher of prudent, scientific warfare. Rome, which conquered Greece in 146 BC, adopted Greek deities into its own pantheon; by evoking Pallas as a symbol of Roman imperial supremacy Blind may be gesturing toward another kind of cultural conquest and plunder.

[29] The Nubians, originally inhabitants of the central Nile valley, are indigenous to the region which is present-day northern Sudan and southern Egypt.

[30] The Druids were fiercely independent members of the high-ranking class in ancient Celtic culture, residing in parts of Britain and Gaul (modern-day France). Beginning with the reign of Julius Caesar in the first century BC, the Romans launched a military campaign against the Celts, killing them by the thousands and destroying their culture in much of mainland Europe.

A trembling people waits
As, surging through its gates,
Break the fierce Goths with trumpet-blasts of doom;[31]
    And many a glorious shrine
    Begins to flare and shine,
And many a palace flames up through the gloom,
Kindled like torches by relentless wrath
To light the Spoiler on destruction's path.

    Yea, with Rome's ravished walls,
    The old world tottering falls
And crumbles into ruin wide and vast;
    The Empire seems to rock
    As with an earthquake's shock,
And vassal provinces look on aghast;
As realms are split and nation rent from nation,
The globe seems drifting to annihilation.

v.

'Peace on earth and good will unto Men!'[32]
Came the tidings borne o'er wide dominions;
   The glad tidings thrilled the world as when
Spring comes fluttering on the west wind's pinions,
    When her voice is heard
    Warbling though each bird,
    And a new-born hope
Throbs through all things infinite in scope.

'Peace on earth and good will!' came the word
Of the Son of Man, the Man of Sorrow —
   But the peace turned to a flaming sword,
Turned to woe and wailing on the morrow
    When with gibes and scorns,
    Crowned with barren thorns,
    Gashed and crucified,
On the Cross the tortured Jesus died.

And the world, once full of flower-hung shrines,
Now forsakes old altars for the new,

---

[31] A description of the Sack of Rome on 24 August 410 AD, when the city, which was no longer the capital of the Western Roman Empire, was attacked by the Visigoths, a Germanic people, who, along with the Ostrogoths, were a major political entity within the Roman Empire. They occupied territory in southern France and the Iberian Peninsula.

[32] Luke 2. 14. This section of the poem demythologizes Christianity, here described as a 'wondrous story' emerging after the fall of Rome as 'Zeus grows faint and Venus' star declines'. Initially answering to the needs of humans for a 'heaven of love | Which their homesick lives are dying of', this new faith devolves into 'fury fiercer than a leopard's' as the Inquisition reveals the will to power of organized religion (see below, note 35), and the one faith is fragmented into warring creeds.

Zeus grows faint and Venus' star declines
As Jehovah glorifies the Jew,
   He whom — lit with awe —
   God-led Moses saw,
   Graving with firm hand
In his people's heart his Lord's command.

Holding Hells and Heavens in either hand
Comes the priest and comes the wild-eyed prophet,
   Tells the people of some happier land,
Terrifies them with a burning Tophet;
   Gives them creeds for bread
   And warm roof o'erhead,
   Gives for life's delight
Passports to the kingdom, spirit-bright.

And the people groaning everywhere
Hearken gladly to the wondrous story,
   How beyond this life of toil and care
They shall lead a life of endless glory:
   Where beyond the dim
   Earth-mists Seraphim,
   Love-illumined, wait —
Hierarchies of angels at heaven's gate.

Let them suffer while they live below,
Bear in silence weariness and pain;
   For the heavier is their earthly woe,
Verily the heavenlier is their gain
   In the mansions where
   Sorrow and despair,
   Yea, all moan shall cease
With the moan of immemorial seas.[33]

And to save their threatened souls from sin,
Save them from the world, the flesh, the devil,
   Men and Women break from bonds of kin
And in cloistered cell draw bar on evil,
   Worship on their knees

---

[33] The first six stanzas of this section of the poem echo Swinburne, especially the poems 'Hymn to Proserpine' and 'Before a Crucifix' (*The Poems of Algernon Charles Swinburne*, 6 vols (London: Chatto & Windus, 1904), I, pp. 67–73; II, pp, 81–87). In 'Hymn' Swinburne argues that Christianity, like the Greco-Roman religion Blind's earlier stanzas allude to, is fated to die out, which Blind implies here by representing Christianity as one belief system in a historical procession of other once-living faiths. Like Swinburne, she employs a mordant irony throughout these stanzas when emphasizing the suffering and bloodshed Christianity has sanctioned (note the rhyming of 'word' and 'sword' in the second stanza). Stanzas three through five allude to 'Before a Crucifix' in emphasizing that the corrupt and oppressive Church subjugates the poor, giving them 'creeds for bread'.

  Sacred Images,
  And all Saints above,
The Madonna, mystic Rose of love.³⁴

 Mystic Rose of Maiden Motherhood,
Moon of Hearts immaculately mild,
 Beaming o'er the turbulent times and rude
With the promise of her blessèd Child:
  Whom pale Monks adore,
  Pining evermore
  For the heaven of love
Which their homesick lives are dying of.

 But the flame of mystical desires
Turns to fury fiercer than a leopard's,
 Holy fagots blaze with kindling fires
As the priests, the people's careful shepherds,
  In Heaven's awful name,
  Set the pile on flame
  Where, for Conscience' sake,
Heretics burn chaunting at the stake.

 Subterranean secrets of the prison,
Throbs of anguish in the crushing cell,
 Torture-chambers of the Inquisition³⁵
Are the Church's antidotes to Hell.
  Better rack them here,
  Mutilate and sear,
  Than their souls should go
To the place of everlasting woe.

 And a lurid universal night,
Lit by quenchless fires for unquenched sages,
 Thick with spectral broods that shun the light,
Looms impervious o'er the stifled ages
  Where the blameless wise
  Fall a sacrifice,
  Fall as fell of old
The unspotted firstlings of the fold.

 And the violent feud of clashing creeds
Shatters empires and breaks realms asunder;
 Cities tremble, sceptres shake like reeds

---

³⁴ 'Mystical Rose' is one of the Madonna's titles in the Litany of the Blessed Virgin Mary, a form of prayer used in church services and processions.
³⁵ Beginning in the twelfth century and continuing for hundreds of years, the Inquisition was an office set up within the Catholic Church to discover and punish heresy throughout Europe and the Americas. It is infamous for the severity of its tortures and its persecution of Jews and Muslims.

At the swift bolts of the Papal thunder;
      Yea, the bravest quail,
      Cast from out the pale
      Of all Christendom
By the dread anathemas of Rome.[36]

And like one misled by marish gleams
When he hears the shrill cock's note of warning,
    Europe, starting from its trance of dreams,
Sees the first streak of the clear-eyed morning
      As it broadening stands
      Over ravaged lands
      Where mad nations are
Locked in grip of fratricidal war.

Castles burn upon the vine-clad knolls,
Huts glow smouldering in the trampled meadows;
    And a hecatomb of martyred souls
Fills a queenly town with wail of widows
      In those branded hours
      When red-guttering showers
      Splash by courts and stews[37]
To the Bells of Saint Bartholomew's.[38]

Seed that's sown upon the wanton wind
Shall be harvested in whirlwind rages,
    For revenge and hate bring forth their kind,
And black crime must ever be the wages
      Of a nation's crime
      Time transmits to time,
      Till the score of years
Is wiped out in floods of staunchless tears.

Yea, the anguish in a people's life
May have eaten out its heart of pity,
    Bred in scenes of scarlet sin and strife,
Heartless splendours of a haughty city;
      Dark with lowering fate,
      At the massive gate

---

[36] 'Anathema' was initially used in its ecclesiastical sense by St Paul to mean the expulsion of someone from the Christian community. The liturgical meaning evolved to signify a formal ecclesiastical curse of excommunication and the condemnation of heretical doctrines, which was often issued from Rome by Catholic cardinals or the pope. Blind evokes it here to describe the increasing schisms within Christianity which ultimately led to the Reformation (see also note 40).
[37] British colloquialism for brothel.
[38] The St Bartholomew's Day massacre in 1572 was a targeted group of assassinations and a wave of Catholic mob violence directed against the Huguenots (Protestants) during the French Wars of Religion in the period of the Reformation.

Of its kings it may
Stand and knock with tragic hand one day.

For the living tomb gives up its dead,[39]
Bastilles yawn,[40] and chains are rent asunder,
   Little children now and hoary head,
Man and maiden, meet in joy and wonder;
      Throng on radiant throng,
      Brave and blithe and strong,
      Gay with pine and palm,
Fill fair France with freedom's thunder-psalm.

Free and equal — rid of king and priest —
The rapt nation bids each neighbour nation
   To partake the sacramental feast
And communion of the Federation:
      And electrified
      Masses, far and wide,
      Thrill to hope and start
Vibrating as with one common heart.

From the perfumed South of amorous France[41]
With her wreath of orange bloom and myrtle,
   From old wizard woods of lost Romance
Soft with wail of wind and voice of turtle,
      From the roaring sea
      Of grey Normandy,
      And the rich champaigns
Where the vine gads o'er Burgundian plains;

---

[39] The remaining stanzas in this section of the poem recount the Enlightenment dream of liberation from the 'mind-forg'd manacles' of church and state, the French Revolution that sought to make the dream a reality, the Reign of Terror that turned the dream into a nightmare, and the defeat of Napoleon at Waterloo. It is important to note that Blind and her fellow republicans, including William Morris, William Michael Rossetti, Eleanor Marx, and Olive Schreiner, considered the French Revolution the beginning of an unfinished revolutionary movement. As Rossetti wrote in his edition of Shelley's poetry, Shelley's most productive years 'were years of revolution', and he completed this sentence in terms that made it clear the revolution had not yet run its course: 'indeed what years, since the great disintegration of 1789–93, have not been so? And how many more are we not destined to see until the world of those mighty days shall be in some approximate degree openly accepted and firmly constituted?' (William Michael Rossetti, 'Memoir', in *The Complete Poetical Works of Percy Bysshe Shelley*, 3 vols (London: Constable, 1870) I, p. cxxx).
[40] The 14 July 1789 storming of the Paris Bastille, a medieval armoury, fortress, and political prison that represented royal authority, was the flashpoint of the French Revolution.
[41] This and the next stanza describe the major regions of France, and specifically those which participated in the French Revolution, from the warm south where France borders Spain to cool Normandy in the north, which faces England. The 'wizard woods' is the Forest of Orléans in the Loire Valley; the Rhône River is in south-eastern France and empties into the Mediterranean Sea; Gascony is a region in south-western France with a coast on the Atlantic Ocean.

From the banks of the blue arrowy Rhone,
And from many a Western promontory,
From volcanic crags of cloven stone
Crowned with castles ivy-green in story;
    From gay Gascon coasts
    March fraternal hosts,
    Equal hosts and free,
Pilgrims to the shrine of liberty.[42]

But king calls on king in wild alarms,
Troops march threatening through the vales and passes,
    Barefoot Faubourgs[43] at the cry to arms
On the frontier hurl their desperate masses:
    The deep tocsin's boom[44]
    Fills the streets with gloom,
    And with iron hand
The red Terror guillotines[45] the land.

For the Furies of the sanguine past
Chase fair Freedom, struggling torn and baffled,
    Till infuriate — turned to bay at last —
Rolled promiscuous on the common scaffold,
    Vengeful she shall smite
    A Queen's head bleached white,[46]
    And a courtesan's[47]
Whose light hands once held the reins of France.

---

[42] Throughout her 1886 biography of the French writer, *salonnière*, and revolutionary Madame Roland, Blind sides with the revolutionaries of the eighteenth and nineteenth centuries (see p. 11).

[43] Residents of the Faubourg Saint-Antoine, a Paris suburb to the east of the Bastille, who stormed the Bastille on 14 July 1789. They were among the most zealous supporters of the Revolution in its early years, and many fought against invading armies as European monarchies revolted against France, beginning with Austria and Prussia. They were subject to persecution and execution during Robespierre's Reign of Terror.

[44] A bell rung to sound alarms during the Revolution.

[45] Blind turns the noun 'guillotine', a device designed to speed up the process of beheading, into a verb to express the country-wide killings during a two-year period when, following the creation of the First French Republic in 1792, a series of massacres and numerous public executions took place. By 1794, when Robespierre himself died on the guillotine, over 16,000 official death sentences had been carried out in France. The executions were decreed by Robespierre and the Committee of Public Safety, which became the de facto wartime government in France in 1793.

[46] Marie Antoinette became the last queen of France before the Revolution. She was convicted of high treason and sent to the guillotine on 16 October 1793, less than a year after Louis was executed. According to folklore, her hair turned white overnight while she awaited her fate.

[47] Blind follows the description of Marie Antoinette's fate with that of Madame Du Barry, the official mistress of Marie Antoinette's husband, who was also sent to the guillotine, on 7 December 1793. In the extended metaphor of the stanza, 'fair Freedom' is driven to vengeful violence by the Furies (three goddesses of vengeance in Greek mythology) unleashed by the Reign of Terror. The word 'sanguine' in the first line is used in its etymological meaning: blood-red.

She shall smite and spare not — yea, her own,
Her fair sons so pure from all pollution,
   With their guiltless life-blood must atone
To the goddess of the Revolution;
      Dying with a song
      On their lips, her young
      Ardent children end,
Meeting death even as one meets a friend.

And her daughter, in heroic shame,
Turned to Freedom's Moloch statue, crying:
   'Liberty, what crimes done in thy name!'[48]
Spake, and with her Freedom's self seemed dying
      As she bleeding lay
      'Neath Napoleon's sway:
      Europe heard her knell
When on Waterloo the Empire fell.[49]

            VI.[50]

Woe, woe to Man and all his hapless brood!
 No rest for him, no peace is to be found;
 He may have tamed wild beasts and made the ground
Yield corn and wine and every kind of food;
 He may have turned the ocean to his steed,
 Tutored the lightning's elemental speed
To flash his thought from Ætna to Atlantic;[51]

---

[48] The last words spoken by Madame Roland, who became a leader of the Girondist faction during the Revolution (the Girondists were opposed by Robespierre and his Jacobin allies). She was the first Girondin to be arrested during the Reign of Terror and was guillotined on 8 November 1793. She was 39. In her 1886 biography of Madame Roland, Blind writes: 'Standing on the scaffold, her shining eyes turned to the statue of Liberty lately erected near it, she said, bowing to the goddess of her worship, "O Liberty! what crimes are committed in thy name!"' (*Madame Roland*, p. 249). In this stanza Blind has her evoke Moloch, the biblical name of a Canaanite god associated with child sacrifice through fire or war, to decry the evil committed in the name of freedom.

[49] A battle fought on 18 June 1815, near Waterloo in Belgium, where Napoleon Bonaparte's French army was defeated by a British-led coalition that included units from the United Kingdom, the Netherlands, Hanover, Brunswick, and Nassau, all under the command of the Duke of Wellington, and a Prussian army under the command of Field Marshal von Blücher. Marking the end of the Napoleonic Wars, the defeat also ended Napoleon's rule as Emperor of France, as well as the First French Empire. Finally, it definitively ended the series of wars that had convulsed Europe and other regions of the world since the French Revolution.

[50] As she moves toward an affirmation of the power of imagination and art, Blind forsakes the octet stanzas of the previous section. Like many Romantic poets, she creates an experimental verse form, this one consisting of seventeen-line stanzas mixing iambic pentameter and tetrameter lines, making use of enjambment to increase the rhythm of the stanzas, which mimics the urgency of her quest for release from 'immemorial strife' (see p. 76).

[51] A reference to the invention of the telegraph, which allowed communication to travel from the Mediterranean to the New World.

He may have weighed the stars and spanned the stream,[52]
And trained the fiery force of panting steam[53]
To whirl him o'er vast steppes and heights gigantic:
  But the storm-lashed world of feeling —
  Love, the fount of tears unsealing,
  Choruses of passion pealing —
    Lust, ambition, hatred, awe,
    Clashing loudly with the law,
    But the phantasms of the mind
    Who shall master, yea, who bind!

What help is there without, what hope within
  Of rescue from the immemorial strife?
What will redeem him from the spasm of life,
  With all its devious ways of shame and sin?
  What will redeem him from ancestral greeds,
  Grey legacies of hate and hoar misdeeds,
Which from the guilty past Man doth inherit —
  The past that is bound up with him, and part
  Of the pulsations of his inmost heart,
And of the vital motions of his spirit?
  Ages mazed in tortuous errors,
  Ghostly fears, and haunting terrors,
  Minds bewitched that served as mirrors
    For the foulest fancies bred
    In a fasting hermit's head,
    Such as cast a sickly blight
    On all shapes of life and light.

Yea, panting and pursued and stung and driven,
  The soul of Man flies on in deep distress,
  As once across the world's harsh wilderness
Latona fled, chased by the Queen of heaven;[54]
  Flying across the homeless Universe
  From the inveterate stroke of Juno's curse;

---

[52] English scientists and close friends Henry Cavendish (1731–1810) and John Michell (1724–1793), remarkable in their own right (Cavendish discovered hydrogen and Michell postulated the existence of black holes), worked both separately and together on experiments designed to measure the weight of the earth and other celestial bodies.
[53] The steam engine, designed and developed by James Watt (in collaboration with Matthew Boulton) between 1763 and 1775 (and patented by Watt in 1784), was one of the main engines of the industrial revolution.
[54] Latona, known as Leto in Greek mythology, the daughter of the Titan couple Coeus and Phoebe. After conceiving two children by Jupiter, Latona was exiled from the universe by Jupiter's wife Juno, who forbade any land from allowing her to give birth there. Latona thus began an endless sojourn across the earth, eventually finding temporary refuge on the island of Delos, where she gave birth to her twin children Apollo and Artemis. Blind calls Artemis Diana in 'The Ascent of Man', after her Roman name.

On whom even mother earth closed all her portals,
  Refusing shelter in her cooing bowers,
  Or rest upon her velvet couch of flowers,
To the most weary of all weary mortals.
    Within whose earth-encumbered form,
    Like two fair stars entwined in storm,
    Or wings astir within the worm,
      Feeling out for light and air,
      Struggled that celestial pair,
      Phœbus[55] of unerring bow,
      And chaste Dian fair as snow.

Ah, who will harbour her? Ah, who will save
  The fugitive from pangs that rack and tear;
  Who, finding rest nor refuge anywhere,
Seems doomed to be her unborn offspring's grave;
  The seed of Jove, murdered before their birth —
  Did not the sea, more merciful than earth,
Bid Delos stand — that wandering isle of Ocean —
  Stand motionless upon the moving foam,[56]
  To be the exile's wave-encircled home,
And lull her pains with leaves in drowsy motion,
    Where the soft-boughed olive sighing
    Bends above the woman lying
    And in spasms of anguish crying,
      Shuddering through her mortal frame,
      As from dust is struck the flame
      Which shall henceforth beam sublime
      Through the firmament of Time?[57]

Oh, balmy Island on the brine,[58]
  Harbour of refuge on the tumbling seas,
  The fabulous bowers of the Hesperides[59]

---

[55] A synonym for Apollo.

[56] Delos is a Greek island in the Cyclades archipelago; in Greek mythology it was originally a floating island. After granting Zeus's request to give him Delos so Latona could find refuge there, the sea god Poseidon positioned the floating island in the middle of the Aegean Sea and fastened it with four diamond chains.

[57] This stanza describes Latona's birth pangs and the birth of the twin gods Apollo and Artemis, symbolizing enlightenment and nature respectively (Artemis was the goddess of the wilderness).

[58] Delos was considered a holy sanctuary and site even before Greek mythology sanctified it as Apollo and Artemis's birthplace, and today it is one of the most important archaeological sites in all of Greece. This stanza emphasizes its status as an Edenic paradise where nature, mind, and art exist in exquisite harmony.

[59] The bower or garden of the Hesperides, near the Atlas Mountains in Africa, belonged to the goddess Hera. Its name derived from the nymphs of the sunset who cared for it and guarded the grove of trees that bore golden apples said to bestow immortality on all who consumed them.

Ne'er bore such blooming gold as glows in thine:
  Thou green Oasis on the tides of Time
  Where no rude blast disturbs the azure clime;
Thou Paradise whence man can ne'er be driven,
  Where, severed from the world-clang and the roar,
  Still in the flesh he yet may reach that shore
Where want is not, and, like the dew from heaven,
    There drops upon the fevered soul
    The balm of Thought's divine control
    And rapt absorption in the whole:
      Delivery in the realm of art
      Of the world-racked human heart —
      Forms and hues and sounds that make
      Life grow lovelier for their sake.

By sheer persistence, strenuous and slow,
  The marble yields and, line by flowing line
  And curve by curve, begins to swell and shine
Beneath the ring of each far-sighted blow:
  Until the formless block obeys the hand,
  And at the mastering mind's supreme command
Takes form and radiates from each limb and feature
  Such beauty as ne'er bloomed in mortal mould,
  Whose face, out-smiling centuries, shall hold
Perfection's mirror up to 'prentice nature.
    Not from out voluptuous ocean
    Venus rose in balanced motion,
    Goddess of all bland emotion;
      But she leaped a shape of light,
      Radiating love's delight,
      From the sculptor's brain to be
      Sphered in immortality.

New spirit-yearnings for a heavenlier mood
  Call for a love more pitiful and tender,
  And 'neath the painter's touch blooms forth in splendour
The image of transfigured motherhood.
  All hopes of all glad women who have smiled
  In adoration on their first-born child
Here smile through one glad woman made immortal;
  All tears of all sad women through whose heart
  Has pierced the edge of sorrow's sevenfold dart[60]
Lie weeping with her at death's dolorous portal.
    For in married hues whose splendour
    Bodies forth the gloom and grandeur

---

[60] A reference to the Virgin Mary; 'The Seven Sorrows of Mary' is a popular Roman Catholic devotion, and some paintings of Mary depict her body pierced by seven swords.

Of life's pageant, tragic, tender,
    Common things transfigured flush
    By the magic of the brush,
    As when sun-touched raindrops glow,
    Blent in one harmonious bow.

But see, he comes, Lord of life's changeful shows,
  To whom the ways of Nature are laid bare,
  Who looks on heaven and makes the heavens more fair,
And adds new sweetness to the perfumed rose;
  Who can unseal the heart with all its tears,
  Marshal loves, hates, hopes, sorrows, joys, and fears
In quick procession o'er the passive pages;
  Who has given tongue to silent generations
  And wings to thought, so that long-mouldered nations
May call to nations o'er the abyss of ages:
    The poet, in whose shaping brain
    Life is created o'er again
    With loftier raptures, loftier pain;
      Whose mighty potencies of verse
      Move through the plastic Universe,
      And fashion to their strenuous will
      The world that is creating still.

Do you hear it, do you hear it
Soaring up to heaven, or somewhere near it?
From the depths of life upheaving,
Clouds of earth and sorrow cleaving,
From despair and death retrieving,
All triumphant blasts of sound
Lift you at one rhythmic bound
From the thraldom of the ground.

    *   *   *   *   *

All the sweetness which the glowing
Violets waft to west winds blowing,
All the burning love-notes aching,
Rills and thrills of rapture shaking
Through the hearts that throb to breaking
  Of the little nightingales;[61]
Mellow murmuring waters streaming
  Lakeward in long silver trails,
Crooning low while earth lies dreaming
  To the moonlight-tangled vales;

---

[61] These last two stanzas before the sonnets that conclude Part II are pantheistic hymns, and they make use of a common hymn metre, trochaic tetrameter — lines with four stressed syllables that begin on a stressed beat.

Swish of rain on half-blown roses
  Hoarding close their rich perfume,
Which the summer dawn uncloses
  Sparkling in their morning bloom;
Convent peals o'er pastoral meadows,
  Swinging through hay-scented air
When the velvet-footed shadows
  Call the hind to evening prayer.
Yea, all notes of woods and highlands;
Sea-fowls' screech round sphinx-like islands
  Couched among the Hebrides;[62]
Cuckoo calls through April showers,
When the green fields froth with flowers
  And with bloom the orchard trees.
Boom of surges with their hollow
  Refluent shock from cave to cave,
As the maddening spring tides follow
  Moonstruck reeling wave o'er wave.
Yea, all rhythms of air and ocean
Married to the heart's emotion,
To the intervolved emotion
Of the heart for ever turning
  In a whirl of bliss and pain,
  Blending in symphonious strain
All the vague, unearthly yearning
  Of the visionary brain.

* * * * *

All life's discords sweetly blending,
Heights on heights of being ascending,
  Harmonies of confluent sound
  Lift you at one rhythmic bound
  From the thraldom of the ground;
Loosen all your bonds of birth,
Clogs of sense and weights of earth,
  Bear you in angelic legions
  High above terrestrial regions
Into ampler ether, where

---

[62] The Hebrides are an archipelago of hundreds of islands off the west coast of Scotland. This stanza, a pantheistic hymn to nature, draws on Blind's several visits to Scotland, beginning with a trip to the Hebrides in the fall of 1873. The reference here to the 'boom of surges' sounding 'from cave to cave' describes Fingal's cave on Staffa Island, known for its natural acoustics (Felix Mendelssohn's 'Hebrides Overture' was inspired by his 1829 visit to the cave). In a letter to Garnett, Blind describes her experience there: 'I despair of describing to you the cave itself. You hang as it were midway between what looks like the nave of a natural Cathedral paved by the wandering wave. Columns disposed in wonderful symmetry support the lofty arch, and the muffled thunder of the tide resounding from the profoundest recesses of the cavern is a music more sublime than the peal of the finest organ' (Mathilde Blind ALS to Richard Garnett, 26 September 1873, Add. MS 61927, fols 224–28).

Spirits breathe a finer air,
  Where upon world altitudes
  God-intoxicated moods
Fill you with beatitudes;
Till no longer cramped and bound
By the narrow human round,
  All the body's barriers slide,
  Which with cold obstruction hide
The supreme, undying, sole
Spirit struggling though the whole,
And no more a thing apart
From the universal heart
Liberated by the grace
Of man's genius for a space,
Human lives dissolve, enlace
In a flaming world embrace.

A Symbol[63]

Hurrying for ever in their restless flight
  The generations of earth's teeming womb
  Rise into being and lapse into the tomb
Like transient bubbles sparkling in the light;
They sink in quick succession out of sight
  Into the thick insuperable gloom
  Our futile lives in flashing by illume —
Lightning which mocks the darkness of the night.
Nay — but consider, though we change and die,
  If men must pass shall Man not still remain?
  As the unnumbered drops of summer rain
Whose changing particles unchanged on high,
  Fixed, in perpetual motion, yet maintain
The mystic bow emblazoned on the sky.

Time's Shadow[64]

Thy life, O Man, in this brief moment lies:

---

[63] While the octave of this sonnet emphasizes the passing of generations and the fleeting nature of life, the sestet holds out hope for humanity's continued growth. In this sense it offers an affirmative alternative to Tennyson's lament in canto 55 of *In Memoriam* that Darwinian nature cares only for the survival of the species, not the individual: 'Are God and Nature then at strife, | That Nature lends such evil dreams? | So careful of the type she seems, | So careless of the single life'.

[64] This sonnet was originally published in 1882 in Hall Caine's anthology *Sonnets of Three Centuries* (London: Elliot Stock, 1882), p. 237. Caine's volume is intended as an authoritative account of the sonnet's history, and contains two sonnets by Blind (the other is 'The Dead', which originally appeared in Blind's 1881 volume *The Prophecy of St. Oran and Other Poems* and was reprinted in her 1893 volume *Songs and Sonnets*).

Time's narrow bridge whereon we darkling stand,
  With an infinitude on either hand
Receding luminously from our eyes.
Lo, there thy Past's forsaken Paradise
  Subsideth like some visionary strand,
  While glimmering faint, the Future's promised land,
Illusive from the abyss, seems fain to rise.[65]

This hour alone Hope's broken pledges mar,
  And Joy now gleams before, now in our rear,
Like mirage mocking in some waste afar,
  Dissolving into air as we draw near.
  Beyond our steps the path is sunny-clear,
The shadow lying only where we are.

---

[65] The poetic allusions in this part of the sonnet include echoes of Keats' 'Ode to a Nightingale' ('Darkling I listen'), Matthew Arnold's 'Dover Beach' ('we are here as on a darkling plain'), and the opening stanzas of the fourth Canto of Byron's 'Childe Harold' ('I saw or dream'd of such, — but let them go, — | They came like truth, and disappear'd like dreams').

Part II.[66]

'Love is for ever poor, and so far from being delicate and beautiful, as mankind imagined [*sic*: imagine], he is squalid and withered... homeless and unsandalled; he sleeps without covering before the doors, and in the unsheltered streets.' — Plato.[67]

The Pilgrim Soul[68]

Through the winding mazes of windy streets
Blindly I hurried I knew not whither,
Through the dim-lit ways of the brain thus fleets

A fluttering dream driven hither and thither. —
The fitful flare of the moon fled fast,
Like a sickly smile now seeming to wither,

Now dark like a scowl in the hurrying blast
As ominous shadows swept over the roofs

---

[66] The structure of this part of the poem mirrors that of the first — a long poem ('The Pilgrim Soul'), followed by shorter ones — in this case, three sonnets. The subject matter of this part is the current state of human society. While the treatment is allegorical, the shift to the first person allows Blind to register the implications of social crisis and the search for redemption in humanly compelling, emotionally intimate terms.

[67] Blind is quoting here from Shelley's translation of *The Symposium* (Percy Bysshe Shelley, *The Banquet of Plato, and Other Pieces, Translated and Original* (New York: Cassell, 1877), 27–121 (p. 87)). Tellingly, she is quoting the only female voice in this otherwise all-male dialogue, Diotima, whose view of *Êros* (in Greek mythology the offspring of Poverty and Resource) Socrates has come to embrace. Diotima explains that *Êros* or Love is a spirit that serves as an intermediary between gods and humans, between mortality and immortality, and that it rises through levels of closeness to wisdom and true beauty, from carnal attraction to individual bodies to attraction to souls, and eventually union with the truth and virtue. In keeping with its parentage, Love is always resourceful, but always in need. In 'The Pilgrim Soul', a female adrift in modern civilization searches for the banished passions of Love and Sympathy and finds them in a destitute child; Blind thus simultaneously literalizes Diotima's personification of Love and echoes her philosophical perspective, viewing Love as the means of redeeming mankind. The three sonnets that follow in Part III can be productively read in relation to both Diotima's disquisition on Love and, more broadly, Plato's Theory of Forms.

[68] For this section of the poem Blind adopts the terza rima, a verse form originated by Dante for the *Divine Comedy* (1320). The terza rima is composed of three-line stanzas woven into a complex rhyme scheme, with the end-word of the second line in one tercet supplying the rhyme for the first and third lines in the following tercet. The rhyme scheme (aba, bcb, cdc, ded) continues through to the final stanza or line. At the end of her Commonplace Book, Blind recorded that she originally wrote this poem on 22 September 1888 ('The Commonplace book of Mathilde Blind', p. 113). Symons reprinted this section of the poem in *A Selection from the Poems of Mathilde Blind*, pp. 4–15. It is worth noting that Blind's use of allegory here is similar to two of the allegories Olive Schreiner published in *The Woman's World*: 'The Lost', vol. I (1889), pp. 145–46, and 'Life's Gifts', vol. II (1889), p. 408.

Where white as a ghost the scared moonlight had passed.
Curses came mingled with wails and reproofs,
With doors banging to and the crashing of glass,
With the baying of dogs and the clatter of hoofs,

With the rust of the river as, huddling its mass
Of weltering water towards the deep ocean,
'Neath many-arched bridges its eddies did pass.

A hubbub of voices in savage commotion
Was mixed with the storm in a chaos of sound,
And thrilled as with ague in shuddering emotion

I fled as the hunted hare flees from the hound.
Past churches whose bells were tumultuously ringing
The year in, and clashing in concord around;

Past the deaf walls of dungeons whose curses seemed clinging
To the tempest that shivered and shrieked in amazement;
Past brightly lit mansions whence music and singing

Came borne like a scent through the close-curtained casement,
To vaults in whose shadow wild outcasts were hiding
Their misery deep in the gloom of the basement.

By vociferous taverns where the women were biding
With features all withered, distorted, aghast;
Some sullenly silent, some brutally chiding,

Some reeling away into gloom as I passed
On, on, through lamp-lighted and fountain-filled places,
Where throned in rich temples, resplendent and vast,

The Lord of the City is deafened with praises
As worshipping multitudes kneel as of old;
Nor care for the crowds of cadaverous faces,

The men that are marred and the maids that are sold —
Inarticulate masses promiscuously jumbled
And crushed 'neath their Juggernaut idol of gold.[69]

Lost lives of great cities bespattered and tumbled,

---

[69] Originating in Hindu mythology as a word describing an uncouth idol of Krishna, the eighth avatar of Vishnu, 'Juggernaut' has come to figuratively signify an 'institution, practice, or notion to which persons blindly devote themselves, or are ruthlessly sacrificed' ('Juggernaut, n.', OED Online, Oxford University Press, June 2020 <www.oed.com/view/Entry/101949> [accessed 11 January 2021]).

Black rags the rain soaks, the wind whips like a knout,[70]
Were crouched in the streets there, and o'er them nigh stumbled

A swarm of light maids as they tripped to some rout.
The silk of their raiment voluptuously hisses
And flaps o'er the flags as loud laughing they flout

The wine-maddened men they ne'er satiate with kisses
For the pearls and the diamonds that make them more fair,
For the flash of large jewels that fire them with blisses,

For the glitter in the gold of their hair.
They smiled and they cozened, their bold eyes shone brightly
And lightened with laughter, as, lit by the flare

Of the wind-fretted gas-lamps, they footed it lightly,
Or, closely enlacing and bowered in gloom,
With mouth pressed to hot mouth, their parched lips drain nightly

The wine-cup of pleasure red-sealing their doom.
Brief lives like bright rockets which, aridly glowing,
Fall burnt out to ashes and reel to the tomb.

On, on, loud and louder the rough night was blowing,
Shrill singing was mixed with strange cries of despair;
And high overhead the black sky, redly glowing,

Loomed over the city one ominous glare,
As dark yawning funnels from foul throats for ever
Belched smoke grimly flaming, which outraged the air.

On, on, by long quays where the lamps in the river
Were writhing like serpents that hiss ere they drown,
And poplars with palsy seemed coldly to shiver,

On, on, to the bare desert end of the town.
When lo! the wind stopped like a heart that's ceased beating,
And nought but the waters, white foaming and brown,

Were heard as to seaward their currents went fleeting.
But hark! o'er the lull breaks a desolate moan,
Like a little lost lamb's that is timidly bleating

When, strayed from the shepherd, it staggers alone
By tracks which the mountain streams shake with their thunder,

---

[70] A whip or scourge used as an instrument of punishment.

Where death seems to gape from each boulder and stone.

I turned to the murmur: the clouds swept asunder
And wheeled like white sea-gulls around the white moon;
And the moon, like a white maid, looked down in mute wonder

On a boy whose wan eyelids were closed as in swoon.[71]
Half nude on the ground he lay, wasted and chilly,
And torn as with thorns and sharp brambles of June;

His hair, like a flame which at twilight burns stilly,
In a halo of light round his temples was blown,
And his tears fell like rain on a storm-stricken lily

Where he lay on the cold ground, abandoned, alone.
With heart moved towards him in wondering pity,
I tenderly seized his thin hand with my own:

Crying, 'Child, say how cam'st thou so far from the city?
How cam'st thou alone in such pitiful plight,
All blood-stained thy feet, with rags squalid and gritty,

A waif by the wayside, unhoused in the night?'
Then rose he and lifted the bright locks, storm driven,
Which flamed round his forehead and clouded his sight,

And mournful as meres on a moorland at even
His blue eyes flashed wildly through tears as they fell.
Strange eyes full of horror, yet fuller of heaven,

Like eyes that from heaven have looked upon hell.
The eyes of an angel whose depths show where, burning
And lost in the pit, toss the angels that fell.

'Ah,' wailed he in tones full of agonized yearning,
Like the plaintive lament of a sickening dove
On a surf-beaten shore, whence it sees past returning

The wings of the wild flock fast fading above,
As they melt on the sky-line like foam-flakes in motion:
So sadly he wailed, 'I am Love! I am Love!

'Behold me cast out as weed spurned of the ocean,
Half nude on the bare ground, and covered with scars

---

[71] In allegorical terms this abandoned child represents the enfeeblement of Love in a world that has abandoned empathy, morality, and community.

I perish of cold here'; and, choked with emotion,

Gave a sob: at the low sob a shower of stars
Broke shuddering from heaven, pale flaming, and fell
Where the mid-city roared as with rumours of wars.

'Be these God's tears?' I cried, as my tears 'gan to well.
'Ah, Love, I have sought thee in temples and towers,
In shrines where men pray, and in marts where they sell;

'In tapestried chambers made tropic with flowers,
Where amber-haired women, soft breathing of spice,
Lay languidly lapped in the gold-dropping showers

'Which gladdened and maddened their amorous eyes.
I have looked for thee vainly in churches where beaming
The Saints glowed embalmed in a prism of dyes,

'Where wave over wave the rapt music went streaming
With breakers of sound in full anthems elate.
I have asked, but none knew thee, or knew but thy seeming;

'A mask in thy likeness on high seats of state;
And they bound it with gold, and they crowned it with glory,
This thing they called love, which was bond slave to hate.

'And they bowed down before it with brown heads and hoary,
They worshipped it nightly, loud hymning its praise,
While out in the cold blast, none heeding its story,

'Love staggers, an outcast, with lust in its place.'
Love shivered and sighed like a reed that is shaken,
And lifting his hunger-nipped face to my face:

'Nay, if of the world I must needs die forsaken,
Say thou wilt not leave me to dearth and despair.
To thy heart, to thy home, let the exile be taken,

'And feed me and shelter — ' 'Where, outcast, ah, where?
Like thee I am homeless and spurned of all mortals;
The House of my fathers yawns wide to the air.

'Stalks desolation across the void portals,
Hope lies aghast on the ruinous floor,
The halls that were thronged once with star-browed immortals,

'With gods statue-still o'er the world-whirr and roar,

With fauns of the forest and nymphs of the river,
Are cleft as if lightning had struck to their core.

'The luminous ceilings, where soaring for ever
Dim hosts of plumed angels smoked up to the sky,
With God-litten[72] faces that yearned to the giver

'As vapours of morning the sun draws on high,
Now ravaged with rain hear the hollow winds whistle
Through rifts in the rafters which echo their cry.

'Blest walls that were vowed to the Virgin now bristle
With weeds of sick scarlet and plague-spotted moss,
And stained on the ground, choked with thorn and rank thistle,

'Rots a worm-eaten Christ on a mouldering Cross.[73]
From the House of my fathers, distraught, broken-hearted,
With a pang of immense, irredeemable loss,

'On my wearying pilgrimage blindly I started
To seek thee, oh Love, in high places and low,
And instead of the glories for ever departed,

'To warm my starved life in thy mightier glow.
For I deemed thee a Presence ringed round with all splendour,
With a sceptre in hand and a crown on thy brow;

'And, behold, thou art helpless — most helpless to tender
Thy service to others, who needest their care.
Yea, now that I find thee a weak child and slender,

'Exposed to the blast of the merciless air,
Like a lamb that is shorn, like a leaf that is shaken,
What, Love, now is left but to die in despair?

'For Death is the mother of all the forsaken,
The grave a strait bed where she rocks them to rest,
And sleep, from whose silence they never shall waken,

'The balm of oblivion she sheds on their breast.'
Then I seized him and led to the brink of the river,

---

[72] Lit by God ('litten' is a participle of 'light').
[73] An echo of Swinburne's antitheistic 'Before a Cross', particularly this stanza: 'And mouldering now and hoar with moss | Between us and the sunlight swings | The phantom of a Christless cross | Shadowing the sheltered heads of kings | And making with its moving shade | The souls of harmless men afraid' (*The Poems of Algernon Charles Swinburne*, II, p. 86).

Where two storm-beaten seagulls were fluttering west,

And the lamplight in drowning seemed coldly to shiver,
And clasping Love close for the leap from on high,
Said — 'Let us go hence, Love; go home, Love, for ever;

'For life casts us forth, and Man dooms us to die.'
As if stung by a snake the Child shuddered and started,
And clung to me close with a passionate cry:

'Stay with me, stay with me, poor, broken-hearted;
Pain, if not pleasure, we two will divide;
Though with the sins of the world I have smarted,

'Though with the shame of the world thou art dyed,
Weak as I am, on thy breast I'll recover,
Worn as thou art, thou shalt bloom as my bride:

'Bloom as the flower of the World for the lover
Whom thou hast found in a lost little Child.'
And as he kissed my lips over and over —

Child now, or Man, was it who thus beguiled? —
Even as I looked on him, Love, waxing slowly,
Grew as a little cloud, floating enisled,

Which spreads out aloft in the blue sky till solely
It fills the deep ether tremendous in height,
With far-flashing snow-peaks and pinnacles wholly

Invisible, vanishing light within light.
So changing waxed Love — till he towered before me,
Outgrowing my lost gods in stature and might.

As he grew, as he drew me, a great awe came o'er me,
And stammering, I shook as I questioned his name;
But gently bowed o'er me, he soothèd and bore me,

Yea, bore me once again to the haunts whence I came,
By dark ways and dreary, by rough roads and gritty,
To the penfolds of sin, to the purlieus of shame.[74]

---

[74] The archaic words 'penfolds' and 'purlieus', the first referring to an enclosure for livestock and the second to a tract of land under private ownership used for the hunting and killing of game, here take on connotations of sexual enslavement and prostitution. In figurative terms, 'to hunt in purlieu (or purlieus)' means 'to pursue or enter into an illicit relationship, esp. with a prostitute' ('purlieu, n., †b.', OED Online, Oxford University Press, March 2020, <www.oed.com/view/Entry/154933> [accessed 11 August 2021]).

And lo, as we went through the woe-clouded city,
Where women bring forth and men labour in vain,
Weak Love grew so great in his passion of pity
That all who beheld him were born once again.[75]

Saving Love[76]

Would we but love what will not pass away!
  The sun that on each morning shines as clear
  As when it rose first on the world's first year;
The fresh green leaves that rustle on the spray.
The sun will shine, the leaves will be as gay
  When graves are full of all our hearts held dear,
  When not a soul of those who loved us here,
Not one, is left us — creatures of decay.

Yea, love the Abiding in the Universe
Which was before, and will be after us.
  Nor yet for ever hanker and vainly cry
  For human love — the beings that change or die;
Die — change — forget: to care so is a curse,
Yet cursed we'll be rather than not care thus.

Nirvana[77]

Divest thyself, O Soul, of vain desire!
  Bid hope farewell, dismiss all coward fears;[78]
  Take leave of empty laughter, emptier tears,
And quench, for ever quench, the wasting fire
Wherein this heart, as in a funeral pyre,

---

[75] Through secular communion with another suffering soul, and by experiencing pity as a passion, Love is here reborn, assuming god-like grandeur and power.

[76] In keeping with Blind's antitheistic outlook, love is eternal, but those who love are not.

[77] Originally published in 1887 in *Women's Voices*, p. 314. Like 'A Symbol' in Part I, this sonnet considers the loss of individual selfhood a source of affirmation rather than despair. The title comes from the Sanskrit word signifying the realization of the non-existence of self, which frees the individual from all earthly entanglements. The 'All' in the last line signifies the entrance of the 'soul' into what Blind calls in the last poem in *Birds of Passage* the 'vast confederacy of minds' (see p. 235), not personal immortality. In her Commonplace Book, Blind described the rapture she is expressing here this way: 'I felt a great love of everything; [...] for the sun bursting through the clouds + scattering them till the sky was as clear as sapphire; for the light on the time mellowed roofs on the flowing woodland trees. I thought of St. Francis whose heart was perpetually going out in pure adoration to every created thing; whose heart beat in harmony with the world heart. This must be the state which Christians mean by heaven + perhaps Buddhists by Nirvana!' ('The Commonplace book of Mathilde Blind', p. 17).

[78] An echo of the title of Emily Brontë's posthumously published poem 'No Coward Soul is Mine' (1850), about the immersion of the individual soul into the divine soul.

Aye burns, yet is consumed not. Years on years
  Moaning with memories in thy maddened ears —
Let at thy word, like refluent waves, retire.

Enter thy soul's vast realm as Sovereign Lord,
And, like that angel with the flaming sword,
  Wave off life's clinging hands. Then chains will fall
From the poor slave of self's hard tyranny —
And Thou, a ripple rounded by the sea,
  In rapture lost be lapped within the All.

Motherhood[79]

From out the font of being, undefiled,
  A life hath been upheaved with struggle and pain;
  Safe in her arms a mother holds again
That dearest miracle — a new-born child.
To moans of anguish terrible and wild —
  As shrieks the night-wind through an ill-shut pane —
  Pure heaven succeeds; and after fiery strain
Victorious woman smiles serenely mild.

Yea, shall she not rejoice, shall not her frame
  Thrill with a mystic rapture! At this birth,
The soul now kindled by her vital flame
  May it not prove a gift of priceless worth?
Some saviour of his kind whose starry fame
  Shall bring a brightness to the darkened earth.

---

[79] At the end of her Commonplace Book, Blind recorded that she originally wrote this sonnet on 7 May 1886 in Cimiez, a neighbourhood in Nice ('The Commonplace book of Mathilde Blind', p. 113).

Part III.

'Our spirits have climbed high
By reason of the passion of our grief, —
And from the top of sense, looked over sense
To the significance and heart of things
Rather than things themselves.'
                    E. B. Browning.[80]

The Leading of Sorrow[81]

Through a twilight land, a moaning region,
  Thick with sighs that shook the trembling air,
Land of shadows whose dim crew was legion,
  Lost I hurried, hunted by despair.
Quailed my heart like an expiring splendour,
  Fitful flicker of a faltering fire,
Smitten chords which tempest-stricken render
  Rhythms of anguish from a breaking lyre.

Love had left me in a land of shadows,
  Lonely on the ruins of delight,
And I grieved with tearless grief of widows,
  Moaned as orphans homeless in the night.
Love had left me knocking at Death's portal —
  Shone his star and vanished from my sky —
And I cried: 'Since Love, even Love, is mortal,
  Take, unmake, and break me; let me die.'

Then, the twilight's grisly veils dividing,
  Phantom-like there stole one o'er the plain,
Wavering mists for ever round it gliding
  Hid the face I strove to scan in vain.
Spake the veiled one: 'Solitary weeper,
  'Mid the myriad mourners thou'rt but one:
Come, and thou shalt see the awful reaper,

---

[80] Elizabeth Barrett Browning, 'A Drama of Exile', in *A Drama of Exile: and Other Poems*, vol. 1 (New York: H. G. Langley, 1845), pp. 13–132 (p. 64). The speaker here is Adam, and the work is a closet drama about Adam and Eve after their exile from Eden. Barrett Browning treats this exile as a fortunate fall into human agency and freedom. Blind was a great admirer of Barrett Browning's poetry, and this work would have especially appealed to her, both for its secular interpretation of the Christian origin story and because Barrett Browning uses the story of Eve to deny the patriarchal myth of female inferiority.

[81] The rhyme scheme of these octet stanzas follows the pattern of the octave in an English or Elizabethan sonnet: ababcdcd. In this section of the poem, which like Part II is allegorical, Love has deserted the Pilgrim Soul, and she is thrown into the arms of Sorrow, whom she follows across the surface of the 'thickly peopled earth' witnessing increasingly grotesque scenes of natural and human violence and chaos.

Evil, reaping all beneath the sun.'

On my hand the clay-cold hand did fasten
  As it murmured — 'Up and follow me;
O'er the thickly peopled earth we'll hasten,
  Yet more thickly packed with misery.'
And I followed: ever in the shadow
  Of that looming form I fared along;
Now o'er mountains, now through wood and meadow,
  Or through cities with their surging throng.

With none other for a friend or fellow
  Those relentless footsteps were my guide
To the sea-caves echoing with the hollow
  Immemorial moaning of the tide.
Laughed the sunlight on the living ocean,
  Danced and rocked itself upon the spray,
And its shivered beams in twinkling motion
  Gleamed like star-motes in the Milky Way.

Lo, beneath those waters surging, flowing,
  I beheld the Deep's fantastic bowers;
Shapes which seemed alive and yet were growing
  On their stalks like animated flowers.
Sentient flowers which seemed to glow and glimmer
  Soft as ocean blush of Indian shells,
White as foam-drift in the moony shimmer
  Of those sea-lit, wave-pavilioned dells.

Yet even here, as in the fire-eyed panther,
  In disguise the eternal hunger lay,
For each feathery, velvet-tufted anther
  Lay in ambush waiting for its prey.
Tiniest jewelled fish that flashed like lightning,
  Blindly drawn, came darting through the wave,
When, a stifling sack above them tightening,
  Closed the ocean-blossom's living grave.

Now we fared through forest glooms primeval
  Through whose leaves the light but rarely shone,
Where the buttressed tree-trunks looked coeval
  With the time-worn, ocean-fretted stone;
Where, from stem to stem their tendrils looping,
  Coiled the lithe lianas[82] fold on fold,

---

[82] Vines rooted in the soil that climb the trunks of trees to gain access to sunlight in the upper stories of a forest canopy.

Or, in cataracts of verdure drooping,
  From on high their billowy leafage rolled.

Where beneath the dusky woodland cover,
  While the noon-hush holds all living things,
Butterflies of tropic splendour hover
  In a maze of rainbow-coloured wings:
Some like stars light up their own green heaven
  Some are spangled like a golden toy,
Or like flowers from their foliage driven
  In the fiery ecstasy of joy.

But, the forest slumber rudely breaking,
  Through the silence rings a piercing yell;
At the cry unnumbered beasts, awaking,
  With their howls the loud confusion swell.
'Tis the cry of some frail creature panting
  In the tiger's lacerating grip;
In its flesh carnivorous teeth implanting,
  While the blood smokes round his wrinkled lip.

'Tis the scream some bird in terror utters,
  With its wings weighed down by leaden fears,
As from bough to downward bough it flutters
  Where the snake its glistening crest uprears:
Eyes of sluggish greed through rank weeds stealing,
  Breath whose venomous fumes mount through the air,
Till benumbed the helpless victim, reeling,
  Drops convulsed into the reptile snare.

Now we fared o'er sweltering wastes whose steaming
  Clouds of tawny sand the wanderer blind.
Herds of horses with their long manes streaming
  Snorted thirstily against the wind;
O'er the waste they scoured in shadowy numbers,
  Gasped for springs their raging thirst to cool,
And, like sick men mocked in fevered slumbers,
  Stoop to drink — and find a phantom pool.

What of antelopes crunched by the leopard?
  What if hounds run down the timid hare?
What though sheep, strayed from the faithful shepherd,
  Perish helpless in the lion's lair?
The all-seeing sun shines on unheeding,
  In the night shines the unruffled moon,
Though on earth brute myriads, preying, bleeding,
  Put creation harshly out of tune.

Cried I, turning to the shrouded figure —
  'Oh, in mercy veil this cruel strife!
Sanguinary orgies which disfigure
  The green ways of labyrinthine life.
From the needs and greeds of primal passion,
  From the serpent's track and lion's den,
To the world our human hands did fashion,
  Lead me to the kindly haunts of men.'

And through fields of corn we passed together,
  Orange golden in the brooding heat,
Where brown reapers in the harvest weather
  Cut ripe swathes of downward rustling wheat.
In the orchards dangling red and yellow,
  Clustered fruit weighed down the bending sprays;
On a hundred hills the vines grew mellow
  In the warmth of fostering autumn days.

Through the air the shrilly twittering swallows
  Flashed their nimble shadows on the leas;
Red-flecked cows were glassed in golden shallows,
  Purple clover hummed with restless bees.
Herdsmen drove the cattle from the mountain,
  To the fold the shepherd drove his flocks,
Village girls drew water from the fountain,
  Village yokels piled the full-eared shocks.

From the white town dozing in the valley,
  Round its vast Cathedral's solemn shade,
Citizens strolled down the walnut alley
  Where youth courted and glad childhood played.
'Peace on earth,' I murmured; 'let us linger —
  Here the wage of life seems good at least':
As I spake the veiled One raised a finger
  Where the moon broke flowering in the east.

Faintly muttering from deep mountain ranges,
  Muffled sounds rose hoarsely on the night,
As the crash of foundering avalanches
  Wakes hoarse echoes in each Alpine height.
Near and nearer sounds the roaring — thunder,
  Mortal thunder, crashes through the vale;
Lightning flash of muskets breaks from under
  Groves once haunted by the nightingale.

Men clutch madly at each weapon — women,
  Children crouch in cellars, under roofs,

For the town is circled by their foemen —
  Shakes the ground with clang of trampling hoofs.
Shot on shot the volleys hiss and rattle,
  Shrilly whistling fly the murderous balls,
Fiercely roars the tumult of the battle
  Round the hard-contested, dear-bought walls.

Horror, horror! The fair town is burning,
  Flames burst forth, wild sparks and ashes fly;
With her children's blood the green earth's turning
  Blood-red — blood-red, too, the cloud-winged sky.
Crackling flare the streets: from the lone steeple
  The great clock booms forth its ancient chime,
And its dolorous quarters warn the people
  Of the conquering troops that march with time.

Fallen lies the fair old town, its houses
  Charred and ruined gape in smoking heaps;
Here with shouts a ruffian band carouses,
  There an outraged woman vainly weeps.
In the fields where the ripe corn lies mangled,
  Where the wounded groan beneath the dead,
Friend or foe, now helplessly entangled,
  Stain red poppies with a guiltier red.

There the dog howls o'er his perished master,
  There the crow comes circling from afar;
All vile things that batten on disaster
  Follow feasting in the wake of war.
Famine follows — what they ploughed and planted
  The unhappy peasants shall not reap;
Sickening of strange meats and fever haunted,
  To their graves they prematurely creep.

'Hence' — I cried in unavailing pity —
  'Let us flee these scenes of monstrous strife,
Seek the pale of some imperial city
  Where the law rules starlike o'er man's life.'
Straightway floating o'er blue sea and river,
  We were plunged into a roaring cloud,
Wherethrough lamps in ague fits did shiver
  O'er the surging multitudinous crowd.

Piles of stone, their cliff-like walls uprearing,
  Flashed in luminous lines along the night;
Jets of flame, spasmodically flaring,
  Splashed black pavements with a sickly light;

Fabulous gems shone here, and glowing coral,
  Shimmering stuffs from many an Eastern loom,
And vast piles of tropic fruits and floral
  Marvels seemed to mock November's gloom.

But what prowls near princely mart and dwelling,
  Whence through many a thundering thorough-fare
Rich folk roll on cushions softly swelling
  To the week-day feast and Sunday prayer?
Yea, who prowl there, hunger-nipped and pallid,
Breathing nightmares limned upon the gloom?
  'Tis but human rubbish, gaunt and squalid,
  Whom their country spurns for lack of room.

In their devious track we mutely follow,
  Mutely climb dim flights of oozy stairs,
Where through the gap-toothed, mizzling roof the yellow
  Pestilent fog blends with the fetid air.
Through the unhinged door's discordant slamming
  Ring the gruesome sounds of savage strife —
Howls of babes, the drunken father's damning,
  Counter-cursing of the shrill-tongued wife.

Children feebly crying on their mother
  In a wailful chorus — 'Give us food!'
Man and woman glaring at each other
  Like two gaunt wolves with a famished brood.
Till he snatched a stick, and, madly staring,
  Struck her blow on blow upon the head;
And she, reeling back, gasped, hardly caring —
  'Ah, you've done it now, Jim' — and was dead.

Dead — dead — dead — the miserable creature —
  Never to feel hunger's cruel fang
Wring the bowels of rebellious nature
  That her infants might be spared the pang.
'Dead! Good luck to her!' The man's teeth chattered,
  Stone-still stared he with blank eyes and hard,
Then, his frame with one big sob nigh shattered,
  Fled — and cut his throat down in the yard.

Dark the night — the children wail forsaken,
  Crane their wrinkled necks and cry for food,
Drop off into fitful sleep, or waken
  Trembling like a sparrow's ravished brood.
Dark the night — the rain falls on the ashes,
  Feebly hissing on the feeble heat,

Filters through the ceiling, drops in splashes
  On the little children's naked feet.

Dark the night — the children wail forsaken —
  Is there none, ah, none, to heed their moan?
Yea, at dawn one little one is taken,
  Four poor souls are left, but one is gone.
Gone — escaped — flown from the shame and sorrow
  Waiting for them at life's sombre gate,
But the hand of merciless to-morrow
  Drags the others shuddering to their fate.

But one came — a girlish thing — a creature
  Flung by wanton hands 'mid lust and crime —
A poor outcast, yet by right of nature
  Sweet as odour of the upland thyme.
Scapegoat of a people's sins, and hunted,
  Howled at, hooted to the wilderness,
To that wilderness of deaf hearts, blunted
  To the depths of woman's dumb distress.[83]

Jetsam, flotsam of the monster city,
  Spurned, defiled, reviled, that outcast came
To those babes that whined for love and pity,
  Gave them bread bought with the wage of shame.
Gave them bread, and gave them warm, maternal
  Kisses not on sale for any price:
Yea, a spark, a flash of some eternal
  Sympathy shone through those haunted eyes.

Ah, perchance through her dark life's confusion,
  Through the haste and taste of fevered hours,
Gusts of memory on her youth's pollution
  Blew forgotten scents of faded flowers.
And she saw the cottage near the wild wood,
  With its lichened and latticed panes,
Strayed once more through golden fields of childhood,
  Hyacinth dells and hawthorn-scented lanes.

---

[83] Here the central example of human violence and degradation is a young woman seduced and abandoned by a nobleman, who in her abasement becomes a Christ-like figure ministering to the poor and abandoned. Blind's evocation of the 'monster city' contains echoes of James ('B. V.') Thomson's 'The City of Dreadful Night' (1880), which Blind heard Thomson read aloud in the late 1870s. Blind and Thomson saw each other frequently from 1876 until Thomson's death in 1882; she was a great admirer of his poetry, though in her biography of George Eliot she called Thomson's radical pessimism 'a disease of the soul' (Blind, *George Eliot*, p. 172). For more on the relationship between the two poets, see Diedrick, *Mathilde Blind*, pp. 151–66.

Heard once more the song of nested thrushes
   And the blackbird's long mellifluous note,
Felt once more the glow of maiden blushes
   Burn through rosy cheek and milkwhite throat
In that orchard where the apple blossom
   Lightly shaken fluttered on her hair,
As the heart was fluttering in her bosom
   When her sweetheart came and kissed her there.

Often came he in the lilac-laden
   Moonlit twilight, often pledged his word;
But she was a simple country-maiden,
   He the offspring of a noble lord.
Fading lilacs May's farewell betoken,
   Fledglings fly and soon forget the nest;
Lightly may a young man's vows be broken,
   And the heart break in a woman's breast.

Gathered like a sprig of summer roses
   In the dewy morn and flung away,
To the girl the father's door now closes,
   Let her shelter henceforth how she may.
Who will house the miserable mother
   With her child, a helpless castaway!
'I, am I the keeper of my brother?'[84]
   Asks smug virtue as it turns to pray!

Lovely are the earliest Lenten lilies,[85]
   Primrose pleiads,[86] hyacinthine sheets;
Stripped and rifled from their pastoral valleys,
   See them sold now in the public streets!
Other flowers are sold there besides posies —
   Eyes may have the hyacinth's glowing blue,
Rounded cheeks the velvet bloom of roses,
   Taper necks the rain-washed lily's hue.

But a rustic blossom! Love and duty
   Bound up in a child whom hunger slays!

---

[84] In response to God asking Cain the whereabouts of his brother, Cain answers: 'Am I my brother's keeper?' (Genesis 4. 9–10).
[85] *Narcissus pseudonarcissus*, the only daffodil native to England.
[86] The Pleiades, a group of more than 800 stars located about 410 light years from Earth in the constellation Taurus, is the only star cluster visible to the naked eye in the night sky. In Greek mythology the Pleiades, or Seven Sisters, were the seven daughters of the Titan Atlas and the Oceanid Pleione. Since there are no varieties of primrose named 'pleiads', Blind is likely using the term to describe a starry mass of the congregated flowers, comparing them to a constellation of 'sister' blossoms.

Ah! but one thing still is left her — beauty
   Fresh, untainted yet — and beauty pays.
Beauty keeps her child alive a little,
   Then it dies — her woman's love with it —
Beauty's brilliant sceptre, ah, how brittle,
   Drags her daily deeper down the pit.

Ruin closes o'er her — hideous, nameless;
   Each fresh morning marks a deeper fall;
Till at twenty — callous, cankered, shameless,
   She lies dying at the hospital.[87]
Drink, more drink, she calls for — her harsh laughter
   Grates upon the meekly praying nurse,
Eloquent about her soul's hereafter:
   'Souls be blowed!' she sings out with a curse.

And so dies, an unrepenting sinner —
   Pitched into her pauper's grave what time
That most noble lord rides by to dinner
   Who had wooed her in her innocent prime.
And in after-dinner talk he preaches
   Resignation — o'er his burgundy —
Till a grateful public dubs his speeches
   Oracles of true philanthropy.

Peace ye call this? Call this justice, meted
   Equally to rich and poor alike?
Better than this peace the battle's heated
   Cannon-balls that ask not whom they strike!
Better than this masquerade of culture
   Hiding strange hyæna appetites,
The frank ravening of the raw-necked vulture
   As its beak the senseless carrion smites.

What of men in bondage, toiling blunted
   In the roaring factory's lurid gloom?
What of cradled infants starved and stunted?
   What of woman's nameless martyrdom?
The all-seeing sun shines on unheeding,
   Shines by night the calm, unruffled moon,
Though the human myriads, preying, bleeding,
   Put creation harshly out of tune.

'Hence, ah, hence' — I sobbed in quivering passion —
   'From these fearful haunts of fiendish men!

---

[87] This account of a dying prostitute infected with syphilis (as the reference to 'cankered' indicates) can be compared to Blind's poem 'The Message', about a dying and unrepentant prostitute, in *Dramas in Miniature* (see p. 143).

Better far the plain, carnivorous fashion
  Which is practised in the lion's den.'
And I fled — yet staggering still did follow
  In the footprints of my shrouded guide —
To the sea-caves echoing with the hollow
  Immemorial moaning of the tide.

Sinking, swelling roared the wintry ocean,
  Pitch-black chasms struck with flying blaze,
As the cloud-winged storm-sky's sheer commotion
  Showed the blank Moon's mute Medusa face[88]
White o'er wastes of water — surges crashing
  Over surges in the formless gloom,
And a mastless hulk, with great seas washing
  Her scourged flanks, pitched toppling to her doom.

Through the crash of wave on wave gigantic,
  Through the thunder of the hurricane,
My wild heart in breaking shrilled with frantic
  Exultation — 'Chaos come again!
Yea, let earth be split and cloven asunder
  With man's still accumulating curse —
Life is but a momentary blunder
  In the cycle of the Universe.

'Yea, let earth with forest-belted mountains,
  Hills and valleys, cataracts and plains,
With her clouds and storms and fires and fountains,
  Pass with all her rolling sphere contains,
Melt, dissolve again into the ocean,
  Ocean fade into a nebulous haze!'
And I sank back without sense or motion
  'Neath the blank Moon's mute Medusa face.

Moments, years, or ages passed, when, lifting
  Freezing lids, I felt the heavens on high,
And, innumerable as the sea-sands drifting,
  Stars unnumbered drifted through the sky.
Rhythmical in luminous rotation,
  In dædalian[89] maze they reel and fly,
And their rushing light is Time's pulsation
  In his passage through Eternity.

---

[88] See p. 61, note 16.
[89] A reference to the craftsman and artist of Greek mythology who created the Labyrinth, a massive maze under the court of Crete's King Minos, designed to imprison the Minotaur. The adjectival form as used here has a derived meaning of 'intricate' and 'confusing'.

Constellated suns, fresh lit, declining,
  Were ignited now, now quenched in space,
Rolling round each other, or inclining
  Orb to orb in multi-coloured rays.
Ever showering from their flaming fountains
  Light more light on each far-circling earth,
Till life stirred crepuscular seas, and mountains
  Heaved convulsive with the throes of birth.

And the noble brotherhood of planets,
  Knitted each to each by links of light,
Circled round their suns, nor knew a minute's
  Lapse or languor in their ceaseless flight.
And pale moons and rings and burning splinters
  Of wrecked worlds swept round their parent spheres,
Clothed with spring or sunk in polar winters
  As their sun draws nigh or disappears.

Still new vistas of new stars — far dwindling —
  Through the firmament like dewdrops roll,
Torches of the Cosmos which enkindling
  Flash their revelation on the soul.
Yea, One spake there — though nor form nor feature
  Shown — a Voice came from the peaks of time: —
'Wilt thou judge me, wilt thou curse me, Creature
  Whom I raised up from the Ocean slime?[90]

'Long I waited — ages rolled o'er ages —
  As I crystallized in granite rocks,
Struggled dumb through immemorial stages,
  Glacial æons, fiery earthquake shocks.
In fierce throbs of flame or slow upheaval,
  Speck by tiny speck, I topped the seas,
Leaped from earth's dark womb, and in primeval
  Forests shot up shafts of mammoth trees.

'Through a myriad forms I yearned and panted,
  Putting forth quick shoots in endless swarms —
Giant-hoofed, sharp-tusked, or finned or planted
  Writhing on the reef with pinioned arms.
I have climbed from reek or sanguine revels
  In Cimmerian[91] wood and thorny wild,

---

[90] This 'Voice' is a kind of evolving world-spirit (reminiscent of Swinburne's 'Hertha'), as old as the planet, who here re-enacts earth history before calling the speaker from despair to her mission: bringing forth a new era of transformative poetics.
[91] The Cimmerians were a nomadic people of antiquity and the earliest known inhabitants of the Crimea.

Slowly upwards to the dawnlit levels
  Where I bore thee, oh my youngest Child!

'Oh, my heir and hope of my to-morrow,
  I — I draw thee on through fume and fret,
Croon to thee in pain and call through sorrow,
  Flowers and stars take for thy alphabet.
Through the eyes of animals appealing,
  Feel my fettered spirit yearn to thine,
Who, in storm of will and clash of feeling,
  Shape the life that shall be — the divine.

'Oh, redeem me from my tiger rages,
  Reptile greed, and foul hyæna lust;
With the hero's deeds, the thoughts of sages,
  Sow and fructify this passive dust;
Drop in dew and healing love of woman
  On the bloodstained hands of hungry strife,
Till there break from passion of the Human
  Morning-glory of transfigured life.

'I have cast my burden on thy shoulder;
  Unimagined potencies have given
That from formless Chaos thou shalt mould her
  And translate gross earth to luminous heaven.
Bear, oh, bear the terrible compulsion,
  Flinch not from the path thy fathers trod,
From Man's martyrdom in slow convulsion
  Will be born the infinite goodness — God.'

Ceased the Voice: and as it ceased it drifted
  Like the seashell's inarticulate moan;
From the Deep, on wings of flame uplifted,
  Rose the sun rejoicing and alone.
Laughed in light upon the living ocean,
  Danced and rocked itself upon the spray,
And its shivered beams in twinkling motion
  Gleamed like star-motes of the Milky Way.

And beside me in the golden morning
  I beheld my shrouded phantom-guide;
But no longer sorrow-veiled and mourning —
  It became transfigured by my side.
And I knew — as one escaped from prison
  Sees old things again with fresh surprise —
It was Love himself, Love re-arisen
  With the Eternal shining though his eyes.

Poems of the Open Air

'Therefore all seasons shall be sweet to thee,
Whether the summer clothe the general earth
With greenness, or the redbreast sit and sing
Betwixt the tufts of snow on the bare branch.'
                                        S. T. Coleridge.[92]

The Sower

The winds had hushed at last as by command;
    The quiet sky above,
With its grey clouds spread o'er the fallow land,
    Sat brooding like a dove

There was no motion in the air, no sound
    Within the tree-tops stirred,
Save when some last leaf, fluttering to the ground,
    Dropped like a wounded bird:

Or when the swart[93] rooks in a gathering crowd
    With clamorous noises wheeled,
Hovering awhile, then swooped with wranglings loud
    Down on the stubbly field.

For now the big-thewed[94] horses, toiling slow
    In straining couples yoked,
Patiently dragged the ploughshare to and fro
    Till their wet haunches smoked.

Till the stiff acre, broken into clods,
    Bruised by the harrow's tooth
Lay lightly shaken, with its humid sods
    Ranged into furrows smooth.

There looming lone, from rise to set of sun,
    Without or pause or speed,
Solemnly striding by the furrows dun,
    The sower sows the seed.

The sower sows the seed, which mouldering,
    Deep coffined in the earth,
Is buried now, but with the future spring
    Will quicken into birth.

---

[92] The first four lines of the last stanza of Coleridge's 'Frost at Midnight' (1798).
[93] Dark.
[94] Muscular.

Oh, poles of birth and death! Controlling Powers
    Of human toil and need!
On this fair earth all men are surely sowers,
    Surely all life is seed!

All life is seed, dropped in Time's yawning furrow,
    Which with slow sprout and shoot,
In the revolving world's unfathomed morrow,
    Will blossom and bear fruit.

A Spring Song

Dark sod pierced by flames of flowers,
    Dead wood freshly quickening,
Bright skies dusked with sudden showers,
    Lit by rainbows on the wing.

Cuckoo calls and young lambs' bleating
    Nimble arts which coyly bring
Little gusts of tender greeting
    From shy nooks where violets cling.

Half-fledged buds and birds and vernal
    Fields of grass dew-glistening;
Evanescent life's eternal
    Resurrection, bridal Spring!

April Rain

    The April rain, the April rain,
Comes slanting down in fitful showers,
    Then from the furrow shoots the grain,
And banks are fledged with nestling flowers;
And in grey shaw[95] and woodland bowers
    The cuckoo through the April rain
        Calls once again.

    The April sun, the April sun,
Glints through the rain in fitful splendour,
    And in grey shaw and woodland dun
The little leaves spring forth and tender
Their infant hands, yet weak and slender,
    For warmth towards the April sun,
        One after one.

And between shower and shine hath birth

---

[95] A Scottish term for a small group of trees; a thicket.

The rainbow's evanescent glory;
  Heaven's light that breaks on mists of earth!
Frail symbol of our human story,
It flowers through showers where, looming hoary,
    The rain-clouds flash with April mirth,
        Like Life on earth.

The Sleeping Beauty

There was intoxication in the air;
  The wind, keen blowing from across the seas,
  O'er leagues of new-ploughed land and heathery leas,
Smelt of wild gorse[96] whose gold flamed everywhere.
An undertone of song pulsed far and near,
  The soaring larks filled heaven with ecstasies,
  And, like a living clock among the trees,
The shouting cuckoo struck the time of year.

For now the Sun had found the earth once more,
  And woke the Sleeping Beauty with a kiss;
Who thrilled with light of love in every pore,
  Opened her flower-blue eyes, and looked in his.
Then all things felt life fluttering at their core —
  The world shook mystical in lambent bliss.

Apple-Blossom

Blossom of the apple trees!
  Mossy trunks all gnarled and hoary,
  Grey boughs tipped with rose-veined glory,
Clustered petals soft as fleece
Garlanding old apple trees!

How you gleam at break of day!
  When the coy sun, glancing rarely,
  Pouts and sparkles in the pearly
Pendulous dewdrops, twinkling gay
On each dancing leaf and spray.

Through your latticed boughs on high,
  Framed in rosy wreaths, one catches
  Brief kaleidoscopic snatches
Of deep lapis-lazuli[97]
In the April-coloured sky.

---

[96] A wild bush with sharp thorns and small, yellow flowers which have a coconut-like fragrance.

[97] A deep-blue semi-precious stone prized for its intense colour. Ground into powder, it makes ultramarine, the best and most expensive of blue pigments.

When the sundown's dying brand
  Leaves your beauty to the tender
  Magic spells of moonlight splendour,
Glimmering clouds of bloom you stand,
Turning earth to fairyland.

Cease, wild winds, O, cease to blow!
  Apple-blossom, fluttering, flying,
  Palely on the green turf lying,
Vanishing like winter snow;
Swift as joy to come and go.

The Music-Lesson

A thrush alit on a young-leaved spray,
    And, lightly clinging,
    It rocked in its singing
As the rapturous notes rose loud and gay;
    And with liquid shakes,
    And trills and breaks,
Rippled through blossoming boughs of May.

Like a ball of fluff, with a warm brown throat
    And throbbing bosom,
    'Mid the apple-blossom,
The new-fledged nestling sat learning by rote
    To echo the song
    So tender and strong,
As it feebly put in its frail little note.

O blissfullest lesson amid the green grove!
    The low wind crispeth
    The leaves, where lispeth
The shy little bird with its parent above;
    Two voices that mingle
    And make but a single
Hymn of rejoicing in praise of their love.

The Teamster[98]

With slow and slouching gait Sam leads the team;

---

[98] While many of the poems in this section of the volume, in contrast to 'The Ascent of Man', seem to embrace a pre-Darwinian conception of nature (as the quotation from Coleridge at the beginning of the section suggests), this narrative poem clearly continues the evolutionary theme. On a first reading it seems incongruous that Blind would present May, the object of desire in this triangle of sexual rivalry, in such passive terms, since so many of Blind's poems assert the independence and sexual agency of women. But if the poem is considered as a rebuttal of Darwin's conception of human females in *The Descent*

He stoops i' the shoulders, worn with work not years;
One only passion has he, it would seem —
 The passion for the horses which he rears:
He names them as one would some household pet,
  May, Violet.

He thinks them quite as sensible as men;
 As nice as women, but not near so skittish;
He fondles, cossets, scolds them now and then,
 Nay, gravely talks as if they know good British:
You hear him call from dawn to set of sun,
  'Goo back! Com on!'

Sam never seems depressed nor yet elate,
 Like Nature's self he goes his punctual round;
On Sundays, smoking by his garden gate,
 For hours he'll stand, with eyes upon the ground,
Like some tired cart-horse in a field alone,
  And still as stone.

Yet, howsoever stolid he may seem,
 Sam has his tragic background, weird and wild
Like some adventure in a drunkard's dream.
 Impossible, you'd swear, for one so mild:
Yet village gossips dawdling o'er their ale
  Still tell the tale.

In his young days Sam loved a servant-maid,
 A girl with happy eyes like hazel brooks
That dance i' the sun, cheeks as if newly made
 Of pouting roses coyly hid in nooks,
And warm brown hair that wantoned into curl:
  A fresh-blown girl.

Sam came a-courting while the year was blithe,
 When wet browed mowers, stepping out in tune,
With level stroke and rhythmic swing of scythe,
 Smote down the proud grass in the pomp of June,

---

of Man, Blind's near caricature of May's passivity can be read as her way of obliquely mocking Darwin's illogic. Late in *Descent*, after presenting ample evidence establishing that female birds select their partners, Darwin writes that 'it would be a strange anomaly if female quadrupeds, which stand higher in the scale and have higher mental powers, did not generally, or at least often, exert some choice' (Darwin, *The Descent of Man*, II, pp. 268–69). Yet later Darwin claims that, because human males are 'more powerful in body and mind' than females, men have 'gained the power of selection' (II, p. 371). 'The Teamster' takes this to an almost comic extreme.

And wagons, half-tipped over, seemed to sway
    With loads of hay.

The elder bush beside the orchard croft
  Brimmed over with its bloom like curds and cream;
From out grey nests high in the granary loft
  Black clusters of small heads with callow scream
Peered open-beaked, as swallows flashed along
    To feed their young.

Ripening towards the harvest swelled the wheat,
  Lush cherries dangled 'gainst the latticed panes;
The roads were baking in the windless heat,
  And dust had floured the glossy country lanes,
One sun-hushed, light-flushed Sunday afternoon
    The last of June.

When, with his thumping heart all out joint,
  And pulses beating like a stroller's drum,
Sam screwed his courage to the sticking point
  And asked his blushing sweetheart if she'd come
To Titsey[99] Fair; he meant to coax coy May
    To name the day.

But her rich master snapped his thumb and swore
  The girl was not for him! Should not go out!
And, whistling to his dogs, slammed-to the door
  Close in Sam's face, and left him dazed without
In the fierce sunshine, blazing in his path
    Like fire of wrath.

Unheeding, he went forth with hot wild eyes
  Past fields of feathery oats and wine-red clover;
Unheeded, larks soared singing to the skies,
  Or rang the plaintive cry of rising plover;
Unheeded, pheasants with a startled sound
    Whirred from the ground.

On, on he went by acres full of grain,
  By trees and meadows reeling past his sight,
As to a man whirled onwards in a train
  The land with spinning hedgerows seems in flight;
At last he stopped and leant a long, long while
    Against a stile.

---

[99] Rural village in Sussex, south-east England.

Hours passed; the clock struck ten; a hush of night,
  In which even wind and water seemed at peace;
But here and there a glimmering cottage light
  Shone like a glowworm though the slumberous trees;
Or from some far-off homestead through the dark
      A watch-dog's bark.

But all at once Sam gave a stifled cry:
  'There's fire,' he muttered, 'fire upon the hills!'
No fire — but as the late moon rose on high
  Her light looked smoke-red as through belching mills:
No fire — but moonlight turning in his path
      To fire of wrath.

He looked abroad with eyes that gave the mist
  A lurid tinge above the breadths of grain
Owned by May's master. Then he shook his fist,
  Still muttering, 'Fire!' and measured o'er again
The road he'd come, where, lapped in moonlight, lay
      Huge ricks of hay.

There he paused glaring. Then he turned and waned
  Like mist into the misty, moon-soaked night,
Where the pale silvery fields were blotched and stained
  With strange fantastic shadows. But what light
Is that which leaps up, flickering lithe and long,
      With licking tongue!

Hungry it darts and hisses, twists and turns,
  And with each minute shoots up high and higher,
Till, wrapped in flames, the mighty hayrick burns
  And sends its sparks on to a neighbouring byre,
Where, frightened at the hot, tremendous glow,
      The cattle low.

And rick on rick takes fire; and next a stye,[100]
  Whence through the smoke the little pigs rush out;
The house-dog barks; then, with a startled cry,
  The window is flung open, shout on shout
Wakes the hard-sleeping farm where man and maid
      Start up dismayed.

And with wild faces wavering in the glare,
  In nightcaps, bedgowns, clothes half huddled on
Some to the pump, some to the duck-pond tear

---

[100] An outdoor enclosure for raising domestic pigs as livestock.

In frantic haste, while others splashing run
With pails, or turn the hose with flame-scorched face
        Upon the blaze.

At last, when some wan streaks began to show
  In the chill darkness of the sky, the fire
Went out, subdued but for the sputtering glow
  Of sparks among wet ashes. Barn and byre
Were safe, but swallowed all the summer math
        By fire of wrath.

Still haggard from the night's wild work and pale,
  Farm-men and women stood in whispering knots,
Regaled with foaming mugs of nut-brown ale;
  Firing his oaths about like vicious shots,
The farmer hissed out now and then: 'Gad damn!
        It's that black Sam.'

They had him up and taxed him with the crime;
  Denying naught, he sulked and held his peace;
And so, a branded convict, in due time,
  Handcuffed and cropped, they shipped him over-seas:
Seven years of shame sliced from his labourer's life
        As with a knife.

But through it all the image of a girl
  With hazel eyes like pebbled waters clear,
And warm brown hair that wantoned into curl,
  Kept his heart sweet through many a galling year,
Like to a bit of lavender long pressed
        In some black chest.

At last his time was up, and Sam returned
  To his dear village with its single street,
Where, in the sooty forge, the fire still burned,
  As, hammering on the anvil, red with heat,
The smith wrought at a shoe with tongues aglow,
        Blow upon blow.

There stood the church, with peals for death and birth,
  Its ancient spire o'ertopping ancient trees,
And there the graves and mounds of unknown earth,
  Gathered like little children round its knees;
There was 'The Bull', with sign above the door,
        And sanded floor.

Unrecognized Sam took his glass of beer,

And picked up gossip which the men let fall:
How Farmer Clow had failed, and one named Steer
  Had taken on the land, repairs and all;
And how the Kimber girl was to be wed
        To Betsy's Ned.

Sam heard no more, flung down his pence, and took
  The way down to the well-remembered stile;
There, in the gloaming by the trysting brook,
  He came upon his May — with just that smile
For sheep-faced Ned, that light in happy eyes:
        Oh, sugared lies!

He came upon them with black-knitted brows
  And clenched brown hands, and muttered huskily:
'Oh, little May, are those your true love's vows
  You swore to keep while I was over-sea?'
Then crying, turned upon the other one,
        'Com on, com on.'

Then they fell to with faces set for fight,
  And hit each other hard with rustic pride;
But Sam, whose arm with iron force could smite,
  Knocked his cowed rival down, and won his bride.
May wept and smiled, swayed like a wild red rose
        As the wind blows.

She married Sam, who loved her with a wild
  Strong love he could not put to words — too deep
For her to gauge; but with her first-born child
  May dropped off, flower-like, into the long sleep,
And left him nothing but the memory of
        His little love.

Since then the silent teamster lives alone,
  The trusted headman of his master Steer;
One only passion seems he still to own —
  The passion for the foals he has to rear;
And still the prettiest, full of life and play,
        Is little May.

A Highland Village

Clear shining after the rain,
  The sun bursts the clouds asunder,
  And the hollow-rumbling thunder
Groans like a loaded wain

As, deep in the Grampians[101] yonder,
He grumbles now and again.

Whenever the breezes shiver
The leaves where the rain-drops quiver,
  Each bough and bush and brier
  Breaks into living fire,
Till every tree is bright
With blossom bursts of light.

From golden roof and spout
  Brown waters gurgle and splutter,
  And rush down the flooded gutter
Where the village children shout,
As barefoot they splash in and out
  The water with tireless patter.

The bald little Highland street
  Is all alive and a-glitter;
The air blows keen and sweet
  From the field where the swallows twitter;
Old wives on the doorsteps meet,
  At the corner the young maids titter.

And the reapers hasten again,
Ere quite the daylight wane
  To shake out the barley sheaves;
  While through the twinkling leaves
  The harvest moon upheaves
Clear shining after the rain.

On a Forsaken Lark's Nest

Lo, where left 'mid the sheaves, cut down by the iron-fanged reaper,
Eating its way as it clangs fast through the wavering wheat,
Lies the nest of a lark, whose little brown eggs could not keep her
As she, affrighted and scared, fled from the harvester's feet.

Ah, what a heartful of song that now will never awaken,
Closely packed in the shell, awaited love's fostering,
That should have quickened to life what, now a-cold and forsaken,
Never, enamoured of light, will meet the dawn on the wing.

Ah, what pæans of joy, what raptures no mortal can measure,
Sweet as honey that's sealed in the cells of the honey-comb,
Would have ascended on high in jets of mellifluous pleasure,

---

[101] A Scottish mountain range dividing the Highlands from the Lowlands.

Would have dropped from the clouds to nest in its gold-curtained home.

Poor, pathetic brown eggs! Oh, pulses that never will quicken!
Music mute in the shell that hath been turned to a tomb!
Many a sweet human singer, chilled and adversity-stricken,
Withers benumbed in a world his joy might have helped to illume.

Reapers

Sun-tanned men and women, toiling there to-gether;
  Seven I count in all, in yon field of wheat,
Where the rich ripe ears in the harvest weather
  Glow an orange gold though the sweltering heat.

Busy life is still, sunk in brooding leisure:
  Birds have hushed their singing in the hushed tree-tops;
Not a single cloud mars the flawless azure;
  Not a shadow moves o'er the moveless crops;

In the glassy shallow, that no breath is creasing,
  Chestnut-coloured cows in the rushes dank
Stand like cows of bronze, save when they flick the teasing
  Flies with switch of tail from each quivering flank.

Nature takes a rest — even her bees are sleeping,
  And the silent wood seems a church that's shut;
But these human creatures cease not from their reaping
  While the corn stands high, waiting to be cut.

Apple-Gathering

Essex flats are pink with clover,
  Kent is crowned with flaunting hops,
Whitely shine the cliffs of Dover,
  Yellow wave the Midland crops;

Sussex Downs the flocks grow sleek on,
  But, for me, I love to stand
Where the Herefordshire beacon[102]
  Watches o'er his orchard land.

---

[102] One of the highest peaks of the Malvern Hills, surrounded by a British Iron Age hill fort earthwork known as British Camp. The Malvern area was one of Blind's favourite places to visit in Great Britain. The town of Malvern was famous in the Victorian era for its 'water cure', which involved drinking from the many springs in the Malvern Hills. In the early 1880s she often visited the spa town of Malvern to seek treatment for her chronic bronchitis. Others who visited the spa town included Charles Darwin, Florence Nightingale, the Prime Minister Lord Aberdeen, and Alfred Tennyson.

Where now sun, now shadow dapples —
   As it wavers in the breeze —
Clumps of fresh-complexioned apples
   On the heavy-laden trees:

Red and yellow, streaked and hoary,
   Russet-coated, pale or brown —
Some are dipped in sunset glory,
   And some painted by the dawn.

What profusion, what abundance!
   Not a twig but has its fruits;
High in air some in the sun dance,
   Some lie scattered near the roots.

These the hasty winds have taken
   Are a green, untimely crop;
Those by burly rustics shaken
   Fall with loud resounding plop.

In this mellow autumn weather,
   Ruddy 'mid the long green grass,
Heaped-up baskets stand together,
   Filled by many a blowsy lass.

Red and yellow, streaked and hoary,
   Pile them on the granary floors,
Till the yule-log's flame in glory
   Loudly up the chimney roars;

Till gay troops of children, lightly
   Tripping in with shouts of glee,
See ripe apples dangling brightly
   On the red-lit Christmas-tree.

The Songs of Summer

The songs of summer are over and past!
   The swallow's forsaken the dripping eaves;
   Ruined and black 'mid the sodden leaves
The nests are rudely swung in the blast:
   And ever the wind like a soul in pain
   Knocks and knock at the window-pane.

The songs of summer are over and past!
   Woe's me for a music sweeter than theirs —
   The quick, light bound of a step on the stairs,
The greeting of lovers too sweet to last:

And ever the wind like a soul in pain
Knocks and knocks at the window-pane.

Autumn Tints

Coral-coloured yew-berries
  Strew the garden ways,
Hollyhocks and sunflowers
  Make a dazzling blaze
  In these latter days.

Marigolds by cottage doors
  Flaunt their golden pride,
Crimson-punctured bramble leaves
  Dapple far and wide
  The green mountain-side.

Far away, on hilly slopes
  Where fleet rivulets run,
Miles on miles of tangled fern,
  Burnished by the sun,
  Glow a copper dun.

For the year that's on the wane,
  Gathering all its fire,
Flares up through the kindling world
  As, ere they expire,
  Flames leap high and higher.

Green Leaves and Sere

Three tall poplars beside the pool
  Shiver and moan in the gusty blast,
The carded clouds are blown like wool,
  And the yellowing leaves fly thick and fast.

The leaves, now driven before the blast,
  Now flung by fits on the curdling pool,
Are tossed heaven-high and dropped at last
  As if at the whim of a jabbering fool.

O leaves, once rustling green and cool!
  Two met here where one moans aghast
With wild heart heaving towards the past:
  Three tall poplars beside the pool.

The Hunter's Moon[103]

The Hunter's Moon rides high,
  High o'er the close-cropped plain;
Across the desert sky
  The herded clouds amain
Scamper tumultuously,
    Chased by the hounding wind
    That yelps behind.

The clamorous hunt is done,
  Warm-housed the kennelled pack;
One huntsman rides alone
With dangling bridle slack;
He wakes a hollow tone,
    Far echoing to his horn
    In clefts forlorn.

The Hunter's Moon rides low,
  Her course in nearly sped.
Where is the panting roe?
Where hath the wild deer fled?
Hunter and hunted now
    Lie in oblivion deep:
    Dead or asleep.

The Passing Year

No breath of wind stirs in the painted leaves,
  The meadows are as stirless as the sky,
  Like a Saint's halo golden vapours lie
Above the restful valley's garnered sheaves.
The journeying Sun, like one who fondly grieves,
  Above the hills seems loitering with a sigh,
  As loth to bid the fruitful earth good-bye,
On these hushed hours of luminous autumn eves.

There is a pathos in his softening glow,
  Which like a benediction seems to hover
O'er the tranced earth, ere he must sink below
  And leave her widowed of her radiant Lover,
A frost-bound sleeper in a shroud of snow
  While winter winds howl a wild dirge above her.

---

[103] The first full moon after a harvest moon.

The Robin Redbreast

The year's grown songless! No glad pipings thrill
  The hedge-row elms, whose wind-worn branches shower
  Their leaves on the sere grass, where some late flower
In golden chalice hoards the sunlight still.
Our summer guests, whose raptures used to fill
  Each apple-blossomed garth and honeyed bower,
  Have in adversity's inclement hour
Abandoned us to bleak November's chill.

But hearken! Yonder russet bird among
  The crimson clusters of the homely thorn
Still bubbles o'er with little rills of song —
A blending of sweet hope and resignation:
  Even so, when life of love and youth is shorn,
One friend becomes its last, best consolation.

The Red Sunsets, 1883[104]

The boding sky was charactered with cloud,
  The scripture of the storm — but high in air,
  Where the unfathomed zenith still was bare,
A pure expanse of rose-flushed violet glowed
And, kindling into crimson light, o'erflowed
  The hurrying wrack with such a blood-red glare,
  That heaven, igniting, wildly seemed to flare
On the dazed eyes of many an awe-struck crowd.

And in far lands folk presaged with blanched lips
Disastrous wars, earthquakes, and foundering ships
  Such whelming floods as never dykes could stem,

---

[104] In this and the following 'Red Sunsets' sonnet, set in Manchester at Christmas time, Blind imagines the Krakatoa eruption of that year as the portent of apocalyptic change in the political order, emerging from an economic system that originated with James Watt's 1784 patent on the double-acting steam engine and led inevitably to the factory system, alienated labour, *The Condition of the Working Class in England*, and *The Communist Manifesto*. These sonnets combine both the generalized end-of-the-world foreboding prevalent during the *fin de siècle* and Blind's dream of a socialist future. When she first visited Manchester in 1876 Blind met Charles Rowley, who in 1875 became a liberal councillor for the Ancoats district of Manchester and in 1878 founded the Ancoats Brotherhood with the Ruskinian aim of bringing art and literature to the working classes. Ancoats was a notorious Manchester slum, and by organizing free lectures, free concerts, and free art exhibitions for exploited workers, Rowley hoped to provide them with the means to gain social and political agency. Rowley attracted leading socialists, including Ford Madox Ford, William Morris, Peter Kropotkin, and George Bernard Shaw to speak at the Sunday gatherings the Brotherhood organized. These two sonnets can be read as companion poems to 'Manchester by Night', published in her 1883 volume *The Prophecy of St. Oran and Other Poems* and reprinted in *Songs and Sonnets*.

Or some proud empire's ruin and eclipse:
    Lo, such a sky, they cried, as burned o'er them
    Once lit the sacking of Jerusalem!

The Red Sunsets, 1883[105]

The twilight heavens are flushed with gathering light,
  And o'er wet roofs and huddling streets below
  Hang with a strange Apocalyptic glow
On the black fringes of the wintry night.
Such bursts of glory may have rapt the sight
  Of him to whom on Patmos long ago
  The visionary angel came to show
That heavenly city built of chrysolite.

And lo, three factory hands begrimed with soot,
  Aflame with the red splendour, marvelling stand,
And gaze with lifted faces awed and mute.
  Starved of earth's beauty by Man's grudging hand,
O toilers, robbed of labour's golden fruit,
  Ye, too, may feast in Nature's fairyland.

On the Lighthouse at Antibes[106]

A stormy light of sunset glows and glares
  Between two banks of cloud, and o'er the brine
  Thy fair lamp on the sky's carnation line[107]
Alone on the lone promontory flares:
Friend of the Fisher who at nightfall fares
  Where lurk false reefs masked by the hyaline[108]
  Of dimpling waves, within whose smile divine

---

[105] This sonnet alludes to several biblical passages. Lines six and seven refer to Revelation 1. 9: 'I John, who also am your brother, and companion in tribulation, and in the kingdom and patience of Jesus Christ, was in the isle that is called Patmos, for the word of God, and for the testimony of Jesus Christ.' Lines seven and eight, where an angel shows 'the city built of chrysolite' (chrysolite is a silicate of magnesia and iron found in lava) allude to Revelation 21. 10: 'and he [an angel] carried me away in the spirit to a great and high mountain, and shewed me that great city, the holy Jerusalem, descending out of heaven from God'. These lines also draw on the description of the city from Revelation 21. 19 and 20: 'And the foundations of the wall of the city were garnished with all manner of precious stones. The first foundation was jasper [...] the seventh, chrysolite'. The sestet then goes on to implicitly compare the three factory hands to the three wise men who attended on Christ's birth, and to imply that, because they can perceive the sublimity of nature, they will be redeemed by the coming apocalypse.
[106] The Antibes lighthouse is on the Mediterranean coast south-west of Nice.
[107] A coloured streak in the sky caused by condensed water vapour.
[108] Glassiness, translucency.

Death lies in wait behind Circean snares.[109]

The evening knows thee ere the evening star;
  Or sees thy flame sole Regent of the bight,[110]
When storm, hoarse rumoured by the hills afar,
  Makes mariners steer landward by thy light,
Which shows through shock of hostile nature's war
  How man keeps watch o'er man through deadliest night.

Cagnes[111]

On the Riviera

In tortuous windings up the steep incline
  The sombre street toils to the village square,
  Whose antique walls in stone and moulding bear
Dumb witness to the Moor. Afar off shine,
With tier on tier, cutting heaven's blue divine,
  The snowy Alps; and lower the hills are fair,
  With wave-green olives rippling down to where
Gold clusters hang and leaves of sunburnt vine.

You may perchance, I never shall forget
  When, between twofold glory of land and sea,
We leant together o'er the old parapet,
  And saw the sun go down. For, oh, to me,
The beauty of that beautiful strange place
Was its reflection beaming from your face.

---

[109] A reference to the sorceress Circe in Greek mythology, who in *The Odyssey* turned Odysseus's men into swine.

[110] The curve in a coastline.

[111] Cagnes-sur-Mer is a town west-south-west of Nice in the Provence-Alpes-Côte d'Azur region in south-eastern France. While visiting this small village in late November 1887 Blind met a Russian relative of Marie Bashkirtseff, the painter whose journal she would translate in 1890. In a 26 November 1887 letter to Garnett, Blind described the walk to the topmost point in the village with this man, which formed the basis of this poem: 'Cagnes the most picturesque place by far which I have seen here, [is] a hill village dating back to the time of the Saracens and with not a modern discord in the way of architecture to destroy the shell. We went in a little cheap 'Bus crowded with holiday folk and then made our way up the steep, narrow street, the walls and roofs of the houses having assimilated in tone with the grey rock, and the sober tinted olive trees. The view from the little Plase at the top of the town took us completely by surprise. White-shining in the distance the snowy peaks of the Maritime Alps rose against the deep blue sky, while the lower hills feathered with pine and olive woods sloped and rose to a mysterious valley with a solitary road flanked by a clump of cypresses and the fragment of a Roman ruin. The terrace gardens with this downward incline were full of golden globed orange trees, only by the roadside one tall and solitary palm reminded one irresistibly of Heine' (Mathilde Blind ALS to Richard Garnett, Add. MS 61929, fol. 157).

A Winter Landscape

All night, all day, in dizzy, downward flight,
  Fell the wild-whirling, vague, chaotic snow,
  Till every landmark of the earth below,
Trees, moorlands, roads, and each familiar sight
Were blotted out by the bewildering white.
  And winds, now shrieking loud, now whimpering low,
  Seemed lamentations for the world-old woe
That death must swallow life, and darkness light.

But all at once the rack was blown away,
  The snowstorm hushing ended in a sigh;
  Then like a flame the crescent moon on high
Leaped forth among the planets; pure as they,
Earth vied in whiteness with the Milky Way:
  Herself a star beneath the starry sky.

The Ascent of Man (1889)

Love in Exile

'Whatever way my days decline,
    I felt and feel, tho' left alone,
    His being working in mine own,
The footsteps of his life in mine.'
                    Lord Tennyson.[112]

Songs

I.

Thou walkest with me as the spirit-light
  Of the hushed moon, high o'er a snowy hill,
Walks with the houseless traveller all the night,
  When trees are tongueless and when mute the rill.
Moon of my soul, O phantasm of delight,
  Thou walkest with me still.

The vestal flame of quenchless memory burns
  In my soul's sanctuary. Yea, still for thee
My bitter heart hath yearned, as moonward yearns
  Each separate wave-pulse of the clamorous sea:
My Moon of love, to whom for ever turns
  The life that aches through me.

II.

I was again beside my love in dream:[113]
  Earth was so beautiful, the moon was shining;
The muffled voice of many a cataract stream
  Came like a love-song, as, with arms entwining,

---

[112] This epigraph is from Canto 85 of *In Memoriam*, and its autobiographical subject is Tennyson's feeling that even after the death of his close friend Arthur Henry Hallam, Hallam's 'being' continued living within his mind and memory. But throughout *In Memoriam*, Tennyson links his lyric speaker's feelings to shared human experiences, and this is worth remembering when analysing Blind's lyric poems in this section. It might be tempting to read 'Love in Exile' as a series of poems lamenting Blind's own lost or unrequited love, as Angela Thirlwell does when she claims that the addressee is Blind's close friend (and perhaps more), the painter Ford Madox Brown (Angela Thirlwell, *Into the Frame: The Four Loves of Ford Madox Brown* (London: Chatto & Windus, 2010), p. 202). However, there are a number of individuals (male and female) that individual poems here could at some level be addressing, from Blind's dead brother Ferdinand, whose loss she mourned all her life, to Symons, to Mona Caird, whose beauty and attractiveness she celebrates explicitly in her Commonplace Book. It is important to stress that the speaker in the 'Love in Exile' lyrics is a desiring subject, but not identical to the poet herself. As Louise Chandler Moulton said of these verses in her review of *The Ascent of Man*, '[n]othing can be more absurd than to consider love poems as the direct result of personal experience' (see p. 265).
[113] When Blind expanded this sequence for her omnibus volume *Songs and Sonnets*, she changed its opening line to 'I was again beside thee in a dream'.

Our hearts were mixed in unison supreme.

The wind lay spell-bound in each pillared pine,
  The tasselled larches had no sound or motion,
As my whole life was sinking into thine —
  Sinking into a deep, unfathomed ocean
Of infinite love — uncircumscribed, divine.

Night held her breath, it seemed, with all her stars:
  Eternal eyes that watched in mute compassion
Our little lives o'erleap their mortal bars,
  Fused in the fulness of immortal passion,
A passion as immortal as the stars.

There was no longer any thee or me;
  No sense of self, no wish or incompleteness
The moment, rounded to Eternity,
  Annihilated time's destructive fleetness:
For all but love itself had ceased to be.

III.

I am athirst, but not for wine;
The drink I long for is divine,
Poured only from your eyes in mine.

I hunger, but the bread I want,
Of which my blood and brain are scant,
Is your sweet speech, for which I pant.

I am a-cold, and lagging lame,
Life creeps along my languid frame;
Your love would fan it into flame.

Heaven's in that little word — your love!
It makes my heart coo like a dove,
My tears fall as I think thereof.

IV.

I would I were the glow-worm,[114] thou the flower,
  That I might fill thy cup with glimmering light;
I would I were the bird, and thou the bower,
  To sing thee songs throughout the summer night.

I would I were a pine tree deeply rooted,
  And thou the lofty, cloud-beleaguered rock,

---

[114] A kind of insect larvae or adult larviform female insect that glows because of bioluminescence.

Still, while the blasts of heaven around us hooted,
  To cleave to thee and weather every shock.

I would I were the rill, and thou the river;
  So might I, leaping from some headlong steep,
With all my waters lost in thine for ever,
  Be hurried onwards to the unfathomed deep.

I would — what would I not? O foolish dreaming!
  My words are but as leaves by autumn shed,
That, in the faded moonlight idly gleaming,
  Drop on the grave where all our love lies dead.

V.

Dost thou remember ever, for my sake,
When we two rowed upon the rock-bound lake?
How the wind-fretted waters blew their spray
About our brows like blossom-falls of May
      One memorable day?

Dost thou remember the glad mouth that cried —
'Were it not sweet to die now side by side,
To lie together tangled in the deep
Close as the heart-beat to the heart — so keep
      The everlasting sleep?'

Dost thou remember? Ah, such death as this
Had set the seal upon my heart's young bliss!
But, wrenched asunder, severed and apart,
Life knew a deadlier death: the blighting smart
      Which only kills the heart.

VI.

O moon, large golden summer moon,
  Hanging between the linden trees,
  Which in the intermittent breeze
Beat with the rhythmic pulse of June!

O night-air, scented through and through
  With honey-coloured flower of lime,
  Sweet now as in that other time
When all my heart was sweet as you!

The sorcery of this breathing bloom
  Works like enchantment in my brain,
  Till, shuddering back to life again,
My dead self rises from its tomb.

And, lovely with the love of yore,
  Its white ghost haunts the moon-white ways;
  But, when it meets me face to face,
Flies trembling to the grave once more.

VII.

Why will you haunt me unawares,
  And walk into my sleep,
Pacing its shadowy thoroughfares,
Where long-dried perfume scents the airs,
  While ghosts of sorrow creep,
Where on Hope's ruined altar-stairs,
  With ineffectual beams,
The Moon of Memory coldly glares
  Upon the land of dreams?

My yearning eyes were fain to look
  Upon your hidden face;
Their love, alas! you could not brook,
But in your own you mutely took
  My hand, and for a space
You wrung it till I throbbed and shook,
  And woke with wildest moan
And wet face channelled like a brook
  With your tears or my own.

VIII.

When you wake from troubled slumbers
  With a dream-bewildered brain,
And old leaves which no man numbers
Chattering tap against the pane;
  And the midnight wind is wailing
Till you very life seems quailing
  As the long gusts shudder and sigh:
  Know you not that homeless cry
  Is my love's, which cannot die,
  Wailing through Eternity?

When beside the glowing embers,
  Sitting in the twilight lone,
Drop on drop you hear November's
  Melancholy monotone,
As the heavy rain comes sweeping,
With a sound of weeping, weeping,
  Till your blood is chilled with fears;
  Know you not those falling tears,

Flowing fast through years on years,
For my sobs within your ears?

When with dolorous moan the billows
  Surge around where, far and wide,
Leagues on leagues of sea-worn hollows
  Throb with thunders of the tide,
And the weary waves in breaking
Fill you, thrill you, as with aching
  Memories of our love of yore,
  Where you pace the sounding shore,
  Hear you not, through roll and roar,
    Soul call soul for evermore?

IX.

In a lonesome burial-place
Crouched a mourner white of face;
  Wild her eyes — unheeding
Circling pomp of night and day —
Ever crying, 'Well away,
  Love lies a-bleeding!'

And her sighs were like a knell,
And her tears for ever fell,
  With their warm rain feeding
That purpureal flower, alas!
Trailing prostrate in the grass,
  Love lies a-bleeding.[115]

Through the yews' black-tufted gloom
Crimson light fell on the tomb,
  Funeral shadows breeding:
In the sky the sun's light shed
Dyed the earth one awful red —
  Love lies a-bleeding.

Came grey mists, and blanching cloud
Bore one universal shroud;
  Came the bowed moon leading,
From the infinite afar
Star that rumoured unto star —
  Love that lies a-bleeding.

---

[115] 'Love-lies-bleeding' is the common name for the flower of the amaranth plant. In *Paradise Lost*, John Milton describes Amaranth as 'immortal' because its flowers generally do not wither and retain their reddish tones (ranging from maroon to crimson) even when dried.

X.

On life's long round by chance I found
  A dell impearled with dew;
Where hyacinths, gushing from the ground,
  Lent to the earth heaven's native hue
    Of holy blue.

I sought that plot of azure light
  Once more in gloomy hours;
But snow had fallen overnight
And wrapped in mortuary white
  My fairy ring of flowers.

XI.

Ah, yesterday was dark and drear,
  My heart was deadly sore;
Without thy love it seemed, my Dear,
  That I could live no more.

And yet I laugh and sing to-day;
  Care or care not for me,
Thou canst not take the love away
  With which I worship thee.

And if to-morrow, Dear, I live,
  My heart I shall not break:
For still I hold it that to give
  Is sweeter than to take.

XII.

Yea, the roses are still on fire
  With the bygone heat of July,
    Though the least little wind drifting by
Shake a rose-leaf or two from the brier,
  Be it never so soft a sigh.

Ember of love still glows and lingers
  Deep at the red heart's smouldering core;
    With the sudden passionate throb of yore
We shook as our eyes and clinging fingers
  Met once only to meet no more.

XIII.

We met as strangers on life's lonely way,
  And yet it seemed we knew each other well;
There was no end to what thou hadst to say,
  Or to the thousand things I found to tell.

My heart, long silent, at thy voice that day
  Chimed in my breast like to a silver bell.

How much we spoke, and yet still left untold
  Some secret half revealed within our eyes:
Didst thou not love me once in ages old?
  Had I not called thee with importunate cries,
And, like a child left sobbing in the cold,
  Listened to catch from far thy fond replies?

We met as strangers, and as such we part;
  Yet all my life seems leaving me with thine;
Ah, to be clasped once only heart to heart,
  If only once to feel that thou wert mine!
These lips are locked, and yet I know thou art
  That all in all for which my soul did pine.

XIV.

You make the sunshine of my heart
  And its tempestuous shower;
Sometimes the thought of you is like
  A lilac bush in flower,
Yea, honey-sweet as hives in May.
And then the pang of it will strike
My bosom with a fiery smart,
As though love's deeply planted dart
  Drained all its life away.

My thoughts hum round you, Dear, like bees
  About a bank of thyme,
Or round the yellow blossoms of
  The heavy-scented lime.
Ah, sweeter you than honeydew,
Yet dark the ways of love,
For it has robbed my soul of peace,
And marred my life and turned heart's-ease
  Into funereal rue.[116]

XV.

Dear, when I look into your eyes
  My hurts are healed, my heart grows whole;
  The barren places in my soul,
Like waste lands under April skies,
Break into flower beneath your eyes.

---

[116] In addition to the named plants in this poem, it is worth noting of the last two lines that the common name of the pansy (itself a pun on *pensée*) is 'hearts-ease', and that 'rue' is a bitter herb symbolising regret.

Ah, life grows lovely where you are;
  Only to think of you gives light
  To my dark heart, within whose night
Your image, though you bide afar,
Glows like a lake-reflected star.

Dare I crave more than only this:
  A thrill of love, a transient smile
  To gladden all my world awhile?
No more, alas! Is mortal bliss
Not transient as a lover's kiss?

XVI.

Ah, if you knew how soon and late
  My eyes long for a sight of you
Sometimes in passing by my gate
  You'd linger until fall of dew,
      If you but knew!

Ah, if you knew how sick and sore
  My life flags for the want of you,
Straightway you'd enter at the door
  And clasp my hand between your two,
      If you but knew!

Ah, if you knew how lost and lone
  I watch and weep and wait for you,
You'd press my heart close to your own
  Till love had healed me through and through,
      If you but knew!

XVII.

Your looks have touched my soul with bright
      Ineffable emotion;
As moonbeams on a stormy night
Illume with transitory light
A seagull on her lonely flight
      Across the lonely ocean.

Fluttering from out the gloom and roar,
      On fitful wing she flies,
Moon-white above the moon-washed shore;
Then, drowned in darkness as before,
She's lost, as I when lit no more
      By your beloved eyes.

XVIII.

Oh, brown Eyes with long black lashes,
    Young brown Eyes,
Depths of night from which there flashes
  Lightning as of summer skies,
  Beautiful brown Eyes!

In your veiled mysterious splendour
    Passion lies
Sleeping, but with sudden tender
  Dreams that fill with vague surmise
  Beautiful brown Eyes.

All my soul, with yearning shaken,
    Asks in sighs —
Who will see your heart awaken,
  Love's divine sunrise
  In those young brown Eyes?

XIX.

Once on a golden day,
In the golden month of May,
I gave my heart away —
  Little birds were singing.

I culled my heart in truth,
Wet with the dews of youth,
For love to take, forsooth —
  Little flowers were springing.

Love sweetly laughed at this,
And between kiss and kiss
Fled with my heart in his:
  Winds warmly blowing.

And with his sun and shower
Love kept my heart in flower,
As in the greenest bower
Rose richly glowing.

Till, worn at evensong,
Love dropped my heart among
Stones by the way ere long;
  Misprizèd token.

There in the wind and rain,
Trampled and rent in twain,

Ne'er to be whole again,
  My heart lies broken.

XX.

What magic is there in thy mien,
  What sorcery in thy smile,
Which charms away all cark and care,
Which turns the foul days into fair,
  And for a little while
Changes this disenchanted scene
From the sere leaf into the green,
  Transmuting with love's golden wand
  This beggared life to fairyland?

My heart goes forth to thee, oh friend,
  As some poor pilgrim to a shrine,
A pilgrim who has come from far
To seek his spirit's folding star,
  And sees the taper shine;
The goal to which his wanderings tend,
Where want and weariness shall end,
  And kneels ecstatically blest
  Because his heart hath entered rest.

Heart's-Ease

As opiates to the sick on wakeful nights,
  As light to flowers, as flowers in poor men's rooms,
  As to the fisher when the tempest glooms
The cheerful twinkling of his village lights;
As emerald isles to flagging swallow flights,
  As roses garlanding with tendrilled blooms
  The unweeded hillocks of forgotten tombs,
As singing birds on cypress-shadowed heights,

Thou art to me — a comfort past compare —
  For thy joy-kindling presence, sweet as May
  Sets all my nerves to music, makes away
With sorrow and the numbing frost of care,
  Until the influence of thine eyes' bright sway
Has made life's glass go up from foul to fair.

Untimely Love

Peace, throbbing heart, nor let us shed one tear
  O'er this late love's unseasonable glow;
  Sweet as a violet blooming in the snow,
The posthumous offspring of the widowed year,

That smells of March when all the world is sere,
  And, while around the hurtling sea-winds blow —
  Which twist the oak and lay the pine tree low —
Stands childlike in the storm and has no fear.

Poor helpless blossom orphaned of the sun,
  How could it thus brave winter's rude estate?
  Oh love, more helpless love, why bloom so late,
Now that the flower-time of the year is done?
Since thy dear course must end when scarce begun,
  Nipped by the cold touch of untoward fate.

The After-Glow

It is a solemn evening, golden-clear —
  The Alpine summits flame with rose-lit snow
  And headlands purpling on wide seas below,
And clouds and woods and arid rocks appear
Dissolving in the sun's own atmosphere
  And vast circumference of light, whose slow
  Transfiguration — glow and after-glow —
Turns twilight earth to a more luminous sphere.

Oh heart, I ask, seeing that the orb of day
Has sunk below, yet left to sky and sea
  His glory's spiritual after-shine:
I ask if Love, whose sun hath set for thee,
May not touch grief with his memorial ray,
  And lend to loss itself a joy divine?

L'envoi

Thou art the goal for which my spirit longs;
        As dove on dove,
Bound for one home, I send thee all my songs
        With all my love.

Thou art the haven with fair harbour lights;
        Safe locked in thee,
My heart would anchor after stormful nights
        Alone at sea.

Thou art the rest of which my life is fain,
        The perfect peace;
Absorbed in thee the world, with all its pain
        And toil, would cease.

Thou art the heaven to which my soul would go!
        O dearest eyes,
Lost in your light you would turn hell
        To Paradise.

Thou all in all for which my heart-blood yearns!
        Yea, near or far —
Where the unfathomed ether throbs and burns
        With star on star,

Or where, enkindled by the fires of June,
        The fresh earth glows,
Blushing beneath the mystical white moon
        Through rose on rose —

Thee, thee I see, thee feel in all live things,
        Beloved one;
In the first bird which tremulously sings
        Ere peep of sun;

In the last nestling orphaned in the hedge,
        Rocked to and fro,
When dying summer shudders in the sedge,
        And swallows go;

When roaring snows rush down the mountain
        March floods with rills,
Or April lightens through the living grass
        In daffodils;

When poppied cornfields simmer in the heat
        With tare and thistle,
And, like winged clouds above the mellow wheat
        The starlings whistle;

When stained with sunset the wide moorland glare
        In the wild weather,
And clouds with flaming craters smoke and flare
        Red o'er red heather;

When the bent moon, on frostbound midnights waking,
        Leans to the snow
Like some world-mother whose deep heart is breaking
        O'er human woe.

As the round sun rolls red into the ocean,
        Till all the sea

Glows fluid gold, even so life's mazy motion
    Is dyed with thee:

For as the wave-like years subside and roll,
    O heart's desire,
Thy soul glows interfused within my soul,
    A quenchless fire.

Yea, thee I feel, all storms of life above,
    Near though afar;
O thou my glorious morning star of love,
    And evening star.

Dramas in Miniature (1891)

Dramas in Miniature

The Russian Student's Tale[1]

The midnight sun with phantom glare
Shone on the soundless thoroughfare
Whose shuttered houses, closed and still,
Seemed bodies without heart or will;
Yea, all the stony city lay
Impassive in that phantom day,
As amid livid wastes of sand
The sphinxes of the desert stand.

* * * * *

And we, we two, turned night to day,
As, whistling many a student's lay,
We sped along each ghostly street,
With girls whose lightly tripping feet
Well matched our longer, stronger stride,
In hurrying to the water-side.
We took a boat; each seized an oar,
Until on either hand the shore
Slipped backwards, as our voices woke
Far echoes, mingling like a dream
With swirl and tumult of the stream.
On — on — away, beneath the ray
Of midnight in the mask of day;
By great wharves where the masts at peace
Look like the ocean's barren trees;
Past palaces and glimmering towers,
And gardens fairy-like with flowers,
And parks of twilight green and closes,
The very Paradise of roses.
The waters flow; on, on we row,
Now laughing loud, now whispering low;
And through the splendour of the white

---

[1] In this dramatic monologue Blind inhabits the callow sensibility of a privileged male student who thinks he is taking advantage of an inexperienced young woman he has just met during a holiday excursion with his college friend. Blind undercuts the speaker's sophistries in many ways, including her strategic use of the verb 'seem' in the lines 'I told her [...] | How I was hers, seemed to be | Her own to all eternity'. Of all the 'dramas' in this section of the volume, 'The Russian Student's Tale' most strikingly illustrates David W. Shaw's point that '[t]he vocative is the defining trope of the Victorian monologue, which naturalizes the apostrophes of Coleridge's conversation poems by transforming them into a speaker's seduction of a silent listener' ('Lyric Displacement in the Victorian Monologue: Naturalizing the Vocative', *Nineteenth-Century Literature*, 52.3 (1997), 302–25 (p. 308)).

Electrically glowing night,
Wind-wafted from some perfumed dell,
Tumultuously there loudly rose
Above the Neva's[2] surge and swell,
With amorous ecstasies and throes,
And lyric spasms of wildest wail,
The love-song of a nightingale.

*   *   *   *   *

I see her still beside me. Yea,
As if it were but yesterday,
I see her — see her as she smiled;
Her face that of a little child
For innocent sweetness undefiled;
And that pathetic flower-like blue
Of eyes which, as they look at you,
Seemed yet to stab your bosom through.
I rowed, she steered; oars dipped and flashed,
The broadening river roared and splashed,
So that we hardly seemed to hear
Our comrades' voices, though so near;
Their faces seeming far away,
As still beneath that phantom day
I looked at her, she smiled at me!
And then we landed — I and she.

*   *   *   *   *

There's an old Café in the wood;
A students' haunt on summer eves,
Round which responsive poplar leaves
Quiver to each æolian[3] mood
Like some wild harp a poet smites
On visionary summer nights.
I ordered supper, took a room
Green-curtained by the tremulous gloom
Of those fraternal poplar trees
Shaking together in the breeze;
My pulse, too, like a poplar tree,
Shook wildly as she smiled at me.
Eye in eye, and hand in hand,
Awake amid the slumberous land,

---

[2] A river in north-western Russia that flows through St Petersburg and empties into the Neva Bay in the Gulf of Finland.
[3] From Aeolus, the Greek god of the winds. An allusion to Samuel Taylor Coleridge's 'The Æolian Harp' (1795). Æolian harps are wooden boxes that feature a sounding board, with strings stretched lengthwise across two bridges, that create musical sounds when wind passes through them.

I told her all my love that night —
How I had loved her at first sight;
How I was hers, and seemed to be
Her own to all eternity.
And through the splendour of the white
Electrically glowing night,
Wind-wafted from some perfumed dell,
Tumultuously there loudly rose
Above the Neva's surge and swell
With amorous ecstasies and throes,
And lyric spasms of wildest wail,
The love-song of the nightingale.

* * * * *

I see her still beside me. Yea,
As if it were but yesterday,
I hear her tell with cheek aflame
Her ineradicable shame —
So sweet flower in such vile hands!
Oh, loved and lost beyond recall!
Like one who hardly understands,
I heard the story of her fall.[4]
The odious barter of her youth,
Of beauty, innocence and truth,
Of all that honest women hold
Most sacred — for the sake of gold.
A weary seampstress, half a child,
Left unprotected in the street,
Where, when so hungry, you would meet
All sorts of tempters that beguiled.
Oh, infamous and senseless clods,
Basely to taint so pure a heart,
And make a maid fit for the gods
A creature of the common mart!
She spoke quite simply of things vile —
Of devils with an angel's face;
It seemed the sunshine of her smile
Must purify the foulest place.
She told me all — she would be true —
Told me things too sad, too bad;
And, looking in her eyes' clear blue
My passion nearly drove me mad!
I tried to speak, but tried in vain;

---

[4] As in D. G. Rossetti's 1870 dramatic monologue 'Jenny', spoken by a man spending the night with a prostitute, the speaker in this poem does all the talking for the woman. Blind restores speech to another prostitute in 'The Message' (see p. 143).

A sob rose to my throat as dry
As ashes — for between us twain
A murdered virgin seemed to lie.
And through the splendour of the white
Electrically glowing night.
Wind-wafted from some perfumed dell,
Tumultuously there loudly rose
Above the Neva's surge and swell,
With amorous ecstasies and throes,
And lyric spasms of wildest wail,
The love-song of a nightingale.

* * * * *

Poor craven creature! What was I,
To sit in judgment on her life,
Who dared not make this child my wife,
And lift her up to love's own sky?
This poor lost child we all — yes, all —
Had helped to hurry to her fall,
Making a social leper of
God's creature consecrate to love.
I looked at her — she smiled no more;
She understood it all before
A syllable had passed my lips;
And like a horrible eclipse,
Which blots the sunlight from the skies,
A blankness overspread her eyes —
The blankness as of one who dies.
I knew how much she loved me — knew
How pure and passionately true
Her love for me, which made her tell
What scorched her like the flames of hell.
And I, I loved her too, so much,
So dearly, that I dared not touch
Her lips that had been kissed in sin;
But with a reverential thrill
I took her work-worn hand and thin,
And kissed her fingers, showing still
Where needle-pricks had marred the skin.
And, ere I knew, a hot tear fell,
Scalding the place which I had kissed,
As between clenching teeth I hissed
Our irretrievable farewell.
And through the smouldering glow of night,
Mixed with the shining morning light
Wind-wafted from some perfumed dell,
Above the Neva's surge and swell,

With lyric spasms, as from a throat
Which dying breathes a faltering note,
There faded o'er the silent vale
The last sob of a nightingale.

The Mystic's Vision

I.

Ah! I shall kill myself with dreams!
  These dreams that softly lap me round
Through trance-like hours, in which, meseems,
  That I am swallowed up and drowned;
Drowned in your love which flows o'er me
As o'er the seaweed flows the sea.

II.

In watches of the middle night,
  'Twixt vesper and 'twixt matin bell,
With rigid arms and straining sight,
  I wait within my narrow cell;
With muttered prayers, suspended will,
I wait your advent — statue-still.

III.

Across the Convent garden walls
  The wind blows from the silver seas;
Black shadow of the cypress falls
  Between the moon-meshed olive trees;
Sleep-walking from their golden bowers,
Flit disembodied orange flowers.

IV.

And in God's consecrated house,
  All motionless from head to feet,
My heart awaits her heavenly Spouse,
  As white I lie on my white sheet;
With body lulled and soul awake,
I watch in anguish for your sake.

V.

And suddenly, across the gloom,
  The naked moonlight sharply swings;
A Presence stirs within the room,
  A breath of flowers and hovering wings:
Your Presence without form and void,
Beyond all earthly joys enjoyed.

VI.

My heart is hushed, my tongue is mute,
  My life is centred in your will;
You play upon me like a lute
  Which answers to its master's skill,
Till passionately vibrating,
Each nerve becomes a throbbing string.

VII.

Oh, incommunicably sweet!
  No longer aching and apart,
As rain upon the tender wheat,
  You pour upon my thirsty heart;
As scent is bound up in the rose,
Your love within my bosom glows.

VIII.

Unseen, untouched, unheard, unknown,
  You take possession of your bride;
I lose myself to live alone
  In you, who once were crucified
For me, that now would die in you,
As in the sun a drop of dew.

IX.

Fish may not perish in the deep,
  Nor sparrow fall though yielding air,
Pure gold in hottest flame will keep;
  How should I fail and falter where
You are, O Lord, in whose control
For ever lies my living soul?

X.

Ay, break through every wall of sense,
  And pierce my flesh as nails did pierce
Your bleeding limbs in anguish tense,
  And torture me with bliss so fierce,
That self dies out, as die it must,
Ashes to ashes, dust to dust.

XI.

Thus let me die, so loved and lost,
  Annihilated in my dreams!
Nor force me, an unwilling ghost,
  To face the loud day's brutal beams;
The noisy world's inanities,
All vanities of vanities.

The Message[5]

From side to side the sufferer tossed
  With quick impatient sighs;
Her face was bitten as by frost,
The look as of one hunted crossed
  The fever of her eyes.

All seared she seemed with life and woe,
  Yet scarcely could have told
More than a score of springs or so;
Her hair had girlhood's morning glow,
  And yet her mouth looked old.

Not long for her the sun would rise,
  Nor that young slip of moon,
Wading through London's smoky skies,
Would dwindling meet those dwindling eyes,
  Ere May was merged in June.

May was it somewhere? Who, alas!
  Could fancy it was May?
For here, instead of meadow grass,
You saw, through naked panes of glass,
  Bare walls of whitish grey.

Instead of songs, where in the quick
  Leaves hide the blackbirds' nests,
You heard the moaning of the sick,
And tortured breathings harsh and thick
  Drawn from their labouring chests.

She muttered, 'What's the odds to me?'
  With an old cynic's sneer;
And looking up, cried mockingly,
'I hate you, nurse! Why, can't you see
  You'll make no convert here?'

And then she shook her fist at Heaven,
  And broke into a laugh!
Yes, though her sins were seven times seven,

---

[5] When she conceived the idea for this poem in 1886, Blind wrote to Ford Madox Brown's physician, John Marshall, asking his help in conducting research. 'I should much like to have a look at a hospital where the poorer class of women are as I want to describe such a place. Could you get me admitted?' (Mathilde Blind ALS to John Marshall, 24 August 1886, Exeter, University of Exeter Library, EUL MS 31a/3/319). No further evidence exists about whether Blind visited such a hospital.

Let others pray to be forgiven —
  She scorned such canting chaff.

Oh, it was dreadful, sir! Far worse
  In one so young and fair;
Sometimes she'd scoff and swear and curse;
Call me bad names, and vow each nurse
  A fool for being there.

And then she'd fall back on her bed,
  And many a weary hour
Would lie as rigid as one dead;
Her white throat with the golden head
  Like some torn lily flower.

We could do nothing, one and all
  How much we might beseech;
Her girlish blood had turned to gall:
Far lower than her body's fall
  Her soul had sunk from reach.

Her soul had sunk into a slough
  Of evil past repair.
The world had been against her; now
Nothing in heaven or earth should bow
  Her stubborn knees in prayer.

Yet I felt sorry all the same,
  And sometimes, when she slept,
With head and hands as hot as flame,
I watched beside her, half in shame,
  Smoothed her bright hair and wept.

To die like this — 'twas awful, sir!
  To know I prayed in vain;
And hear her mock me, and aver
That if her life came back to her
  She'd live her life again.

Was she a wicked girl? What then?
  She didn't care a pin!
She was not worse than all those men
Who looked so shocked in public, when
  They made and shared her sin.

'Shut up, nurse, do! Your sermons pall;
  Why can't you let me be?

Instead of worrying o'er my fall,
I wish, just wish, you sisters all
   Turned to the likes of me.'

I shuddered! I could bear no more,
   And left her to her fate;
She was too cankered at the core;
Her heart was like a bolted door,
   Where Love had knocked too late.

I left her in her savage spleen,
   And hoarsely heard her shout,
'What does the cursed sunlight mean
By shining in upon this scene?
   Oh, shut the sunlight out!'

Sighing, I went my round once more,
   Full heavy for her sin;
Just as Big Ben was striking four,
The sun streamed through the open door,
   As a young girl came in.

She held a basket full of flowers —
   Cowslip and columbine;
A lilac bunch from rustic bowers,
Strong-scented after morning showers,
   Smelt like some cordial wine.

There, too, peeped Robin-in-the-hedge,
   There daisies pearled with dew,
Wild parsley from the meadow's edge,
Sweet-william and the purple vetch,
   And hyacinth's heavenly blue.

But best of all the spring's array,
   Green boughs of milk-white thorn;
Their petals on each perfumed spray
Looked like the wedding gift of May
   On nature's marriage morn.

And she who bore those gifts of grace
   To our poor patients there,
Passed like a sunbeam through the place:
Dull eyes grew brighter for her face,
   Angelically fair.

She went the round with elf-like tread,

And with kind words of cheer,
Soothing as balm of Gilead,[6]
Laid wild flowers on each patient's bed,
 And made the flowers more dear.

At last she came where Nellie Dean
 Still moaned and tossed about —
'What does the cursed sunlight mean
By shining in upon this scene?
 Will no one shut it out?'

And then she swore with rage and pain,
And moaning tried to rise;
 It seemed her ugly words must stain
The child who stood with heart astrain,
 And large blue listening eyes.

Her fair face did not blush or bleach,
 She did not shrink away;
Alas! she was beyond the reach
Of sweet or bitter human speech —
 Deaf as the flowers of May.

Only her listening eyes could hear
 That hardening in despair,
Which made that other girl, so near
In age to her, a thing to fear
 Like fever-tainted air.

She took green boughs of milk-white thorn
 And laid them on the sheet,
Whispering appealingly, 'Don't scorn
My flowers! I think, when one's forlorn,
 They're like a message, Sweet.'

How heavenly fresh those blossoms smelt,
 Like showers on thirsty ground!
The sick girl frowned as if repelled,
And with hot hands began to pelt
 And fling them all around.

But then some influence seemed to stay
 Her hands with calm control;

---

[6] Balm of Gilead is a medicinal herb named after the area of ancient Palestine east of the Jordan River where the herb is found. It is mentioned in the Old Testament, where it is described as a kind of universal cure. By the nineteenth century the phrase symbolized salvation through Jesus Christ, as in Washington Glass's 1854 hymn 'The Sinner's Cure'.

Her stormy passion cleared away,
The perfume of the breath of May
  Had passed into her soul.[7]

A nerve of memory had been thrilled,
  And, pushing back her hair,
She stretched out hungry arms half filled
With flower and leaf, and panting shrilled,
  'Where are you, mother, where?'

And then her eyes shone darkly bright
  Through childhood in a mist,
As if she suddenly caught sight
Of some one hidden in the light
  And waited to be kissed.

'Oh, mother dear!' we heard her moan,
  'Have you not gone away?
I dreamed, dear mother, you had gone,
And left me in the world alone,
  In the wild world astray.

'It was a dream; I'm home again!
  I hear the ivy-leaves
Tap-tapping on the leaded pane!
Oh, listen! how the laughing rain
  Runs from our cottage eaves!

'How very sweet the things do smell!
  How bright our pewter shines!
I am at home; I feel so well:
I think I hear the evening bell
  Above our nodding pines.

'The firelight glows upon the brick,
  And pales the rising moon;
And when your needles flash and click,
My heart, my heart, that felt so sick,
  Throbs like a hive in June.

'If only father would not stay
  And gossip o'er his brew;
Then, reeling homewards, lose his way,
Come staggering in at break of day

---

[7] This scene is the basis of the frontispiece Ford Madox Brown provided for *Dramas in Miniature* (see Introduction, p. 35).

And beat you black and blue!

'Yet he can be as good as gold,
　When mindful of the farm,
He tills the field and tends the fold:
But never fear; when I'm grown old
　I'll keep him out of harm.

'And then we'll be as happy here
　As kings upon their throne!
I dreamed you'd left me, mother dear;
That you lay dead this many a year
　Beneath the churchyard stone.

'Mother, I sought you far and wide,
　And ever in my dream,
Just out of reach you seemed to hide;
I ran along the streets and cried,
　'Where are you, mother, where?'

'Through never-ending streets in fear
　I ran and ran forlorn;
And through the twilight yellow-drear
I saw blurred masks of loafers leer,
　And point at me in scorn.

'How tired, how deadly tired, I got;
　I ached through all my bones!
The lamplight grew one quivering blot,
And like one rooted to the spot,
　I dropped upon the stones.

'A hard bed make the stones and cold,
　The mist a wet, wet sheet;
And in the mud, like molten gold,
The snaky lamplight blinking rolled
　Like guineas at my feet.

'Surely there were no mothers when
　A voice hissed in my ear,
'A sovereign! Quick! Come on!' — and then
A knowing leer! There were but men,
　And not a creature near.

'I went — I could not help it. Oh,
　I didn't want to die!
　With now a kiss and now a blow,

Strange men would come, strange men would go;
  I didn't care — not I.

'Sometimes my life was like a tale
  Read in a story-book;
Our blazing nights turned daylight pale,
Champagne would fizz like ginger-ale,
  Red wine flow like a brook.

'Then like a vane my dream would veer:
  I walked the street again;
And through the twilight yellow-drear
Blurred clouds of faces seemed to peer,
  And drift across the rain.'

She started with a piercing scream
  And wildly rolling eye:
'Ah me! it was no evil dream
To pass with the first market-team —
  That thing of shame am I.

'Where were you that you could not come?
  Were you so far above —
Far as the moon above a slum?
Yet, mother, you were all the sum
  I had of human love.

'Ah yes! you've sent this branch of May.
  A fair light from the past.
The town is dark — I went astray.
Forgive me, mother! Lead the way;
  I'm going home at last.'

In eager haste she tried to rise,
  And struggled up in bed,
With luminous, transfigured eyes,
As if they glassed the opening skies,
  Fell back, sir, and was dead.

A Mother's Dream[8]

I.

The snow was falling thick and fast

---

[8] In a 29 January 1891 letter to Garnett, Blind writes that she has nearly finished writing all the poems that make up *Dramas in Miniature*, adding 'I shall have no peace till they are done. I was writing at one, "A Mother's Dream", till five o'clock in the morning last week.

On Christmas Eve;
Across the heath the distant blast
Wailed wildly like a soul in grief,
As waste soul or a windy leaf
Whirled round and round without reprieve,
    And lost at last.

II.

Lisa woke shivering from her sleep
    At break of day,
And felt her flesh begin to creep.
'My child, my child!' she cried; 'now may
Our blessed Lord, whose hand doth stay
The wild-fowl on their trackless way,
    Thee guard and keep.'

III.

'Dreams! dreams!' she to herself did say,
And shook with fright.
    'I saw her plainly where I lay
Fly past me like a flash of light;
Fly out into the wintry night,
Out in the snow as snowy white,
    Far, far away.

IV.

'Her cage hung empty just above
    Your chair, *ma mie*;[9]
Empty as is my heart of love
Since you, my child, dwell far from me —
Dwell in the convent over sea;
All of you left to love Marie,
    Your darling dove.'

V.

Hark to that fond, familiar coo!
    Oh, joy untold!
It falls upon her heart like dew.
There safely perching as of old,
The dove is calling through the cold
And ghastly dawn o'er wood and wold,[10]

I didn't mean to but could not help I had to start up and go on again. I paid for it with two days of sickness and suffering, however if the poems should be really fine I must not grudge it; as nothing worth doing was ever done without pain' (Mathilde Blind ALS to Richard Garnett, Add. MS 61929, fols 55–57).

[9] My beloved.
[10] Uncultivated land or moor.

'Coo-whoo! Coo-whoo!'

VI.

The snow fell softly, flake by flake,
    This Christmas Day,
And whitened every bush and brake;
And o'er the hills so ashen grey
The wind was wailing far away,
Was wailing like a child astray
    Whose heart must break.

VII.

'I miss my child,' she wailed; 'I miss
    Her everywhere!
That's why I have such dreams as this.
I miss her step upon the stair,
I miss her laughter in the air,
I miss her bonnie face and hair,
    And oh — her kiss!

VIII.

'Christmas! Last Christmas, oh how fleet,
    With lark-like trill,
She danced about on fairy feet!
Her eyes clear as a mountain rill,
Where the blue sky is lingering still;
Her rosebud lips the dove would bill
    For something sweet.

IX.

'My dove! my dear! my undefiled!
    Oh, heavy doom!
My life has left me with the child.
She was a sunbeam in my room,
She was a rainbow on the gloom,
She was the wild rose on a tomb
    Where weeds run wild.

X.

'And yet — 'tis better thus! 'Tis best,
    They tell me so.
Yes, though my heart is like a nest,
Whence all the little birds did go —
An empty nest that's full of snow —
Let me take all the wail and woe,
    So she be blest.

XI.

'Let me take all the sin and shame,
    And weep for two,
That she may bear no breath of blame.
"Sin — sin!" they say; what sin had you,
Pure as the dawn upon the dew?
Child — robbed of a child's rightful due,
    Her father's name.

XII.

'I gave her life to live forlorn!
    Oh, let that day
Be darkness wherein I was born!
Let not God light it, let no ray
Shine on it; let it turn away
Its face, because my sin must weigh
    Her down with shame.

XIII.

'I? I? Was I the sinner? I,
Not *he*, they say,
    Who told me, looking eye in eye,
We'd wed far North where grand and gray
His fair ancestral castle lay,
Amid the woods of Darnaway — [11]
    And told a lie.

XIV.

'But I was young; and in my youth
    I simply thought
That English gentlemen spoke truth,
Even to a Norman maid, who wrought
The blush-rose shells the tide had brought
To fairy toys which children bought
    Before my booth.

XV.

'"Those fairy fingers," he would say,
    "With shell-pink nails,
Shall shame the pearls of Darnaway!"
And in his yacht with swelling sails
We flew before the favouring gales,
Where leagues on leagues his woods and vales
    Stretched dim and grey.

---

[11] Darnaway is in northern Scotland, near the North Sea.

XVI.

'Grim rose his castle o'er the wood;[12]
    Its hoary halls
Frowned o'er the Findhorn's[13] roaring flood;
Where, winged with spray and water-galls,
The headlong torrent leaps and falls
In thunder through its tunnelled walls,
    Streaked as with blood.'

XVII.

It all came back in one wild flash
    Of cruel light,
And memory smote her like a lash: —
The foolish trust, the fond delight,
The helpless rage, the fevered flight,
The feet that dragged on through the night,
    The torrent's splash.

XVIII.

The long, long sickness bred of lies
    And lost belief;
The short, sharp pangs and shuddering sighs;
The new-born babe, that in her grief
Bore her wrecked spirit such relief
As the dove-carried olive-leaf
    To Noah's eyes.[14]

XIX.

It all came back, and lit her soul
    With lurid flame;
How she — she — she — from whom he stole
Her virgin love and honest name —
Must, for the ailing child's sake, tame
Her pride, and take — oh, shame of shame! —
    His lordship's dole.

XX.

Like one whom grief hath driven wild,
    She cried again,
'My snowdrop shall not be defiled,

---

[12] Presumably based on Darnaway Castle, just north of the forest of Darnaway, which lies along the banks of the Findhorn river.
[13] One of the longest rivers in Scotland, the Findhorn flows into the Moray Firth on the north coast.
[14] In Genesis 8.11 a dove is released by Noah after the flood in order to find land; it returns carrying a freshly plucked olive leaf, which signifies God bringing Noah, his family, and the animals in the ark to land.

Nor catch the faintest soil or stain,
Reared in the shadow of my pain!
How should a guilty mother train
    A guiltless child?

XXI.

'You shall be spotless, you!' said she,
    'Whate'er my woe;
Even as the snow on yonder lea.
You shall be spotless!' Faint and low,
The wind in dying seemed to blow,
To breathe across the hills of snow,
    'Marie! Marie!'

XXII.

A voice was calling far away,
    O'er fields and fords,
Across the Channel veiled and grey;
A voice was calling without words,
Touching her nature's deepest chords;
Drawing her, drawing her as with cords —
    She might not stay.

XXIII.

Uprose the sun and still and round,
    Shorn of his heat,
Glared bloodshot o'er the frosty ground,
As down the shuttered village street
Fast, fast walked Lisa, and her feet
Left black tracks in earth's winding-sheet
    And made no sound.

XXIV.

Then on, on, by the iron way —
    With whistling scream —
Piercing hard rocks like potter's clay,
She flashed as in a shifting dream
Through flying town, o'er flowing stream,
Borne on by mighty wings of steam,
    Away, away.

XXV.

A sound of wind, and in the air
    The sea-gull's screech,
And waves lap-lapping everywhere;
A rush of ropes and volleyed speech,
And white cliffs sinking out of reach,
Then rising on the rival beach,

Boulogne-sur-Mer.[15]

XXVI.

Above the ramparts on the hill,
    Whence like a chart
It saw the low land spreading chill,
Within its cloistered walls apart
The Convent of the Sacred Heart[16]
Rose o'er the noise of street and mart,
    Serenely still.

XXVII.

Above the unquiet sea it rose,
    A quiet nest,
Severed from earthly wants and woes.
There might the weary find his rest;
There might the pilgrim cease his quest;
There might the soul with guilt oppressed
    Implore repose.

XXVIII.

The day was done, the sun dropped low
    Behind the mill
That swung within its blood-red glow;
And up the street and up the hill
Lisa walked fast and faster still,
Her sable shadow lengthening chill
    Across the snow.

XXIX.

Hark! heavenly clear, with holy swell,
    She hears elate
The greeting of the vesper bell,
And, knocking at the convent gate,
Sighs, 'Here she prays God early and late;
Walled in from love, walled in from hate;
    All's well! All's well!'

XXX.

A sweat broke from her every pore,
    And yet she smiled,

---

[15] This stanza recounts Lisa taking her daughter Marie across the English Channel to France; Boulogne-sur-Mer is a city and major fishing port on France's north coast.
[16] Blind likely modelled this convent on the Convent of Nazareth, located in Boulogne-sur-Mer, which during this time took in the daughters of the poor, mostly from England and Ireland. See Cashel Hoey, *Nazareth*, with a preface by the Rev. W. Humphrey (London: Burns and Oates, 1873), pp. 25–28.

As, stumbling through the clanging door,
She faced a nun of aspect mild.
Like some starved wolf's her eyes gleamed wild:
'My child!' she gasped; 'I want my child.'
    And nothing more.

XXXI.

The nun looked at her, shocked to see
    The violent sway
Of love's unbridled agony;
And calmly queried on the way,
'Your child, Madame? What child, I pray?'
Still, still the mother could but say,
    'Marie! Marie!'

XXXII.

The nun in silence bowed her head,
    And then aloud,
'Christ Jesus knows our needs,' she said.
'Madame, far from the sinful crowd,
The maiden to the Lord you vowed;
There is no safeguard like a shroud —
    Your child is dead.

XXXIII.

'Upon the night Christ saw the light
    She passed away,
As snow will when the sun shines bright.
We heard her moaning where she lay,
"Come, mother, come, while yet you may";
Then like a dove, at break of day,
    Her soul took flight.'

XXXIV.

As from a blow the mother fell,
No moan made she;
    They bore her to the little cell:
There in her coffin lay Marie,
Spotless as snow upon the lea,
Beautiful exceedingly:
    All's well! All's well!

A Carnival Episode[17]

Nice, '87

I.

We two there together alone in the night,
   Where its shadow unconsciously bound us;
My beautiful lady all shrouded in white,
She and I looking down from the balcony's height
On the maskers below in the flickering light,
   As they revelled and rioted round us.

II.

Such a rush, such a rage, and a rapture of life
   Such shouts of delight and of laughter,
On the quays that I watched with the General's wife;
Such a merry-go-reeling of figures was rife,
Turning round to the tune of gay fiddle and fife,
   As if never a morning came after.

III.

The houses had emptied themselves in the streets,
   Where the maskers bombarded each other
With a shower of confetti and hailstorm of sweets.
Till the pavements were turning the colour of sheets;
Where a prince will crack jokes with a pauper he meets,
   For the time like a man and a brother.

IV.

The Carnival frolic was now at its height;
   The whole population in motion
Stood watching the swift constellations of light
That crackling flashed up on their arrowy flight,

---

[17] Originally published as 'The Carnival, Nice', *Black & White* (16 June 1891), p. 574. The Nice Carnival, founded in 1873, is a two-week celebration featuring masquerades, 'flower battles', and parades. It is now held in February, but in the nineteenth century it was held in March. Blind was in Nice during the 1886 carnival, which forms the setting for both 'A Carnival Episode' and 'The Battle of Flowers'. It was during her November 1887 stay in Nice that she met a relative of Marie Bashkirtseff, learned about her recently published journal (in French), and formed the idea of writing about her. Oscar Wilde had taken up the editorship of *The Woman's World* that month and wrote asking Blind to write something for the magazine; her two-part essay 'Marie Bashkirtseff, The Russian Painter' appeared in the July and August 1888 issue of the magazine. Bashkirtseff's journal entries about her several stays in Nice likely inspired the subject matter of 'A Carnival Episode'; her journal opens in Nice, in 1873, where she meets and becomes infatuated with a young Italian, the nephew of a powerful Cardinal, about whom she later writes 'I was never really in love, excepting at Nice, when I was a child, and then it was from ignorance' (*The Journal of Marie Bashkirtseff*, II, 368).

Then spreading their fairy-like fires on the night,
  Fell in luminous rain on the ocean.

V.

And now and again the quick dazzle would flare,
  Glowing red on black masks and white dresses.
We two there together drew back from the glare;
Drew in to the room, and her hood unaware
Fell back from the plaits of her opulent hair,
  That uncoiled the brown snakes of its tresses.[18]

VI.

How fatally fair was my lady, my queen,
  As that wild light fell round her in flashes;
How fatally fair with that mutinous mien,
And those velvety hands all alive with the sheen
Of her rings, and her eyes that were narrowed between
  Heavy lids darkly laced with long lashes!

VII.

Almost I hated her beauty! The air
  I was breathing seemed steeped in her presence.
How maddening that waltz was! Ah, how came I there
Alone with that woman so fatally fair,
With the scent of her garments, the smell of her hair,
  Passing in to my blood like an essence?

VIII.

Her eyes seemed to pluck at the roots of my heart,
  And to put all my blood in a fever;
My soul was on fire, my veins seemed to start,
To hold her, to fold her but once to my heart,
I'd have willingly bared broad chest to the dart,
  And been killed, ay, and damned too for ever.

IX.

I forgot, I forgot! — oh, disloyal, abhorred,
  With the spell of her eyes on my eyes —
That her husband, the man of all men I adored,
Might be fighting for us at the point of the sword;
Might be killing or killed by an African horde,
  Afar beneath African skies.[19]

---

[18] The speaker readily renders the General's wife as a Medusa figure and demon lover out to entice him to betray her husband, though he is the one whose lustful imagination is conjuring this imagery. In Greek mythology, Medusa was a winged human female with living venomous snakes for hair. Those gazing into her eyes turned to stone.

[19] Blind is using this erotically charged drama to critique not only gender relations and

X.

I forgot — nay, I cared not! What cared I to-night
  For aught but my lady, my love,
As she toyed with her mask in the flickering light,
Then suddenly dropped it, perchance, at the sight
Of my passion now reaching its uttermost height,
  As a tide with the full moon above!

XI.

Yet I knew, though I loved her so madly, I knew
  She was only just playing her game.
She would toy with my heart all the Carnival through;
She would turn to a traitor a man who was true;
She would drain him of love and then break him in two,
  And wash her white hands of his shame.[20]

XII.

Yet beware, O my beautiful lady, beware!
  You must cure me of love or else kill.
That fire burns longest that's slowest to flare:
My love is a force that will force you to care;
Nay, I'll strangle us both in the ropes of your hair
  Should you dream you can drop me at will.[21]

XIII.

And then — how I know not — delirious delight!
  Her lips were pressed close upon mine;
My arms clung about her as when in affright
Wrecked men cling to spars in a tempest at night;
So madly I clung to her, crushed her with might
  To my heart which her heart made divine.

---

imperialism, but the submerged interdependencies of the two. Throughout the poem the state of domestic relations is appropriated as a symptom of the state of the nation. The woman here is identified only as 'the General's wife', and the General is the 'man of all men I adored'. As the speaker contemplates acting on his overwhelming desire for the woman, his primary concern is not violating the bond between the woman and spouse, but between himself and the General. Blind draws an implicit parallel between the possessive lust of the speaker for the woman and France's colonial activities in Africa (and, by extension, England's own colonial projects). Moreover, the speaker's erotic imagination — the way he thinks of love as frenzy, strangulation, and force — is congruent with an imperial ideology that brings force to bear on its ostensible mission of Christian love.

[20] Here the speaker suggests that the woman, whom he earlier accused of possessing a 'mutinous mien', is even more cold-blooded than Lady Macbeth.

[21] Unlike the murderer in Robert Browning's 'Porphyria's Lover', to which this section of the poem alludes, this speaker acknowledges his madness is a pose rather than a pathology. Or rather, as Blind represents it, a symptom of the pathological potential of male power and privilege.

XIV.

Oh, merciful Heavens! What drove us apart
  With a shudder of sundering lives?
Oh, was it the throb of my passionate heart
That made the doors tremble, the windows to start;
Or was it my lady just playing her part,
  Most indignant, most outraged of wives?

XV.

She was white as the chalk in the streets — was she fain
  To turn on me now with a sneer?
All the blood in my body surged up to my brain,
And my heart seemed half bursting with passion and pain,
As I seized her slim hands — but I dropped them again!
  Ah! treason is mother to fear.

XVI.

Had it come upon us at that magical hour,
  The judgment of God the Most High?
The floor 'gan to heave and the ceiling to lower,
The dead walls to start with malevolent power,
Till your hair seemed to rise and your spirit to cower,
  As the very stones shook with a sigh.

XVII.

'With you in my arms let the world crack asunder;
  Let us die, love, together!' I cried.
Then, with a clatter and boom as of thunder,
A beam crashed between us and drove us asunder,
And all things rocked round us, above us and under,
  Like a boat that is rocked on a tide.

XVIII.

She sprang like a greyhound — no greyhound more fleet —
  And ran down the staircase in motion;
And blindly I followed her into the street,
All choked up with people in panic retreat
From the houses that scattered their plaster like sleet
  On the crowd in bewildered commotion.

XIX.

Black masks and white dominoes,[22] hale men and dying,
  Scared women that shook as with fever

---

[22] A reference to the masks and costumes donned by carnival participants, featuring black or white and blue domino patterns. Such costumes expressed the atmosphere of mystery, intrigue, and secrecy surrounding carnival; in this stanza they reduce their wearers to objects caught up in the chaos and disorder engendered by the earthquake (which itself represents the moral disorder engendered by the speaker's lust).

Poor babes in their bedgowns all piteously crying,
Tiles hurled from the housetops — all flying, all flying,
As I, wild with passion, implored her with sighing
   To fly with me now and for ever.

XX.

'Go, go!' and she waved me away as she spoke,
   Carried on by the crowd like a feather;
'You forget that it was but a Carnival joke.
Now blest be the terrible earthquake that broke
In between you and me, and has saved at a stroke
   Us two in the night there together.'[23]

The Battle of Flowers[24]

I.

The battle raged, no blood was spilled,
   Though missiles flew in showers;
Hard though they hit, they never killed
Or maimed the merry throwers:
   Or if they killed, those wingèd darts,
They killed but unprotected hearts;
For flowers from flower-like hands can slay
     Jeanne Ray! Jeanne Ray!

II.

Like humming-birds upon the breeze
   So swiftly shot the posies;
Glory of red anemones,
   Pink buds of curled-up roses,
Lilacs and lilies of the vale;
Yea, every flower that scents the gale
Yielded up incense to its day,
     Jeanne Ray! Jeanne Ray!

---

[23] Whereas 'Porphyria's Lover' ends, 'And yet God has not said a word', God is replaced here with a natural intervention as an earthquake brings the couple's liaison to an end, preserving the woman's marriage and the speaker's threatened military fellowship. The fact that the poem takes place during carnival, which ends with Lent, points to a disciplining of desires by the ultimate higher authority. (The late Latin expression 'carne levare' means 'remove meat', with its connotations of carnal consumption, whereas the folk etymology of the word comes from 'carne vale', 'farewell to flesh'; both meanings are apposite here.) By preventing their liaison, the earthquake assures that the woman will resume the role European wives were expected to play in support of empire by preserving order and discipline in the domestic space.

[24] The 'Battle of Flowers' became a central ritual of the Nice Carnival in 1876, three years after the establishment of the carnival itself. A parade of carriages covered in flowers, it also featured the throwing of flowers from and at the passing carriages.

III.

How gallantly along the course,
　Stepping with conscious glances,
Each flower-decked, gaily harnessed horse,
　In rank and file advances!
Even as green boughs and daisy-chains
Enwreathe their bits and bridle-reins,
Bright pleasure hides black grief away
　　　Jeanne Ray! Jeanne Ray!

IV.

The people humming like a hive,
　Swarm closely pressed together,
To watch high fashion's crowded drive
　With flirt of fan and feather;
And nosegays thrown up high in air,
Now hitting grey, now golden hair,
Now deftly caught upon their way,
　　　Jeanne Ray! Jeanne Ray!

V.

And past the eager jostling crowd,
　　Watching their guests from far lands,
Gigs flash by in a violet cloud,
　　And drags with rose-red garlands;
There meet crowned heads from many zones,
And princes who have lost their thrones,
With gifts from Ind and far Cathay,[25]
　　　Jeanne Ray! Jeanne Ray!

VI.

Ah, who shall bear away the prize
　In this bewitching battle,
Where shafts are hurled from brightest eyes,
　And Cupid's arrows rattle;
In that fair fight where flowers alone
By fairer flowers are overthrown?
Who shall be victor in this fray?
　　　Jeanne Ray! Jeanne Ray!

VII.

And people bet with buzz of tongue
　As the gay pageant passes;
Now runs a murmur through the throng

---

[25] India and China. In the Middle Ages, 'Cathy' was the name for North China, thought to be separate and culturally distinct from China, but as knowledge of East Asia increased, it became a poetic term for all of China.

And stirs the thrilling masses.
All heads are turned, all necks astrain,
As through the thickening floral rain,
'Look! look! She comes!' you hear them say —
    Jeanne Ray! Jeanne Ray![26]

VIII.

No turn-out in that festive throng
  Is half so bright and airy;
Your cream-white ponies prance along
  As if they drew a fairy;
They step along with heads held high,
And favours blue to match the sky:
They know theirs is the winning way,
    Jeanne Ray! Jeanne Ray!

IX.

A queen in exile might you be,
  Or leader of the fashion?
Some Jenny Lind from over sea
  Melting all hearts with passion?[27]
Some tragic Muse whose mighty spell
Unlocks the gates of heaven and hell?
What sceptre is it that you sway?
    Jeanne Ray! Jeanne Ray!

X.

All by yourself in spotless white,
  You sit there in your glory;
Your black eyes scintillate with light —
  Eyes that may hide a story.
In spotless white with ribbons blue,
You look fresh from a bath of dew
That sparkles in the rising day,[28]
    Jeanne Ray! Jeanne Ray!

---

[26] Midway through the poem, the speaker shifts to the personal pronoun, which marks a shift in focus to speculation about Jeanne Ray's identity beyond her role in a carnival ritual, how she perceives herself, and what she is thinking.

[27] One of the most highly regarded opera singers in Europe in the mid-nineteenth century, Swedish-born Johanna Maria 'Jenny' Lind was called the 'Swedish Nightingale'. She performed in soprano roles in Sweden, across Europe, and in the United States. She is buried in the Great Malvern Cemetery in the Malvern Hills District of Worcestershire, an area Blind visited in the fall of 1883.

[28] A possible allusion to Sandro Botticelli's painting *The Birth of Venus* (c. 1484–1486), depicting the goddess Venus arriving at the shore after her birth. In the painting Venus stands nude in a giant scallop shell; on her left the wind god Zephyr blows at her, with the wind shown by lines radiating from his mouth.

XI.

Triumphant — without shame or fear —
  You air a thousand graces;
Though women turn when you appear
  With cold, averted faces;
Though men at sight of you will stop,
As if they looked into a shop;
Shall both for this not doubly pay?
     Jeanne Ray! Jeanne Ray![29]

XII.

And with a smile upon your lips,
  Perhaps a shade too rosy,[30]
You shake two dainty finger-tips
  And lightly fling a posy:
So might a high-born dame perchance,
In days of tourneys and romance,
Have flung her glove into the fray,
     Jeanne Ray! Jeanne Ray!

XIII.

As with that little careless sign
  You fling your bouquet lightly,
Three graybeards, flushing as with wine,
  Lift hats and bow politely;
And one, the grandest of the three,
Stoops low with stiff, rheumatic knee;
Out of the dust he picks your spray,
     Jeanne Ray! Jeanne Ray!

XIV.

His coat is all ablaze with stars
  For deeds of martial daring;
His name, a watchword in the wars,
  Kept soldiers from despairing.
Now see beside his orders rare
Your mignonette and maidenhair;[31]

---

[29] The speaker of this poem slowly reveals that the 'queen of exile' at the centre of this parade is a proud courtesan. The fact that she embodies commodified sexuality is indicated by the rhyming couplet noting that men 'stop' to look at her as if they were peering into a 'shop'.

[30] By implication Jeanne Ray is wearing makeup and is thus a 'painted woman'.

[31] Two kinds of symbolically suggestive plants: a mignonette is a herbaceous plant with spikes of small fragrant greenish flowers, and also the diminutive form of 'mignon', the French word for 'darling'; 'maidenhair' is a fern that represents purity and innocence, which derives from the legend that anyone who can hold a branch of maidenhair fern without the leaves moving is still a virgin.

With just a nod you turn away,
    Jeanne Ray! Jeanne Ray!

XV.

You turn to meet the wintry face
  Of an old beggar-woman,
Just there beyond the railed-in space,
  Brown, bony, hardly human;
Who in her tatters seems at least
The skeleton of Egypt's feast;
A ghastly emblem of decay,
    Jeanne Ray! Jeanne Ray![32]

XVI.

With palsied head and shaking hand,
  As if it were December,
Grim by the barrier see her stand,
  Just mumbling a 'Remember!
Remember in thy days of lust,
That fairest flesh must come to dust;
Then have some pity while you may,'
    Jeanne Ray! Jeanne Ray!

XVII.

Why do you shiver at her glance,
  As if the wind blew chilly?
Why does your rosy countenance
  Turn pale as any lily?
The sun is warm, the sky is bright,
The sea dissolving into light
Breaks into blossom-bells of spray;
    Jeanne Ray! Jeanne Ray!

XVIII.

Ah, could some instinct in your breast
  Reveal that beggar's story,
Would not your gay life lose its zest,
  Your empire lose its glory?
Or would you only care to waste
Life's bounty in yet hotter haste?
For is the world not beauty's prey?
    Jeanne Ray! Jeanne Ray![33]

---

[32] Presumably an Egyptian woman seduced and abandoned by a soldier in the army of Napoleon Bonaparte during his campaign in the Ottoman territories of Egypt and Syria (1798–1801), proclaimed to defend French trade interests and weaken Britain's access to India.

[33] Here Jeanne Ray is confronted with the reality that like the beggarwoman, and like the

XIX.

Alighting at the beggar's feet,
  A bright Napoleon flashes![34]
Then gaily through the dust and heat
  Your light Victoria dashes.[35]
Again your face is rosy clear,
As with a loud and ringing cheer
They hail you winner of the day,
     Jeanne Ray! Jeanne Ray!

XX.

And gloriously at set of sun,
  In triumph now departing,
The golden prize your flowers have won
  Leaves rival bosoms smarting.
How many deem you half divine,
Where amid bouquets you recline —
Proud beauty in the devil's pay,
     Jeanne Ray! Jeanne Ray!

XXI.

Down, down beneath the rolling wheels,
  The flowers, so fresh this morning,
Lie trampled under careless heels,
  Vile stuff for all men's scorning.
The roses crushed, the lilies soiled,
The violets of their sweets despoiled,
In dusty heaps defile your way,
     Jeanne Ray! Jeanne Ray!

Napoleonic campaign that brought her to France as one of the spoils of empire, she will eventually lose her allure and power. This implication is made manifest in the final stanza, where the flowers associated with Jeanne Ray's beauty lie 'crushed' and 'spoiled' beneath the wheels of her carriage.

[34] The 'napoleon' is the colloquial term for a French gold coin worth twenty francs, issued during the reign of Napoleon Bonaparte and in use throughout the nineteenth century. Later French gold coins in the same denomination were generally referred to as 'napoleons'.

[35] A symbolically appropriate form of conveyance for Jeanne Ray, the Victoria was a French carriage known for its elegance — a low, light, four-wheeled, doorless vehicle with a forward-facing seat for two persons covered with a folding top. It featured an elevated coachman's seat above the front axle.

The Song of the Willi[36]

According to a widespread Hungarian superstition — showing the ingrained national passion for dancing — the Willi or Willis were the spirits of young affianced girls who, dying before marriage, could not rest in their graves. It was popularly believed that these phantoms would nightly haunt lonely heaths in the neighbourhood of their native villages till the disconsolate lovers came as if drawn by a magnetic charm. On their appearance the Willi would dance with them without intermission till they dropped dead from exhaustion.[37]

---

[36] Originally published in the *Dark Blue* (August 1871), pp. 741–45 as 'The Song of The Willi. A Ballad'. The word 'villi' first appeared in Hungarian in 1821; it means 'supernatural young girls clad in a thin white dress, good and evil alike, living among rocks and mountains' (Lorand Benko, *A Magyar nyelv történeti-etimológiai szótára*, 4 vols (Budapest: Akadémiai Kiadó, 1967–84), III, p. 1148). The German equivalent is 'willi', meaning a girl who dies when a bride. Blind likely encountered the willi legend in the German collection *Magyarische Sagen und Märchen*, written by the German-Hungarian aristocrat and amateur ethnographer János Majláth (1786–1855) and published in Germany in 1825. This collection contains a story titled 'Der Willi-Tanz', Majláth's version of this legend. In this narrative a baron's daughter falls in love with her father's page; when her father banishes him and she hears a false report of his death, she falls into a mortal illness. Her nanny tells her the story of the willi just before her father returns from a trip to announce that he has married her to a nearby lord. She dies shortly after hearing this news, and her lover returns to mourn at her grave. When he arrives one evening in the forest where she is buried, he sees a circle of dancing spirits; his lover emerges from the group, embraces him, and he dies as she kisses him. Although this legend became quite popular in Hungary (the first edition of Majláth's collection was translated into Hungarian by Ferenc Kazinczy and published in 1864) and appears in many Hungarian poems in the first half of the century, the legend itself is Slovakian in origin. Because of Majláth's collection, Blind was one of many writers — including Hungarian writers — who mistakenly located the origins of the legend in Hungary.

[37] Blind's headnote does not appear in the version of the poem published in the *Dark Blue* (she also made several wording and rhyme scheme changes to the poem itself for its republication in *Dramas*). While Blind claims that 'The Song of the Willi' derives from an existing Hungarian superstition, the story as she tells it does not exist in any of the classic studies or indexes of Hungarian folklore or ballad traditions. It does, however, represent an imaginative fusion and revision of two existing motifs. Ninon Leader describes two ballads that share some elements with 'The Song of the Willi', one a classic Hungarian ballad, the other a fragment deriving from the Lenore legend. The first, 'The Girl Who Was Danced to Death', which 'is still popular in Hungary, especially in the western and in the north-eastern parts [...] tells the story of a girl who rejected her suitor, or loved two young men at the same time, and was therefore punished by a most cruel death: she had to dance with the suitor till she died'. While the discovery and merciless punishment of female sexual infidelity lies at the ideological heart of this ballad, the most the speaker of 'The Song of the Willi' can be accused of is unrequited love and sexual longing, which is presented positively in the poem. In the second, 'The Dead Bridegroom', the bridegroom, like the fiancé in Blind's poem, returns after death to seek the fulfilment of vows his lover made. Leader notes that in many versions of this story, most notably the Lenore legend, the bridegroom is the devil in disguise, but that this is 'a Christian rationalization of the original form of the story' (Ninon Leader, *Hungarian Classical Ballads and their Folklore* (Cambridge: Cambridge University

I.

The wild wind is whistling o'er moorland and heather,
        Heigh-ho, heigh-ho!
I rise from my bed, and my bed has no feather,
        Heigh-ho!
My bed is deep down in the brown sullen mould,
  My head is laid low on the clod;
So wormy the sheets, and the pillow so cold,
  Of clammy and moist clinging sod.

II.

The lone livid moon rides alone high in heaven,
        Heigh-ho, heigh-ho!
The stars' cutting glitter their dull shrouds hath riven,
        Heigh-ho!
I rise and I glide out far into the night,
  A shadow so swift and so still;
Bleak, bleak is the moonshine all ghastly and white,
  The dank morass drinketh its fill.

III.

And down in yon valley in wan vapour shrinking,
        Heigh-ho, heigh-ho!
The bare moated town cowers fitfully blinking,
        Heigh-ho!
There, warm under shelter, the fire burning bright,
  My lover sleeps sound in his bed;
But I flit alone in the pitiless night,
  Unpitied, unloved, and unwed.

IV.

And hast thou forgotten the deep troth we plighted?
        Heigh-ho, heigh-ho!
Too warm was thy love by cold death to be blighted,
        Heigh-ho!
My sweetheart! and mind'st thou that this is the night,
  The night that we should have been wed?
And while I flit restless, a low wailing sprite,
  Ah, say, canst thou sleep in thy bed?

V.

A week, but a week, and a wreath of gay flowers,
        Heigh-ho, heigh-ho!
I wore as I vied with the fleet-footed hours,

Press, 1967), pp. 292, 326–27). Devils are conspicuously absent from 'The Song of the Willi'; the speaker's supernatural existence registers in the poem as a metaphor for deeply human desires, not as a marker of evil.

Heigh-ho!
As I vied with the hours in dancing them down
   Till the stars reeled low in the sky,
And sweet came thy whispers as rose-leaves when blown
   About in the breeze of July.

VI.

'Thou'rt light, O my chosen; a bird is not lighter,
       O love, my love!
I'd dance into death with thee; death would be brighter,
       My love!'
And they struck up a wild and a wonderful measure;
   Quick, quick beat our hearts to the tune;
Quick, quick the feet flew in a frenzy of pleasure,
   To the sound of the fife and bassoon.

VII.

On, on whirled the pairs on the swift music driven,
       Heigh-ho, heigh-ho!
Like gossamer vapours afloat in high heaven,
       Heigh-ho!
Like gossamer vapours, in silence they fled,
   With a shifting of face into face;
But fleeter than all the fleet dancers we sped
   In the rush of the rapturous race.

VIII.

How often turned Wanda, the slim, lily-throated,
       Heigh-ho, heigh-ho!
And gazed at us wistful as onward we floated,
       Heigh-ho!
And Bilba, the swarthy, whose eyes had the trick
   Of a stag's, with a glitter of steel;
She lifted her lashes, so long and so thick,
   To stare at my true love and leal.[38]

IX.

But he, he saw none o' them, brown-faced or rosy,
       Heigh-ho, heigh-ho!
Tho' maidens bloomed bright like a fresh-gathered posy,
       Heigh-ho!
For his eyes that shone black as the sloes[39] of the hedges,
   They shone like two stars over me;
And his breath, thrilling o'er me as wind over sedges,
   Stirred my hair till I tingled with glee.

---

[38] Loyal, honest, true; from Scottish northern dialect.
[39] The bluish-black fruit of the blackthorn bush.

X.

Now slow as two down-bosomed swans, we were sliding,
  Heigh-ho, heigh-ho!
O'er the low heaving swell of the silver sounds gliding,
  Heigh-ho!
Now hollowly booming drums rumbled apace,
 Flashed sharp clatt'ring cymbals around,
And swung like loose leaves in a stormy embrace
 We whirled in a tumult of sound.

XI.

But pallid our cheeks grew, late flushing with pleasure,
  Heigh-ho, heigh-ho!
As slowly away swooned the languishing measure,
  Heigh-ho!
For shrill crew the cock as the sun 'gan to rise,
 And it rang from afar like a knell;
Our kisses grew bitter and sweet grew our sighs,
 As sadly we murmured, 'Farewell!'

XII.

High up in the chambers the maidens together,
  O love, my love!
Were piling bleached linen as white as swan's feather
  My love!
Were weaving and spinning and singing aloud,
 While broidering my bride-veil of lace;
But the three fatal sisters they wove me my shroud,
 And death kissed me cold on the face.

XIII.

The wild wind is whistling o'er moorland and heather,
  Heigh-ho, heigh-ho!
I rise from my bed, and my bed has no feather,
  Heigh-ho!
The snow driveth grisly and ghostly, and gleams
 In the glare of the moon's chilly glance;
What pale flitting phantoms aroused by her beams,
 Are circling in shadowy dance!

XIV.

Mayhap ye were maidens death plucked in your flower,
  Heigh-ho, heigh-ho!
As clustering you glowed in love's murmuring bower,
  Heigh-ho!
Who, delirious for life from the gloom of your graves,
 Are driven to wander with me,

And you rise from your tombs like the white-crested waves
  From the depths of the dolorous sea.

XV.

Ah, maidens, pale maidens, o'er moorland and heather,
        Heigh-ho, heigh-ho!
The bridegroom is coming athwart the wild weather,
        Heigh-ho!
Full shines the fair moon on his beautiful face,
  He walketh like one in a trance;
Nay, is running like one who is running a race
  Against death, with his dead bride to dance.

XVI.

At the sound of thy footfall my numb heart is shaken,
        O love, my love!
Once again all its pulses to new life awaken,
        My love!
It leaps like a stag that is borne as on wings
  To the brooks thawing thick through the noon,
Like a lark from the glebe, like a lily that springs
  From its bier to the bosom of June.

XVII.

'I hold thee, I hold thee, I drink thy caresses,
        O love, my love!'
Round thy face, round thy throat, I roll my dank tresses,
        My love!
'I hold thee, I hold thee! Eight nights, wan and weeping',
  I wandered loud sobbing thy name!
'Thy lips are as cold as the snowdrift a-sweeping';
  But thy breath soon shall fan them to flame!

XVIII.

Blow up for the dance now o'er moorland and heather!
        Heigh-ho, heigh-ho!
Blow, blow you wild winds, while we two dance together,
        Heigh-ho!
Till the clouds dance above with tempestuous embraces
  Of maidenly moonbeams in flight;
In the silvery rear of whose fugitive traces
  Reel the stars through the revelling night!

XIX.

'Cocks crow, and the breath on thy sweet lip is failing,
        O love, my love!'
Stars swoon, and the flame in thy dark eye is quailing,
        My love!

'Oh, brighter the night than the fires of the day'
  When thine eyes shine as stars over me!
'Oh, sweeter thy grave than the soft breath of May!'
  Then down, Love to death, but with thee.

Scherzo[40]

Oh, beloved, come and bring
All the flowery wealth of spring!
Though the leaf be in the sere,
Icy winter creeping near;
Though the trees like mourners all
Standing at a funeral,
Black against the pallid air
Toss their wild arms in despair,
With their bald heads sadly bowed
O'er dead summer in her shroud.
Yea, though golden days be o'er,
If you enter at my door,
Spring, dear spring, will come once more.
There will break upon the night
That glad flash of dewy light
Which, like young love in a pet,
Once with sunny tears would wet
Many a wild-wood violet;
And the hyacinth will arise
In the April of your eyes.
Blossoms of the apple tree?
Rarer blossoms bloom for me

---

[40] In music, a 'scherzo' is a vigorous, playful movement in a symphony or sonata, and here Blind employs a series of rhyming tetrameter couplets to emphasize the passion and intensity of the speaker's feelings. Among other things 'Scherzo' expresses Blind's sexual nonconformism, and reflects her associations with such supporters of free monogamous unions as Karl Pearson, a fellow freethinker and the founder of the radical Men and Women's Club. Along with his fellow club member (and future wife) Maria Sharpe, Pearson explored the intersection of positivist science and sexuality in papers and publications. In a letter to Pearson, written four years before 'Scherzo' was published, Blind notes that she has read his essays 'The Woman Question' and 'Socialism and Sex', adding that the latter 'gives food for a great deal of reflection and controversy' (Mathilde Blind ALS to Karl Pearson, 24 March 1887, London, UCL Special Collections, Pearson Papers, 638/6). In 'Socialism and Sex', Pearson imagines a future in which men and women will be physical and intellectual equals, and 'a non-child-bearing woman will be the economic equal of man'. When this occurs, what Pearson calls the 'sex-relationship' will become 'a pure question of taste, a simple matter of agreement between the man and her, in which neither society nor the state would have any need or right to interfere' (Karl Pearson, 'Socialism and Sex', in *The Ethic of Freethought: A Selection of Essays and Lectures* (London: T. Fisher Unwin, 1887). pp. 427–46 (p. 442)). 'Scherzo' is one of several poems of the period (there are others by Michael Field, Edith Nesbit, Dora Sigerson Shorter) featuring women as desiring subjects.

In the cunning white and red,
Most felicitously wed,
On your cheek. And then your brow —
Can a snow-white cherry-bough
Match its bland, unsullied hue,
Where, like threads of silky blue,
Little veins show here and there
Through broad temples where your hair,
Clustering, hangs a tender brown
Softer than the fluffy down
Which before the leaf in March
Beards the lime tree and the larch?
Shall I grieve because the rose,
The red rose, no longer blows,
Since all roses you eclipse
With the roses of your lips?
And what matter, O my sweet,
Though the genial light and heat
Have departed for a while!
Only let me see you smile,
Let me see that dulcet curve
Like a dimpling wavelet swerve
Round the coral of your mouth,
And the North will change to South:
To the happy South, whose clear
Light o'er-brimming atmosphere,
Flowing in at every pore,
Sets life glowing to the core.
You are light and life in sooth,
Fair as was that Grecian youth
Who in her cold sphere above
Drove poor Dian mad with love —
When she saw him where he lay,
White and golden like a spray
Of tall jonquils whose intense
Sweetness faints upon the sense;
When she saw him swathed in light,
Couched on the aërial height
Of hoar Latmos, hushed and warm;
While, to shield him from all harm,
Like a woman's rounded arm,
A fresh creeper wildly fair
Twined around his throat and hair.[41]

[41] In comparing her would-be lover to Endymion, who in some versions of the classical myth inflamed Diana's desire, the speaker (along with Blind) is expressing a thoroughly pagan vision of human love. In her introduction to her translation of Marie Bashkirtseff's journal Blind links Bashkirtseff directly with her friend Rosamund Marriott Watson (1860–

And the goddess clean forgot
Her fair fame without a blot,
And untarnished reputation,
Free from faintest imputation
Of such frailties as the fair
Dwellers in Elysian air
Find recorded to their shame,
Chronicled with date and name,
In the annals of the skies.
She forgot in her surprise,
When her empyrean[42] eyes
Saw Endymion where he lay
Slumbering, and she cast away
Her immortal honour, clear
As her own unclouded sphere,
For the palpitating bliss
Of a surreptitious kiss.[43]

Oh, beloved, come and bring
All the flowery wealth of spring —
All its blossoms, buds, and bells,
And wind-coaxing violet smells —
All its miracle of grace
In the blossom of your face.

1911), whose exercise of sexual freedom had made her notorious in many circles. Describing Bashkirtseff's unrepentant hedonism, Blind alludes to Watson's poem 'Of the Earth, Earthy' (1891), a militantly secular paean to sensuous existence: 'no rapt and saintly vision clothed in the purity of dawn passes across her vision; this child of the nineteenth century is of the earth earthy' (Blind, 'Introduction', *The Journal of Marie Bashkirtseff*, I, xii). The speaker of this poem shares this 'earthy' vision. The male gaze is inverted in the description of Diana gazing at Endymion here, as it is in several nineteenth-century paintings (see for instance 'Diana and Endymion' by Jérôme-Martin Langlois, *circa* 1822). In selectively retelling this myth in pagan, antitheistic terms, Blind is following John Keats's 'Endymion', whose lush, aesthetic paganism she echoes. Keats also alludes to Diana in 'Ode to a Nightingale', presenting her as a mythological image of feminine sexuality.

[42] From the Ancient Greek 'empyros', meaning 'in or on the fire'. In ancient cosmologies, the Empyrean was the highest point in heaven, and the realm of the element of fire.

[43] Although she willingly gives up 'her immortal honour' to transform herself from virgin goddess to desiring woman, Diana's embrace of sexuality is not associated with any sacrifice of human honour (her own 'sphere' remained 'unclouded').

Lyrics

Love's Somnambulist[44]

Like some wild sleeper who alone at night
Walks with unseeing eyes along a height,
  With death below and only stars above;
I, in broad daylight, walk as if in sleep,
Along the edges of life's perilous steep,
  The lost somnambulist of love.

I, in broad day, go walking in a dream,
Led on in safety by the starry gleam
  Of thy blue eyes that hold my heart in thrall;
Let no one wake me rudely, lest one day,
Startled to find how far I've gone astray,
  I dash my life out in my fall.

A Meeting

A twilight glow diffused on high
  Flushed all the autumn land beneath;
Like love that lights your azure eye,
  The pond's blue goblet on the heath
    Was brimful of the sky.

We met by chance, and heaven's rich hue
  Leaped to your face in rosy flame;
Ah, is it possible you knew
  The wild delight that filled my frame
    As I caught sight of you?
Ah, is it possible, my love,
  That your delight can equal mine?
Nay, then, the burning sky above
  Grows pale beside this bliss divine,
    And the deep glow thereof.

---

[44] The sleepwalker was a common figure in Victorian literature, a visible and often sensational embodiment of the divided or multi-layered self that became the accepted model of the mind over the course of the nineteenth century. In an 1875 lecture, Blind's friend W. K. Clifford claimed that '[w]hat we commonly call self is an aggregate of feelings and of objects related to them which hangs together as a conception by virtue of long and repeated association. My self does not include all my feelings, because I habitually separate off some of them, say they do not properly belong to me, and treat them as my enemies' (W. K. Clifford, 'On the Scientific Basis of Morals' (London: Metaphysical Society, 1875), p. 7). Sleepwalking features prominently in late-century fiction by Wilkie Collins, Thomas Hardy, Bram Stoker, and Sheridan Le Fanu.

Your Face

I took your face into my dreams,
  It floated round me like a light;
Your beauty's consecrating beams
  Lay mirrored in my heart all night.
As in a lonely mountain mere,
  Unvisited of any streams,
Supremely bright and still and clear,
  The solitary moonlight gleams,
  Your face was shining in my dreams.

Only a Smile

No butterfly whose frugal fare
  Is breath of heliotrope and clove,
And other trifles light as air,
  Could live on less than doth my love.

That childlike smile that comes and goes
  About your gracious lips and eyes,
Hath all the sweetness of the rose,
  Which feeds the freckled butterflies.

I feed my love on smiles, and yet
  Sometimes I ask, with tears of woe,
How had it been if we had met,
  If you had met me long ago,

Before the fast, defacing years
  Had made all ill that once was well?
Ah, then your smiling breeds such tears
  As Tantalus may weep in hell.[45]

Sometimes I Wonder

Sometimes I wonder if you guess
The deep impassioned tenderness
  Which overflows my heart;

---

[45] A son of Zeus and Pluto, Tantalus became a wealthy king but suffered an unending posthumous punishment. Zeus invited him to his table and shared his divine counsels with him, which Tantalus subsequently divulged. Later, and in order to test the gods' omniscience, Tantalus invited them to a feast, where he cooked and fed them his third son Pelops. The gods then punished him by placing him in the deepest part of the Underworld in the midst of a lake, which he could never drink from because the water always receded when he stooped. Branches laden with fruit hung over his head, but when he stretched out his hand to reach them, they withdrew. The verb 'tantalize' derives from this myth, and appears in the first stanza of 'Seeking'.

The love I never dare confess;
Yet hard, yea, harder to repress
  Than tears too fain to start.

Sometimes I ponder, O my sweet,
The things I'll tell you when we meet;
  But straightway at your sight
My heart's blood oozes to my feet
Like thawing waters in the heat,
  Confused with too much light.

I hardly know, when you are near,
If it is love, or joy, or fear
  Which fills my languid frame;
Enveloped in your atmosphere,
My dark self seems to disappear,
  A moth entombed in flame.

Many Will Love You

Many will love you; you were made for love;
For the soft plumage of the unruffled dove
  Is not so soft as your caressing eyes.
You will love many; for the winds that veer
Are not more prone to shift their compass, dear,
  Than your quick fancy flies.

Many will love you; but I may not, no;
Even though your smile sets all my life aglow,
  And at your fairness all my senses ache.
You will love many; but not me, my dear,
Who have no gift to give you but a tear
  Sweet for your sweetness' sake.

A Dream

Only a dream, a beautiful baseless dream;
    Only a bright
Flash from your eyes, a brief electrical gleam,
    Charged with delight.

Only a waking, alone, in the moon's last gleam
    Fading from sight;
Only a flooding of tears that shudder and stream
    Fast through the night.

Rose d'Amour

I planted a rose tree in my garden,
  In early days when the year was young;
I thought it would bear me roses, roses,
  While nights were dewy and days were long.

It bore but once, and a white rose only —
  A lovely rose with petals of light;
Like the moon in heaven, supreme and lonely;
  And the lightning struck it one summer night.

Sonnet

Even as on some black background full of night,
  And hollow storm in cloudy disarray,
  The forceful brush of some great master may
More brilliantly evoke a higher light;
So beautiful, so delicately white,
  So like a very metaphor of May,
  Your loveliness on my life's sombre grey
In its perfection stands out doubly bright.[46]

And yet your beauty breeds a strange despair,
  And pang of yearning in the helpless heart,
To shield you from time's fraying wear and tear
  That from yourself yourself would wrench apart;
How save you, fairest, but to set you where
  Mortality kills death in deathless art?

A Parting

The year is on the wing, my love,
  With tearful days and nights;
The clouds are on the wing above
  With gathering swallow-flights.

The year is on the wing, my sweet,
  And in the ghostly race,
With patter of unnumbered feet,
  The dead leaves fly apace.

---

[46] The allusion here is to chiaroscuro (literally 'light-dark'), a term originally applied to a technique for making woodcut prints in which effects of light and shade are produced by printing each tone from a different wood block. Initially employed in sixteenth-century Italy, probably by the printmaker Ugo da Carpi, it later became associated with the dramatic effects achieved by Leonardo da Vinci and Caravaggio in their oil paintings.

The year is on the wing, and shakes
  The last rose from its tree;
And I, whose heart in parting breaks,
  Must bid adieu to thee.

My Lady

Like putting forth upon a sea
  On which the moonbeams shimmer,
Where reefs and unknown perils be
To wreck, yea, wreck one utterly,
It were to love you, lady fair,
In whose black braids of billowy hair
  The misty moonstones glimmer.

Oh, misty moonstone-coloured eyes,
  Latticed behind long lashes,
Within whose clouded orbs there lies,
Like lightning in the sleeping skies,
A spark to kindle and ignite,
And set a fire to love alight
  To burn one's heart to ashes.

I will not put forth on this deep
  Of perilous emotion;
No, though your hands be soft as sleep,
They shall not have my heart to keep,
Nor draw it to your fatal sphere.
Lady, you are as much to fear
  As is the fickle ocean.

On a Viola d'Amore[47]

Carved with a Cupid's head, and played on
for the first time after more than a century

What fairy music clear and light,
  Responsive to your fingers,

---

[47] Originally published in *Black & White* (15 August 1891), p. 237. The viola d'amore is a seven- or six-stringed instrument from the baroque period, played like a violin. In this quintessentially aesthetic poem, with its thematic echoes of Keats's 'Ode on a Grecian Urn', the 'dormant music' of the viola awakens to new life and distinctly Romantic strains. Significantly, this awakening transcends the calcified tropes of both rococo artificiality and fairy-tale romance used as successive metaphors; when played again the viola burns with a distinctively Paterian flame. Synaesthesia functions here to express connections among art forms; in the penultimate stanza the music the viola makes takes on a visionary power akin to that of a painter or poet as 'like the Sleeping Beauty' its 'eyes' blue fire' revivify the world, giving it voice and restoring its 'soul'.

Swells rippling on the summer night,
  And amorously lingers
Upon the sense, as long ago
In days of rouge and rococo!

A century of silence lay
  On strings that had not spoken
Since powdered lords to ladies gay
  Gave, for a lover's token,
Fans glowing fresh from Watteau's art,[48]
Well worth a marchioness's heart.

Your dormant music tranced and bound
  Was like the Sleeping Beauty
Prince Charming in the forest found,
  And kissed in loyal duty:
And when she woke her eyes' blue fire
Turned the dumb forest to a lyre.

Thus Amor with the bandaged eyes,
  Fit symbol of hushed numbers,
Most musically wakes and sighs
  After an age of slumbers:
Beneath your magic bow's control
The Viol has regained her soul.

A Child's Fancy

'Hush, hush! Speak softly, Mother dear,
So that the daisies may not hear;
For when the stars begin to peep,
The pretty daisies go to sleep.

'See, Mother, round us on the lawn;
With soft white lashes closely drawn,
They've shut their eyes so golden-gay,
That looked up through the long, long day.

'But now they're tired of all the fun —
Of bees and birds, of wind and sun
Playing their game at hide-and-seek; —
Then very softly let us speak.'

A myriad stars above the child
Looked down from heaven and sweetly smiled;

---

[48] Jean-Antoine Watteau (1684–1721) invented the genre of *fêtes galantes*, highly artificial and theatrical scenes of bucolic ease and elegance. Watteau drew on the world of Italian comedy and ballet for many of his scenes.

But not a star in all the skies
Beamed on him with his Mother's eyes.

She stroked his curly chestnut head,
And whispering very softly, said,
'I'd quite forgotten they might hear;
Thank you for that reminder, dear.'

Lassitude

I laid me down beside the sea,
Endless in blue monotony;
The clouds were anchored in the sky,
Sometimes a sail went idling by.

Upon the shingles on the beach
Grey linen was spread out to bleach,
And gently with a gentle swell
The languid ripples rose and fell.

A fisher-boy, in level line,
Cast stone by stone into the brine:
Methought I too might do as he,
And cast my sorrows on the sea.

The old, old sorrows in a heap
Dropped heavily into the deep;
But with its sorrow on that day
My heart itself was cast away.

Seeking[49]

In many a shape and fleeting apparition,
   Sublime in age or with clear morning eyes,
Ever I seek thee, tantalizing Vision,
      Which beckoning flies.

Ever I seek Thee, O evasive Presence,
   Which on the far horizon's utmost verge,

---

[49] The spirit of Shelley (and Shelley's Neoplatonism) pervades this poem. In her 1872 'Memoir' of the poet Blind writes that 'if we would seek for a being in whom the spiritual tendencies completely triumphed over the more material parts of nature, [...] let us turn [...] to Percy Bysshe Shelley', whose poetry 'possesses a power for setting the soul in motion which at a time when traditional religion has lost its vivid actual hold on men's minds, is simply the most sovereign promoter of the inner life' (*A Selection from the Poems of Percy Bysshe Shelley, Edited With a Memoir by Mathilde Blind* (Leipzig: Bernhard Tauchnitz, 1872), pp. xxxvii–xxxviii).

  Like some wild star in luminous evanescence,
    Shoots o'er the surge.

Ever I seek Thy features ever flying,
 Which ne'er beheld I never can forget:
Lightning which flames through love, and mimics dying
   In souls that set.

Ever I seek Thee through all clouds of error;
 As when the moon behind earth's shadow slips,
She wears a momentary mask of terror
   In brief eclipse.

Ever I seek Thee, passionately yearning;
 Like altar-fire on some forgotten fane,
My life flames up irrevocably burning,
   And burnt in vain.

Birds of Passage

Songs of the Orient and Occident (1895)

> 'The Bird of Time has but a little way
> To flutter — and the bird is on the wing.'
>
> Omar Khayyám[1]

---

[1] *Rubáiyát of Omar Khayyám* is the title Edward FitzGerald gave to his 1859 translation from Persian to English of a selection of quatrains (rubāʿiyāt) attributed to Omar Khayyam (1048–1131), dubbed 'the Astronomer-Poet of Persia'. Although commercially unsuccessful at first, FitzGerald's work was popularized from 1861 onward by Whitley Stokes, and came to be greatly admired by the Pre-Raphaelites in England. FitzGerald had a third edition printed in 1872, which increased interest in the work in the United States (Blind's epigraph comes from the fourth edition, published in 1879). By the 1880s, the book was extremely popular throughout the English-speaking world; numerous 'Omar Khayyam clubs' were formed and a *fin-de-siècle* cult of the Rubáiyát emerged. In 1889 Justin Huntly McCarthy, the son of Blind's friend Justin McCarthy (Irish nationalist, novelist, and MP from 1879 to 1900), published his prose translations of 466 quatrains of the Rubáiyát.

Prelude[2]

What a twitter! what a tumult! what a whirr of wheeling wings!
Birds of Passage hear the message which the Equinoctial[3] brings.

Birds of Passage hear the message and beneath the flying clouds,
Mid the falling leaves of autumn, congregate in clamorous crowds.

Shall they venture on the voyage? are the nestlings fledged for flight;
Fit to face the fluctuant storm-winds and the elemental night?

What a twitter! what a tumult! to the wild wind's marching song
Multitudinous Birds of Passage round the cliffs of England throng.

And o'er tempest-trodden Ocean, cloud-entangled day and night,
Birds on birds, in corporate motion, wing a commonwealth in flight.

Waves, like hollow graves beneath them, hoarsely howling, yawn for prey;
And the welkin[4] glooms above them shifting formless, grey in grey.

And across the Bay of Biscay[5] on undaunted wing they flee,
Where mild seas move musically murmuring of the Odyssey;

Where the gurgling whirlpools glitter and by soft Circean Straits,[6]
Fell Charybdis lies in ambush, and the ravenous Scylla waits;[7]

Where a large Homeric laughter lingers in the echoing caves,
And in playful exultation Dolphins leap from dimpling waves;

Where, above the fair Sicilian, flock-browsed, flower-pranked meadows, looms
Ætna — hoariest of Volcanoes — ominously veiled in fumes;

---

[2] Blind employs the trochaic octometer in this Prelude to the volume, a metre also used by Robert Browning in 'A Toccata of Galuppi's' (1855), Alfred Tennyson in 'Locksley Hall' (1842), and Rudyard Kipling in 'Mandalay' (1890). Blind's long poetic lines also call to mind William Blake, whose aphorism from *Milton*, 'Time is the mercy of eternity', is carved on her marble monument in the St Pancras and Islington Cemetery in London.

[3] The adjectival form of 'equinox', the time in the spring or autumn when the sun crosses the celestial equator and day and night are of equal length. Here Blind is referring to the migration of birds during the autumn equinox, which becomes a metaphor for her own imaginative flight in the volume from the 'orient' to the 'occident', and for much else.

[4] From the Old English 'wolcen', meaning the sky or firmament.

[5] A wide gulf of the north-east Atlantic Ocean lying along the western coast of France and reaching to the northern coast of Spain.

[6] During Odysseus' journey back to Ithaca following the Trojan war in Homer's *Odyssey*, the enchantress Circe lured him onto her island on the west coast of Italy and turned many of his men to swine. The Circean Straits are the straits of Messina between Italy and the island of Sicily.

[7] Scylla and Charybdis are two monsters from Greek mythology, living on the opposite sides of the Circean Straits, who together sought to destroy ships and their crew, notably the ships of Odysseus and Aeneas. Colloquially, being 'between Scylla and Charybdis' means being confronted by two equally terrible alternatives. Later scholarship established that the myth derived from a dangerous whirlpool in the straits of Messina.

Where the seas roll blue and bluer, high and higher arch the skies,
And as measureless as ocean new horizons meet the eyes;

Where at night the ancient heavens bend above the ancient earth,
With the young-eyed Stars enkindled fresh as at their hour of birth;

Where old Egypt's desert, stretching leagues on leagues of level land,
Gleams with threads of channelled waters, green with palms on either hand;

Where the Fellah[8] strides majestic through the glimmering dourah plain,
And in rosy flames flamingoes rise from rustling sugar-cane; —

On and on, along old Nilus,[9] seeking still an ampler light,
O'er its monumental mountains, Birds of Passage take their flight.

Where the sacred Isle of Philæ,[10] twinned within the sacred stream,
Floats, like some rapt Opium-eater's labyrinthine lotos dream,

Birds on birds take up their quarters in each creviced capital,
In each crack of frieze and cornice, in each cleft of roof and wall.

And within those twilight-litten,[11] holy halls of Death and Birth,
Even the gaily twittering swallows, even the swallows, hush their breath.

And they cast the passing shadows of their palpitating wings
O'er the fallen gods of Egypt and the prostrate heads of Kings.

Even as shadows Birds of Passage cast upon their onward flight
Have men's generations vanished, waned and vanished into night.[12]

---

[8] Literally a farmer or agricultural labourer in the Middle East and North Africa, but because of the similarities in beliefs and cultural practices with those of their predecessors, used here to refer to Ancient Egyptians.
[9] In Greek mythology, a son of Oceanus and Tethys and the god of the Nile River.
[10] Originally an island in the Nile, located near the expansive First Cataract of the Nile in Upper Egypt, and the site of an Egyptian temple complex. At the time of Blind's visit the survival of Philae, which contained irreplaceable temples and monuments, was under threat by the Aswan dam project, and was in fact destroyed when the project went forward in 1898. While the project provided some benefit to the Egyptian people, the irrigation it made possible would primarily increase the cultivation of cotton, the crop that was the main Egyptian export and was bound largely for the textile mills of England. Blind submitted an essay on this project to the *Fortnightly* in 1894, but it was never published. It may have fallen victim to the changing of the guard at the journal: sometime in 1894 owner Frederick Chapman fired Frank Harris, who in 1891 had published Blind's 'Recollections of Mazzini', and replaced him with W. L. Courtney, who may have misplaced Blind's submission or objected to its point of view.
[11] The shadowy light cast by the setting sun ('litten' is a participle of 'light').
[12] These last two stanzas allude to the subject and theme of Percy Shelley's sonnet 'Ozymandias', whose title is a form of the Greek name of the Egyptian pharaoh Ramesses II. Shelley describes a 'shattered visage' that is 'half sunk' in the sand, which makes a mockery of the words inscribed on the pedestal: 'My name is Ozymandias, King of Kings; | Look on my Works, ye Mighty, and despair!'

Songs of the Orient

Welcome to Egypt

The Palms stood motionless as Pyramids
  Against the golden halo of the sky;
  Interminable crops of wheat and rye
  Mantled the plain with downy coverlids
Of silken green, where little freckled kids
  Frolicked beneath the staid maternal eye;
  And babe-led buffaloes plashed trampling by,
Sprinkling cool water on their dusty lids.

Spake the grave Arab, as his flashing glance
Swept the large, luminous verdure's dewy sheen,
Sedately, with a bronze-like countenance:
  'Nehârak Saîd!'[13] Lo, this happy day,
My country decks herself in sumptuous green,
  And smiling welcome, Lady, bids you stay.'

The Sphinx

Wanderer, behold Life's riddle writ in stone,
  Fronting Eternity with lidless eyes;
  Of all that is beneath the changing skies,
Immutably abiding and alone.
The handiwork of hands unseen, unknown,
  When Pharaohs of immortal dynasties
  Built Pyramids to brave the centuries,
Cheating Annihilation of her own.

The heart grows hushed before it. Nay, methinks
  That Man, and all on which Man wastes his breath,
  The World, and all the World inheriteth,
With infinite, inexorable links
  Grappling the soul; that love, hate, birth and death
Dwindle to nothingness before thee — Sphinx.

Sphinx Money[14]

Where Pyramids and temple-wrecks are piled
  Confusedly on camel-coloured sands,
  And the mute Arab motionlessly stands,

---

[13] 'May thy day be happy' (Blind's note).
[14] 'Small fossil shells or ammonites, frequently found in some parts of the desert' (Blind's note).

Like some swart god who never wept or smiled, —
I picked up mummy relics of the wild
  (As sea-shells once with clutching baby hands),
And felt a wafture[15] from old Motherlands,
And all the morning wonder of a Child

To find Sphinx-money. So the Beduin[16] calls
  Small fossils of the waste. Nay, poet's gold;
  'Twill give thee entrance to those rites of old,
When hundred-gated Thebes,[17] with storied walls,
  Gleamed o'er her Plain, and vast processions rolled
To Amon-Ra[18] through Karnak's pillared halls.[19]

The Tombs of the Kings

Where the mummied Kings of Egypt, wrapped in linen fold on fold,
Couched for ages in their coffins, crowned with crowns of dusky gold,

Lie in subterranean chambers, biding to the day of doom,
Counterfeit life's hollow semblance in each mazy mountain tomb,

Grisly in their gilded coffins, mocking masks of skin and bone,
Yet remain in change unchanging, balking Nature of her own;

Mured in mighty Mausoleums, walled in from the night and day,
Lo, the mortal Kings of Egypt hold immortal Death at bay.

For — so spake the Kings of Egypt — those colossal ones whose hand
Held the peoples from Pitasa to the Kheta's conquered land;[20]

---

[15] A waving of the hands.
[16] A nomadic Arab of the desert.
[17] Thebes was the capital of Egypt during the period of the New Kingdom (c. 1570- c. 1069 BCE) and was an important centre of worship of the sun god Amon-Ra. Built on either side of the Nile, it is located approximately 675 km south of modern Cairo. Today Luxor and Karnak occupy the site of ancient Thebes, and its surrounding area features some of the most important archaeological sites in Egypt, including the Valley of the Kings, the Valley of the Queens, the Ramesseum (temple of Ramesses II), and the grand temple complex of Queen Hatshepsut. The biblical name for the city is *No-Amon* or *No* (Ezekiel 30. 14, 16; Jeremiah 46. 25; Nahum 3. 8).
[18] A combination of two earlier ancient Egyptian gods, Atum and Ra: the god of the sun and air, and supreme god of the universe. After the rebellion of Thebes against the Hyksos in the sixteenth century BC, Atum acquired national importance, expressed in his fusion with the Sun god Ra, as Amon-Ra or Amun-Re.
[19] The Temple for the worship of Amon, and the original site of the city Thebes, which derives its name from the temple. The Greeks named the city *Thebai* from the Coptic Greek *Ta-opet* — the name of the Karnak Temple.
[20] Between the fifteenth and thirteenth centuries BC, the Hittite Empire (known as the 'Kingdom of Kheta' in the Old Testament, and as enemies of the Israelites and their god)

Who, with flash and clash of lances and war-chariots, stormed and won
Many a town of stiff-necked Syria to high-towering Askalon:[21]

'We have been the faithful stewards of the deathless gods on high;
We have built them starry temples underneath the starry sky.

'We have smitten rebel nations, as a child is whipped with rods:
We the living incarnation of imperishable gods.

'Shall we suffer Death to trample us to nothingness? and must
We be scattered, as the whirlwind blows about the desert dust?

'No! Death shall not dare come near us, nor Corruption shall not lay
Hands upon our sacred bodies, incorruptible as day.

'Let us put a bit and bridle, and rein in Time's headlong course;
Let us ride him through the ages as a master rides his horse.

'On the changing earth unchanging let us bide till Time shall end,
Till, reborn in blest Osiris,[22] mortal with Immortal blend.'

Yea, so spake the Kings of Egypt, they whose lightest word was law,
At whose nod the far-off nations cowered, stricken dumb with awe.

And Fate left the haughty rulers to work out their monstrous doom;
And, embalmed with myrrh and ointments, they were carried to the tomb;

Through the gate of Bab-el-Molouk,[23] where the sulphur hills lie bare,
Where no green thing casts a shadow in the noon's tremendous glare;

Where the unveiled Blue of heaven in its bare intensity
Weighs upon the awe-struck spirit with the world's immensity;

Through the Vale of Desolation, where no beast or bird draws breath,
To the Coffin-Hills of Tuat — the Metropolis of Death.[24]

---

expanded its reach beyond Anatolia (modern-day Turkey) and threatened the established nation of Egypt. The victory of Ramesses II over the Kheta and their allies (which included soldiers from Pitasa) at the Battle of Kadesh in 1274 BC (near the modern Lebanon–Syria border) led to an end to hostilities between the two nations.

[21] A coastal city in the Southern District of Israel that Ramesses II subdued in about 1280 BC.
[22] The Egyptian Lord of the Underworld and Judge of the Dead.
[23] 'The Gate of the Kings. The entrance to the rocky tombs, most of which belong to the eighteenth and nineteenth Dynasties' (Blind's note).
[24] 'The depth of the grave' (Blind's note). 'Tuat', better known as 'Duat', is the realm of the dead in ancient Egyptian mythology. It is represented in hieroglyphs as a star-in-circle.

Down — down — down into the darkness, where, on either hand, dread Fate,
In the semblance of a serpent, watches by the dolorous gate;

Down — down — down into the darkness, where no gleam of sun or star
Sheds its purifying radiance from the living world afar;

Where in labyrinthine windings, darkly hidden, down and down, —
Proudly on his marble pillow, with old Egypt's double crown,

And his mien of cold commandment, grasping still his staff of state,
Rests the mightiest of the Pharaohs, whom the world surnamed the Great.

Swathed in fine Sidonian linen, crossed hands folded on the breast,
There the mummied Kings of Egypt lie within each painted chest.

And upon their dusky foreheads Pleiades[25] of flaming gems,
Glowing through the nether darkness, flash from luminous diadems.[26]

Where is Memphis?[27] Like a Mirage, melted into empty air:
But these royal gems yet sparkle richly on their raven hair.

Where is Thebes in all her glory, with her gates of beaten gold?
Where Syenê,[28] or that marvel, Heliopolis[29] of old?

Where is Edfu?[30] Where Abydos?[31] Where those pillared towns of yore
Whose auroral temples glittered by the Nile's thick-peopled shore?

Gone as evanescent cloudlands, Alplike in the afterglow;
But these Kings hold fast their bodies of four thousand years ago.

Sealed up in their Mausoleums, in the bowels of the hills,
There they hide from dissolution and Death's swiftly grinding mills.

Scattering fire, Uræus serpents[32] guard the Tombs' tremendous gate;

---

[25] A cluster of seven stars in the constellation Taurus, visible to the naked eye in the night sky, here describing seven gems on the kings' crowns.
[26] Jewelled crowns worn by sovereigns.
[27] At one time Memphis was the capital city of ancient Egypt, located south of the Nile delta.
[28] A peninsula in the Nile, near Aswan.
[29] Once a major city of ancient Egypt, now a north-eastern suburb of Cairo.
[30] A city on the west bank of the Nile near Aswan, site of the Ptolemaic Temple of Horus, and about 5 km from the remains of the ancient pyramids.
[31] One of the oldest cities of ancient Egypt, a cult centre for Osiris, and a necropolis for the earliest Egyptian sovereigns. It was located in the low desert west of the Nile River near the modern Egyptian town of Al-Balyanā.
[32] Stylized representations of Egyptian cobras; symbols of sovereignty, royalty, deity, and

While Thoth[33] holds the trembling balance, weighs the heart and seals its fate.[34]

And a multitude of mummies in the swaddling clothes of death,
Ferried o'er the sullen river, on and on still hasteneth.

And around them and above them, blazoned on the rocky walls,
Crowned with stars, enlaced by serpents, in divine processionals,

Ibis-headed,[35] jackal-featured, vulture-hooded, pass on high,
Gods on gods through Time's perspectives — pilgrims of Eternity.

There, revealed by fitful flashes, in a gloom that may be felt,
Wild Chimæras[36] flash from darkness, glittering like Orion's belt.[37]

And on high, o'er shining waters, in their barks the gods sail by,
In the Sunboat and the Moonboat,[38] rowed across the rose-hued sky.

Night, that was before Creation, watches sphinx-like, starred with eyes,
And the hours and days are passing, and the years and centuries.

But these mummied Kings of Egypt, pictures of a perished race,

divine authority in ancient Egypt.

[33] The Egyptian god of writing, magic, wisdom, and the moon.

[34] 'Perhaps of all Egyptian beliefs, none is so widely known as "The Judgment of the Dead". It is frequently represented on tombs and temples, and there is a remarkable wall-painting of it in the beautiful little temple of Dêr-el-Medîneh. After Osiris, Judge of the underworld, Thoth plays the chief part in this impressive ceremony. He is the Moon-god, generally represented as an Ibis or Baboon. "The soul first advanced to the foot of the throne, carrying on its outstretched hands the image of its heart or of its eyes, agents and accomplices of its vices and virtues. It humbly 'smelt the earth,' then arose, and with uplifted hands recited its profession of faith. In the middle of the hall its acts were weighed by the assessors. Like all objects belonging to the gods, the balance is magic. Truth squats upon one of the scales; Thoth places the heart upon the other, and, always merciful, bears upon the side of Truth, that judgment may be favourably inclined. He affirms that the heart is light of offence, inscribes the results of the proceeding upon a wooden tablet, and pronounces the verdict aloud". — *The Dawn of Civilization* by G. Maspero' (Blind's note).

[35] The African sacred ibis (*Threskiornis aethiopicus*) was associated with the god Thoth, who was often represented in the form of a man's body with the head of an ibis.

[36] A fire-breathing lioness was one of the earliest of solar and war deities in Ancient Egypt, pre-dating and possibly influencing the first Greek representations by some 3000 years. In Greek mythology, the Chimæra was a monstrous fire-breathing hybrid creature composed of the parts of more than one animal. The word has come to describe imaginatively dazzling creations composed of disparate parts.

[37] In Greek mythology, a giant huntsman whom Zeus (or Artemis) placed among the stars as the constellation of Orion.

[38] 'The chief barks of Râ, the Sun-god, were called Saktît and Mazît. He entered one on his rising in the East, which carried him along the celestial river; and the other about the middle of his course, which bore him to the land of Manû, which is at the entrance of Hades' (Blind's note).

Lie, of busy Death forgotten, face by immemorial face.

Though the glorious sun above them, burning on the naked plain,
Clothes the empty wilderness with the golden, glowing grain;

Though the balmy Moon above them, floating in the milky Blue,
Fills the empty wildernesses with a silver fall of dew;

Though life comes and flies unresting, like the shadow which a dove
Casts upon the Sphinx, in passing, for a moment from above; —

Still these mummied Kings of Egypt, wrapped in linen, fold on fold,
Bide through the ages in their coffins, crowned with crowns of dusky gold.

Had the sun once brushed them lightly, or a breath of air, they must
Instantaneously have crumbled into evanescent dust.

Pale and passive in their prisons, they have conquered, chained to death;
And their lineaments look living now as when they last drew breath!

Have they conquered? Oh the pity of those Kings within their tombs,
Locked in stony isolation in those petrifying glooms!

Motionless where all is motion in a rolling Universe,
Heaven, by answering their prayer, turned it to a deadly curse.

Left them fixed where all is fluid in a world of star-winged skies;
Where, in myriad transformations, all things pass and nothing dies;

Nothing dies but what is tethered, kept when Time would set it free,
To fulfil Thought's yearning tension upward through Eternity.

Hymn to Horus[39]

Hail, God revived in glory!
   The night is over and done;
Far mountains wrinkled and hoary,
Fair cities great in story,
   Flash in the rising sun.

Behold the Dawn uncloses
   The shutters of the night;
The Waste and her oases

---

[39] 'Horus, the Egyptian Apollo, son of Osiris and Isis, and avenger of his murdered father. He is chiefly associated with the victoriously rising sun, and a slayer of the Serpent, like all Sun-gods. He is generally depicted with the side-lock of infancy, or as hawk-headed, or simply as a great golden Sparrow-Hawk, who puts all other birds to flight' (Blind's note).

Blossoms a rose of roses
      Beneath thy rose-red light.

   Hail, golden House of Horus,
      Lap of heaven's holiest God!
   From lotos-banks before us
   Birds in ecstatic chorus
      Fly, singing, from the sod.

   Up, up, into the shining,
      Translucent morning sky,
   No longer dull and pining,
   With drooping plumes declining,
      The storks and eagles fly.

   The Nile amid his rushes
      Reflects thy risen disk;
   A light of gladness gushes
   Through kindling halls, and flushes
      Each flaming Obelisk.

   Vast Temples catch thy splendour;
   Vistas of columns shine
      Celestial, with a tender
   Rose-bloom on every slender
      Papyrus-pillared shrine.

   In manifold disguises,
      And under many names,
   Thrice-holy son of Isis,[40]
   We worship him who rises
      A child-god fledged in flames.[41]

   Hail, sacred Hawk,[42] who, winging,
      Crossest the heavenly sea!
   With harp-playing, with singing,
   With linen robes, white clinging,
      We come, fair God, to thee.

   Thou whom our soul espouses,
      When weary of the way,
   Enter our golden houses,
   And, with thy mystic spouses,
      Rest from the long, long way.

[40] Mother of Horus, sister and wife of the god Osiris, and ruler of the underworld.
[41] See Introduction, p. 4.
[42] Horus was represented not as a hawk but a falcon, whose right eye was the sun and whose left eye was the moon.

Nuit[43]

The all upholding,
The all enfolding,
The all beholding,
    Most secret Night;
From whose abysses,
With wordless blisses,
The Sun's first kisses,
    Called gods to light.[44]

One god undying,
But multiplying,
Restlessly trying,
    Doing: undone.
Through myriad changes,
He sweeps and ranges;
But life estranges
    Many in one.

In wild commotion,
Out of the ocean,
With moan and motion,
    Wave upon waves,
Mingling in thunder,
Rise and go under:
Break, life, asunder;
    Night has her graves.[45]

---

[43] 'One of the names for the primæval night of Egyptian mythology. She is described as follows in an inscription cut on the floor of the mummy-case of Mykerinos, the builder of the third great Pyramid: "Thy Mother Nuit has spread herself out over thee in her name of Mystery of the Heavens"' (Blind's note). Blind places Nuit at the centre of a radically revisionist cosmology, embodied in the poem's metrical structure, which employs feminine rhymes and subverts the conventionally light or comic tone of dimeter verse. See Introduction, pp. 39–40.

[44] From its first stanza, this poem reflects Blind's awareness and appropriation of Decadent tropes. Here the female source of all religions also exhibits a polymorphous sexuality projected onto the entire universe of matter.

[45] In another deployment of Decadent tropes, Blind ends the poem by imagining that all religions engendered by the primæval night return to embrace their creator, who reappears in the last stanza as a kind of Decadent femme fatale on a cosmic scale.

Egyptian Theosophy[46]

Far in the introspective East
A meditative Memphian Priest

Would solve — such is the Sage's curse —
The riddle of the Universe.

Thought, turning round itself, revolved,
How was this puzzling World evolved?

How came the starry sky to be,
The sun, the earth, the Nile, the sea?

And Man, most tragi-comic Man,
Whence came he here, and where began?

Communing with the baffling sky,
Who twinkled, but made no reply,

He brooded, till his heated brain
Grew fairly addled with the strain.

For in that dim, benighted age
Philosopher and hoary sage

Had not yet had the saving grace
To teach the Schools that Time and Space,

And all the marvels they contain,
Are but the phantoms of the brain.

---

[46] 'The Egyptian imagination was extremely fertile in inventing myths of the creation. "One amongst many was that Sibû was concealed under the form of a colossal gander, whose mate once laid the Sun-Egg, and perhaps still laid it daily. From the piercing cries wherewith he congratulated her, and announced the good news to all who cared to hear it — after the manner of his kind — he had received the flattering epithet of Ngagu-oirû, the Great Cackler. Other versions repudiated the goose in favour of a vigorous bull, the father of gods and men, whose companion was a cow, a large-eyed Hâthor, of beautiful countenance". — *The Dawn of Civilization* by G. Maspero' (Blind's note).

The second half of Blind's title alludes to a late nineteenth-century religious movement (officially established in New York City in 1875) founded by Russian immigrant Helena Blavatsky. This movement was embraced and circulated in England in the 1890s by the socialist, women's rights activist, and birth control advocate Annie Besant. While it draws upon Neoplatonism as well as Hinduism and Buddhism, it shares with Egyptian mythology a belief in the reincarnation of the human soul. Given her own antitheism, it is fitting that Blind's title extends the poem's bemused scepticism concerning a specific Egyptian creation myth to a contemporary manifestation of supernaturalism.

But that profound Egyptian Seer
Maybe — who knows? — came pretty near;

When, after days of strenuous fast,
He hit the startling truth at last;

And on select, mysterious nights,
Veiled in occult, symbolic rites:

He taught — that once upon a time —
To disbelieve it were a crime —

The World's great egg — refute who can,
That meditates on Life and Man —

While deafening cacklings spread the news —
Was laid by an Almighty Goose.

The Moon of Ramadân[47]

The sunset melts upon the Nile,
  The stony desert glows,
Beneath heaven's universal smile,
  One burning damask rose;
And like a Peri's[48] pearly boat,
  No longer than a span,
Look, faint on fiery sky afloat,
  The Moon of Ramadân.

Our boat drifts idly with the Stream,
  Our boatmen ship the oar;
Vistas of endless temples gleam
  On either topaz shore;
And swimming over groves of Palm,
  A crescent weak and wan,
There steals into the perfect calm
  The Moon of Ramadân.

All nature seems to bask in peace
  And hush her lowest sigh;

---

[47] 'The month of Ramadân is the month of fasting, which begins as soon as a Muslim declares that he has seen the new moon. From daybreak to sunset, throughout the month, eating and drinking are absolutely prohibited, but the faithful indemnify themselves by feasting and smoking throughout a great part of the night' (Blind's note).
[48] In Persian mythology, Peri are winged female spirits of exquisite beauty, mischievous creatures that have been denied entry to paradise until they have completed penance for atonement. But as they were taken up by other cultures, they assumed different attributes, and under Islamic influence they were reimagined as benevolent spirits.

Above the river's golden fleece
  The happy Halcyons fly.
And lost in some old lotos dream,
  The pensive Pelican
Sees mirrored in the mazy stream
  The Moon of Ramadân.

Black outlined on the golden air
  A turbaned Silhouette,
The Mueddin[49] invites to prayer
  From many a Minaret.
Our dusky boatmen hear the call,
  And prostrate, man on man,
They bow, adoring, one and all,
  The Moon of Ramadân.

Where Luxor's rose-flushed columns shine
  Above the river's brim,
The priests with incense once, and wine,
  Made sacrifice to Him,
The highest god of Thebes, and head
  Of all the heavenly clan;
But now the Moslem hails instead
  The Moon of Ramadân.

The gods have come, the gods have gone,
  Yet wedded to their walls,
Winged with the serpent of the Sun
  In mute processionals,
They stride from door to massy door,
  Bound nations in their van,
Though Amon's Sun has waned before
  The Moon of Ramadân.

Yea, even proud Egypt's proudest king,
Who chastised rebel lands,
  And brought his gods for offering
  Mountains of severed hands;[50]
Who singly, like a god of War,
  Smote hosts that swerved and ran,
Lies low 'neath Allah's scimetar[51] —
  The Moon of Ramadân.

---

[49] The man who calls Muslims to prayer from the minaret of a mosque.
[50] 'The Pharaohs used to cut off the hands of their conquered enemies, and make them an offering to their gods. The subject is depicted in a striking wall-painting of the Temple at Medinet Haboo' (Blind's note).
[51] Variant of 'scimitar'.

And Isis, Queen, whose sacred disk's
  Horned splendour crowned her brow,
While fires of flashing Obelisks
  Flamed in the Afterglow;
And white-robed priests who served her shrine
  Have turned Mahommedan,
And worship Him who wears for sign
  The Moon of Ramadân.

The rosy lotos, flower and leaf,
  Which wreathed each sacred lake,
With Nature's loveliest bas-relief,
  Has followed in their wake;
Yea, with the last true Pharaoh's death,
  The lotos leaves, grown wan,
Have changed to lily white beneath
  The Moon of Ramadân.

The gods may come, the gods may go,
  And royal realms change hands;
But the most ancient Nile will flow,
  And flood the desert sands;
And nightly will he glass the stars'
  Unearthly caravan,
Nor care if it be Rome's red Mars
  Or Moon of Ramadân.

The sunset fades upon the Nile;
  The desert's stony gloom,
Receding blankly mile on mile,
  Grows silent as a tomb.
All weary wanderers, man and beast,
  Hie, fasting, to the Khan,[52]
While shines above their nightly feast
  The Moon of Ramadân.

The Beautiful Beeshareen Boy[53]

Beautiful, black-eyed boy,

---

[52] In the east, an unfurnished building for the accommodation of travellers. Blind may also be punning on such eastern rulers as Genghis and Kubla Khan.
[53] 'The Beeshareens are a wandering desert tribe of Upper Egypt, reminding one of our Gypsies. Many of them are remarkably handsome, more particularly in childhood. The grace of their movements and charm of manner must strike all travellers on the Nile. The children haunt the shore where boats land, and set up an incessant cry for "backsheesh," and there are few who can resist the winning smiles with which they sweeten their importunities. Conspicuous among the crowd was a lovely boy of sixteen, who attracted

O lithe-limbed Beeshareen![54]
Face that finds no maid coy,
  Page for some peerless queen:
Some Orient queen of old,
Sumptuous in woven gold,
Close-clinging fold on fold,
  Lightning, with gems between.

Bred in the desert, where
  Only to breathe and be
Alive in living air
  Is finest ecstasy;
Where just to ride or rove,
With sun or stars above,
Intoxicates like love,
  When love shall come to thee.

Thy lovely limbs are bare;
  Only a rag, in haste,
Draped with a princely air,
  Girdles thy slender waist.
And gaudy beads and charms,
Dangling from neck and arms,
Ward off dread spells and harms
  Of Efreets[55] of the waste.[56]

Caressed of wind and sun,
  Across the white-walled town

the attention of artists and photographers two or three winters ago. He had the elegant proportions of a Tanagra statuette, and was so constantly asked to sit for his portrait that he must have thought that that was the end and aim of all tourists. Finally, he was carried off to the World's Fair with other curiosities of Egypt. When the Beeshareens returned to Assouan he was not amongst them, and rumour says that he got as far as Marseilles, where he utterly vanished. This tribe dress their profuse black hair in quite an extraordinary fashion. It is worn in countless little plaits, with a high, fuzzy bunch in the centre. I have heard it said that they wear it thus in memory of their descent from one of the lost tribes of Israel' (Blind's note).

In this poem Blind is clearly criticizing the colonial regime, though she displaces her critique onto America. Her political radicalism here is not confined to one country, however, since the poem expresses a pointed critique of the commodity fetishism inherent in capitalism.

[54] A member of the Bishari, an ethnic group inhabiting North-east Africa.
[55] An Efreet, also spelled ifrit or afrit, is a powerful demon in Islamic mythology. In later folklore Efreets developed into independent entities, identified as spirits of the dead who sometimes inhabited desolate places such as ruins and temples.
[56] As this stanza emphasizes, Blind represents this Beeshareen youth as possessing an androgynous beauty, which links this poem with other Decadent fantasies of androgyny, from Swinburne's 'Hermaphroditus' (composed 1863, published 1866) to Michael Field's 'LII' from *Long Ago* (1889). The latter imagines what happened when Tiresias found that 'womanhood was round him thrown'.

Fawnlike we saw thee run,
  Light Love in Mocha brown!
Wild Cupid, without wings,
Twanging thy viol strings;
With crocodiles and rings
  Bartered for half a crown.

Spoilt darling of our bark,
  Smiling with teeth as white
As when across the dark
  There breaks a flash of light.
And what a careless grace
Showed in thy gait and pace;
Eyes starlike in a face
  Sweet as a Nubian night!

Better than Felt or Fez,[57]
  High on thy forehead set,
Countless in lock and tress,
  Waved a wild mane of jet.
Kings well might envy thee
What courts but rarely see,
Curls of rich ebony
  Coiled in a coronet.

Lo — in dim days long since —
  The strolling Almehs tell,[58]
Thou shouldst have been a prince,
  Boy of the ebon fell!
If truth the poet sings,
Thy tribe, oh Beduin,[59] springs
From those lost tribes of Kings,
  Once Kings in Israel.

Ah me! the camp-fires gleam
  Out yonder, where the sands
Fade like a lotos dream
  In hollow twilight lands.
Our sail swells to the blast,
Our boat speeds far and fast,

---

[57] 'Felt or Fez' refers to hats popularized during the Ottoman period — red in colour, conical in shape, and topped with a black tassel. In the nineteenth century they were commonly worn by men in many Muslim countries, including Egypt, but today their use is largely confined to the Balkans and Morocco.
[58] A class of courtesans or female entertainers in Egypt, raised and trained to sing, tell stories, and recite classical poetry.
[59] See p. 187, note 4.

Farewell! And to the last
  Smile, waving friendly hands.

* * * * *

From England's storm-girt isle,
  O'er seas where seagulls wail,
Rocked on the rippling Nile,
  We drift with drooping sail.
On waters hushed at night,
Where stars of Egypt write
In hieroglyphs of light
  Their undeciphered tale.

Forlorn sits Assouan;
  Where is her boy, her pride? —
Now in the lamplit Khan,
  Now by the riverside,
Or where the Soudanese,[60]
Under mimosa trees,
Chaunt mournful melodies,
  We've sought him far and wide.

Oh, desert-nurtured Child,
  How dared they carry thee,
Far from thy native Wild,
  Across the Western Sea?
Packed off, poor boy, at last,
With many a plaster cast
Of plinth and pillar vast,
  And waxen mummies piled!

Ah! just like other ware,
  For a lump sum or so
Shipped to the World's great Fair —
  The big Chicago Show![61]
With mythic beasts and things,

---

[60] Citizens of Sudan.
[61] The World's Columbian Exposition, a world's fair held in Chicago in 1893 to celebrate the 400th anniversary of Christopher Columbus's arrival in the New World in 1492, was also called 'The White City' because its main buildings were clad in white stucco. But white supremacy and Eurocentrism were also everywhere on display, including the 'living exhibits' at the nearby Midway Plaisance (villages representing countries in Europe, the Middle East, Asia, and East Asia). While the European villages were located nearest to the White City, further away and closer to the centre of the Midway were those representing non-European villages and the world's 'lesser races' — including Africans, Asians, American Indians, and Arabs — where the 'beautiful Beeshareen boy' would have been on display.

Beetles and bulls with wings,
And imitation Sphinx,
  Ranged row on curious row!

Beautiful, black-eyed boy;
  Ah me! how strange it is
That thou, the desert's joy,
  Whom heavenly winds would kiss,
With Ching and Chang-hwa ware,[62]
Blue pots and bronzes rare,
Shouldst now be over there
  Shown at Porkopolis.[63]

Gone like a lovely dream,
  Child of the starry smile;
Gone from the glowing stream
  Glassing its greenest isle!
We've sought, but sought in vain;
Thou wilt not come again,
Never for bliss or pain,
  Home to thy orphaned Nile.

The Dying Dragoman[64]

Far in the fiery wilderness,
  Beyond the town of Assouan,
Left languishing in sore distress,
  There lay a dying Dragoman.
Alone amid the waste, alone,
The hot sand burnt him to the bone;
And on his breast, like heated stone,
  The burden of the air did press.

His head was pillowed on a tomb,
  Reared to some holy Sheik of old;
The irresistible Simoom[65]
  Whirled drifts of sand that rose and rolled
Around him, and the panting air

---

[62] Chinese ceramics.
[63] A colloquial name for Chicago, a major meat-processing centre for the United States.
[64] Dragomen are interpreters and guides hired by tourists and tour companies, especially in countries speaking Arabic, Turkish, or Persian. This particular dragoman is an expatriate from south-west Germany (where Blind was born), as indicated by the reference to the 'Black forest clocks' that 'tick day and night' in his consciousness as his homesickness stirs memories of his homeland and family. Such a dragoman would have been hired by tourists like Blind herself.
[65] A hot dry desert wind.

Was one sulphureous spectral glare,
Shot with such gleams as lights the lair
   Of tigers in a jungle's gloom.

Groaning, he closed his bloodshot eyes,
   As if to shut out all he feared;
And greedily a swarm of flies
   Fell on his face and tangled beard.
He lay like one who ne'er would lift
His head above that ashy drift;
When lo, there gleamed across a rift
   The blue oasis of the skies.

Like smoke dispersing far and wide,
   The draggled sands were blown away;
The wild clouds in a refluent tide
   Receded from the face of day.
The lingering airs yet lightly blew
Till the last speck cleared out of view,
And left the hushed Eternal Blue,
   And nothing else beside.

Then once again, with change of moods,
   A mighty shadow, broadening, fell
Across those shadeless solitudes,
   Without a Palm, without a Well.
Wing wedged in wing, an ordered mass
Unnumbered numbers pass and pass,
As if one Will, one only, was
   In all those moving multitudes.

A chord thrilled in the sick man's brain;
   He raised his heavy-lidded eyes,
He raised his heavy head with pain,
   And caught a glimpse of netted skies,
Meshed in ten thousand wings in flight
That cleft the air. Oh wondrous sight!
He gasped, he shrieked in sheer delight:
   'The Storks! The Storks fly home again!'[66]

'I too, O Storks, I too, even I,
   Would see my native land again.

[66] Storks migrate annually in the summer from Europe to the Middle East and Africa, returning the following spring. The storks' spring migration causes the dragoman to yearn for his homeland, engendering a chain of memories. Given the poem's title and narrative arc, Blind is also likely alluding to Egyptian mythology, which associates storks with a person's soul.

Oh, had I wings that I might fly
  With you, wild birds, across the main!
Take, take me to the land, I pray,
The land where nests are full in May,
The land where my young children play:
  Oh, take me with you, or I die.

'My lonely heart blooms like a flower,
  My children, when I think of you,
My love is like an April shower,
  And fills my heart with drops of dew.
Along their unknown tracks, ah me!
The Storks will fly across the sea;
My children soon will hail with glee
  Their red bills on the rain-washed tower.'

Home-sickness seized him for the herds
  That browse upon the fresh green leas;
Home-sickness for the cuckoo birds
  That shout afar in feathery trees;
For running stream and rippling rill
That, racing, turning his woodland mill:
And tears on tears began to fill
  His eyes, confusing all he sees.

Again he doats[67] on rosy cheeks
  Of children rolling in the grass;
Again the busy days and weeks,
  The months and years serenely pass.
Black forest clocks tick day and night,
His board and bed are snowy white,
His humble house is just as bright
  As if it were a house of glass.

Again, beneath the high-peaked roof,
  His wife's unresting shuttle flies
Across the even warp and woof;
  Again his thrifty mother plies
Her wheel, that hums like noontide bees;
And lint-locked babes about her knees
Hark to strange tales of talking trees,
  And Storks deep versed in sage replies.

Again the ring of swinging chimes
  Calls all the pious folk to church,

---

[67] Variant of 'dote'.

With shining Sunday face, betimes,
  Through rustling woods of beech and birch
Full of moist glimmering hollows where
  The pines bow murmuring as in prayer,
And musically through the air
  The forest's mighty Choral swells.

Again, O Lord, again he sees
  The place where Heaven came down one day;
Where, in a space of bloom and bees,
  He won his wife one morn of May.
Warm pulses shook and thrilled his blood,
Wild birds were singing in the wood,
The flowering world in bridal mood
  Joined in the Pinewood's symphonies.

Again, O Lord, in grief and fear,
  He bids good-bye to all he loves;
The waters swell, the woods are sere,
  The Storks are gone, and hushed the doves.
He goes with them; he goes to heal
The sickness whose insidious seal
Is set on him. Ah, tears will steal
  And blur the Storks that disappear.

A furnace fire behind the hill,
  The sun has burnt itself away;
The ghost of light, transparent, chill,
  Yet floats upon the edge of day.
And all the desert holds its breath
As if it felt and crouched beneath
The filmy, flying bat of death
  About a heart for ever still.

And one by one, seraphic, bland,
  The bright stars open in the skies;
And large above the Shadow land
  The white-faced moon begins to rise.
And all the wilderness grows wan
Beneath the stars, that one by one
Look down upon the lifeless man
  As if they were his children's eyes.

A Fantasy

I was an Arab,
  I loved my horse;

Swift as an arrow
  He swept the course.⁶⁸

Sweet as a lamb
  He came to hand;
He was the flower
  Of all the land.

Through lonely nights
  I rode afar;
God lit His lights —
  Star upon star.

God's in the desert;
  His breath the air:
Beautiful desert,
  Boundless and bare!⁶⁹

Free as the wild wind,
  Light as a foal;
Ah, there is room there
  To stretch one's soul.

Far reached my thought,
  Scant were my needs:
A few bananas
  And lotus seeds.⁷⁰

Sparkling as water
  Cool in the shade,
Ibrahim's daughter,⁷¹
  Beautiful maid.

Out of thy Kulleh,⁷²
  Fairest and first,
Give me to drink
  Quencher of thirst.

---

⁶⁸ Nomadic tribes of Arabs who lived in the desert prized and depended on their horses, which were known for their speed, endurance, and intelligence.
⁶⁹ An allusion to Shelley's 'Ozymandias' (1818): 'Round the decay | Of that colossal wreck, boundless and bare | The lone and level sands stretch far away'.
⁷⁰ Blind's choices here may have more to do with the needs of the metre than horticultural practice, since bananas were not found in the Arabian desert. The lotus is a traditional symbol of divine intellect. It also has connotations of forgetfulness of duty and home derived from *The Odyssey*, the subject of Tennyson's poem 'The Lotos-Eaters'. Her spelling here is anomalous, since all other references in 'Songs of the Orient' spell the word 'lotos'.
⁷¹ The Koranic version of Abraham, not a biblical reference.
⁷² A lamb-skin cap.

I am athirst, girl;
  Parched with desire,
Love in my bosom
  Burns as a fire.

Green thy oasis,
  Waving with Palms;
Oh, be no niggard,[73]
  Maid, with thy alms.

Kiss me with kisses,
  Buds of thy mouth,
Sweeter than Cassia[74]
  Fresh from the South.

Bind me with tresses,
  Clasp with a curl;
And in caresses
  Stifle me, girl.

I was an Arab
  Ages ago!
Hence this home-sickness
  And all my woe.

The Desert[75]

Uncircumscribed, unmeasured, vast,
  Eternal as the Sea;
What lacks the tidal sea thou hast —
  Profound stability.

Beneath the sun that burns and brands
  In hushed Noon's halting breath,
Calm as the Sphinx upon thy sands
  Thou art — nay, calm as death.

The desert foxes hide in holes,
  The jackal seeks his lair;
The sombre rocks, like reddening coals,
  Glow lurid in the glare.

---

[73] A miser.
[74] A fragrant plant related to cinnamon.
[75] This poem contains echoes of several others: Samuel Taylor Coleridge's 'The Rime of the Ancient Mariner' (1798); Shelley's 'Ozymandias' (1818); and Matthew Arnold's 'Obermann' (1852), whose metrical pattern it shares (iambic tetrameter stanzas rhyming abab).

Only some vulture far away,
  Bald-headed, harpy-eyed,
Flaps down on lazy wing to prey
  On what has lately died.

No palm tree lifts a lonely shade,
  No dove is on the wing;
It seems a land which Nature made
  Without a living thing,

Or wreckage of some older world,
  Ere children grew, or flowers,
When rocks and hissing stones were hurled
  In hot, volcanic showers.

The solemn Blue bends over all;
  Far as winged thought may flee
Roll ridges of black mountain wall,
  And flat sands like the sea.

No trace of footsteps to be seen,
  No tent, no smoking roof;
Nay, even the vagrant Beeshareen[76]
  Keeps warily aloof.

But yon, mid tumbled hillocks prone,
  Some human form I scan —
A human form, indeed, but stone:
  A cold, colossal Man![77]

How came he here mid piling sands,
  Like some huge cliff enisled,
Osiris-wise, with folded hands,
  Mute spirit of the Wild?

Ages ago the hands that hewed,
  And in the living rock

---

[76] See 'The Beautiful Beeshareen Boy', p. 197

[77] 'This unfinished Colossus of red granite was discovered by two English officers while riding in the desert round Assouan. The scene is one of extraordinary desolation. The ash-coloured sand, broken by blue-black ridges, is a chaos of scattered stones and boulders which might be part of a landscape in the moon. The statue is believed to be that of Amenhotep III., to whom we owe the two Colossi of the Plain, of which one is the famous "Vocal Memnon." He was also the Egyptian Nimrod, and on one of his lion-hunting expeditions to the South is said to have met a beautiful young maiden, whom he married, though she was neither Egyptian nor of royal race. She was that famous Queen Thi who introduced the worship of the Sun's disk into Egypt' (Blind's note).

Carved this Colossus, granite-thewed
And curled each crispy lock:

Ages ago have dropped to rest
  And left him passive, prone,
Forgotten on earth's barren breast,
  Half statue and half stone.

And Persia ruled and Palestine;
  And o'er her violet seas
Arose, with marble gods divine,
  The grace of god-like Greece.

And Rome, the Mistress of the World,
  Amid her diadem
Of Eastern Empires set impearled
  The Scarab's mystic gem.[78]

Perchance he has been lying here
  Since first the world began,
Poor Titan of some earlier sphere
  Of prehistoric Man!

To whom we are as idle flies,
  That fuss and buzz their day;
While still immutable he lies,
  As long ago he lay.

Empurpled in the Afterglow,
  Thou, with the Sun alone,
Of all the stormy waste below,
  Art King, but king of stone!

Uncircumscribed, unmeasured, vast,[79]
  Eternal as the Sea,
The present here becomes the past,
  For all futurity.

Scarabæus Sisyphus[80]

I've watched thee, Scarab! Yea, an hour in vain

---

[78] Scarabs were Egyptian gems cut in the form of a scarab beetle, sometimes depicted with the wings spread, and engraved with hieroglyphs on their flat undersides. See the next poem, 'Scarabæus Sisyphus'.

[79] Perhaps an allusive echo of these lines from Coleridge's 'Kubla Khan': 'Where Alph, the sacred river, ran | Through caverns measureless to man | Down to a sunless sea'.

[80] 'The beetle (*Scarabæus sacer*) was the emblem of the principle of life and creative power,

I've watched thee, slowly toiling up the hill,
  Pushing thy lump of mud before thee still
With patience infinite and stubborn strain.
Strive as thou mayst, spare neither time nor pain,
  To screen thy burden from all chance of ill;
  Push, push, with all a beetle's force of will,
Thy ball, alas! rolls ever down again.

Toil without end! And why? That after thee
  Dim hosts of groping Scarabs too shall climb
This self-same height? Accursèd progeny
  Of Sisyphus, what antenatal crime
Has doomed us too to roll incessantly
  Life's Stone, recoiling from the Alps of time?

The Colossi of the Plain[81]

Ancient of Days! Before the Trojan Wars[82]
  You towered as now in your colossal prime,
  Watching the rosy footed morning climb
O'er far Arabia's flushing mountain bars.
Despite your weird disfigurement and scars
  You dwarf all other monuments. Sublime
  Survivors of old Thebes! you baffle Time,
And sit in silent conclave with the Stars.

Ah, once below you through the glittering plain
  Stretched avenues of Sphinxes to the Nile;
And, flanked with towers, each consecrated fane
Enshrined its god. The broken gods lie prone

---

which the Egyptians worshipped under such manifold forms. It was supposed to have no female, and to roll the eggs which produce its offspring into a kind of ball, sparing no effort to place them in safety' (Blind's note). 'Scarabaeus sacer', which translates as sacred scarab, is the Latin name for the ancient Egyptian dung-beetle. In substituting Sisyphus for sacer, Blind is blending eastern and western mythology. Sisyphus was doomed in hell to roll a large stone uphill, watch it roll down, and endlessly repeat the process. The Egyptian scarabs roll their dung-balls uphill and let them roll down for a creative purpose: to compact the matter around their eggs.

[81] Twin monumental statues of the Pharaoh Amenhotep III (fourteenth century BC), standing about 18 m high, which originally served as guardians to the entrance of Amenhotep's temple. Each statue depicts Amenhotep in a seated position, facing east toward the Nile. They have stood in the Theban Necropolis, located west of the Nile from the modern city of Luxor, since 1350 BCE, though both are so damaged that the figures' features above the waist are now nearly unrecognizable. Though focused on the ephemerality of gods rather than men, this sonnet shares both formal and thematic similarities with Shelley's 'Ozymandias'.

[82] The legendary conflict between the early Greeks and the people of Troy in western Anatolia, dated by later Greek authors to the twelfth or thirteenth century BC, and depicted in Homer's *Iliad* and *Odyssey*, and Virgil's *Aeneid*.

In roofless halls, their hallowed terrors gone,
  Helpless beneath Heaven's penetrating smile.

Mourning Women

All veiled in black, with faces hid from sight,[83]
  Crouching together in the jolting cart,
    What forms are these that pass alone, apart,
In abject apathy to life's delight?
The motley crowd, fantastically bright,
  Shifts gorgeous through each dazzling street and mart;
    Only these sisters of the suffering heart
Strike discords in this symphony of light.

Most wretched women! whom your prophet dooms
  To take love's penalties without its prize!
Yes; you shall bear the unborn in your wombs,
  And water dusty death with streaming eyes,
And, wailing, beat your breasts among the tombs;
  But souls ye have none fit for Paradise.[84]

The Sâkiyeh[85]

'How long shall Man be Nature's fool?' Man cries;
  'Be like those great, gaunt oxen, drilled and bound,
    Inexorably driven round and round
To turn the water-wheel with bandaged eyes?
And as they trudge beneath Egyptian skies,
  Watering the wrinkled desert's beggared ground,
    The hoarse Sâkiyeh's lamentable sound
Fills all the land as with a people's sighs?'

Poor Brutes! Who in unconsciousness sublime,
  Replenishing the ever-empty jars,
    Endow the waste with palms and harvest gold:
  And men, who move in rhythm with moving stars,
    Should shrink to give the borrowed lives they hold:
Bound blindfold to the groaning wheel of Time.

---

[83] The hijab, which can refer to any head, face, or body covering worn by Muslim women that conforms to Islamic standards of modesty, can also serve symbolically to demarcate the human and the divine, which the poem's title foregrounds.

[84] The sestet here alludes to the doctrine (falsely assumed to be set forth in the Qur'ān) that women do not have souls, and thus will be denied entry to paradise. See Jane I. Smith and Yvonne Yazbeck Haddad, 'Women in the Afterlife: The Islamic View as Seen from Qur'ān and Tradition', *Journal of the American Academy of Religion*, 43.1 (1975), 39–50.

[85] 'The ancient Egyptian water-wheel, still in use. It is made of a notch-wheel, fixed vertically on a horizontal axle, and a long chain of earthenware vessels brings the water either from the river itself or from some little branch canal, and empties it into a system of troughs and reservoirs' (Blind's note).

Internal Firesides

Bewilderingly, from wildly shaken cloud,
  Invisible hands, deft moving everywhere,
  Have woven a winding sheet of velvet air,
And laid the dead earth in her downy shroud.
And more and more, in white confusion, crowd
  Wan, whirling flakes, while o'er the icy glare
  Blue heaven that was glooms blackening o'er the bare
Tree skeletons, to ruthless tempest bowed.

Nay, let the outer world be winter-locked;
  Beside the hearth of glowing memories
I warm my life. Once more our boat is rocked,
As on a cradle by the palm-fringed Nile;
And, sharp-cut silhouettes, in single file,
  Lank camels lounge against transparent skies.

On Reading the 'Rubáiyát' of Omar Khayyám

in a Kentish Rose Garden[86]

Beside a Dial[87] in the leafy close,
Where every bush was burning with the Rose,
With million roses falling flake by flake
Upon the lawn in fading summer snows:

I read the Persian Poet's rhyme of old,
Each thought a ruby in a ring of gold —
Old thoughts so young, that, after all these years,
They're writ on every rose-leaf yet unrolled.

You may not know the secret tongue aright
The Sunbeams on their rosy tablets write;
Only a poet may perchance translate
Those ruby-tinted hieroglyphs of light.

---

[86] Blind's poem mirrors the poetic form of the Rubáiyát itself: quatrains employing an aaba rhyme scheme. See also p. 183, note 1.
[87] A sundial, the earliest type of timekeeping, consists of a flat plate (the dial) and a gnomon, which casts a shadow onto the dial, indicating the time when exposed to the sun's rays.

Songs of the Occident

Roman Anemones[88]

The maiden meadows softly blush
  Beneath the enamoured breeze,
And break into one purple flush
  Of frail anemones.

Violet and rose and vermeil white,
  Woven of sun and showers,
They seem to be embodied light
  Transfigured into flowers.

Ave Maria in Rome[89]

Far away dim violet mountains
  Fade away from sight;
Flashing from fantastic fountains,
  Jets the liquid light,
Where from Nymph's or Triton's lip
Bubbling waters drip and drip,
  Bubbling day and night.[90]

Pealed from tower to answering tower,
  O'er the city swells,
Ringing in the hallowed hour,
  Rhythm of bells on bells;
And on wings of Choral Song,
Confluent hearts to Mary throng,
  From low, cloistered cells.

On the golden ground of even,
  Like a half-way home,
On the pilgrim to heaven
  Floats St Peter's Dome;
High, high, in the air alone,
Man's dread Thought transformed to stone,
  Pinnacled o'er Rome.

Pincio.[91]

---

[88] A perennial plant originating from southern France. In Greek mythology, the anemone was said to have grown from the tears that Aphrodite shed over her lost lover Adonis.
[89] Originally published in *The Magazine of Art* (May 1894), p. 17.
[90] Several of Rome's fountains feature Triton, in Greek mythology the son of Poseidon and Amphitrite, and a god of the sea. The Trevi Fountain, the most spectacular of all Rome's fountains, features both Tritons and Sea Nymphs, who surround Oceanus, the personification of all the seas and oceans.
[91] The setting of this poem is the Pincio Gardens, near the Villa Borghese gardens by the

The New Proserpine[92]

Where, countless as the stars of night,
   The daisies made a milky way
Across fresh lawns, and flecked with light,
   Old Ilex groves walled round with bay, —

I saw thee stoop, oh lady sweet,
   And with those pale, frail hands of thine
Gather the spring flowers at our feet,
   Fair as some late-born Proserpine.

Yea, gathering flowers, thou might'st have been
   That goddess of the ethereal brow,
Revisiting this radiant scene
   From realm of dolorous shades below.

Thou might'st have been that Queen of Sighs,
   Love-bound by Hades' dreadful spell;
For veiled within thy heaven-blue eyes,
   There lay the Memory of Hell.

Villa Pamfili Doria.[93]

Soul-Drift

I let my soul drift with the thistledown
   Afloat upon the honeymooning breeze;
My thoughts about the swelling buds are blown,
   Blown with the golden dust of flowering trees.

On fleeting gusts of desultory song,
   I let my soul drift out into the Spring;
The Psyche flies and palpitates among
   The palpitating creatures on the wing.[94]

Go, happy Soul! run fluid in the wave,
   Vibrate in light, escape thy natal curse;

ancient Aurelian Wall in Rome. Blind travelled to Rome in 1893 and 1895, and she stayed at the Palazzo Zuccari, the winter home of her friends and patrons Ludwig and Frida Mond.

[92] Proserpine is the Roman name for the Greek Persephone, the daughter of Zeus and Demeter and goddess of agriculture. She was the wife of Hades, king of the underworld. For the ways in which this poem challenges the male poetic tradition of goddess figures, see Introduction, p. 40.

[93] The Villa Doria Pamphili is a seventeenth-century villa with what is today the largest landscaped public park in Rome.

[94] In formal Greek, the word for butterfly is psyche, meaning the soul. The myth of Psyche signifies the soul achieving immortal union with the divine eros, but not before enduring a series of tribulations.

>   Go forth no longer as my body-slave,
>   But as the heir of all the Universe.

Villa Borghese.[95]

On a Torso of Cupid[96]

>   Peach trees and Judas trees,
>   Poppies and roses,
>   Purple anemones
>   In garden closes!
>   Lost in the limpid sky,
>   Shrills a gay lark on high;
>   Lost in the covert's hush,
>   Gurgles a wooing thrush.
>
>   Look, where the ivy weaves,
>   Closely embracing,
>   Tendrils of clinging leaves
>   Round him enlacing,
>   With Nature's sacredness
>   Clothing the nakedness,
>   Clothing the marble of
>   This poor, dismembered love.
>
>   Gone are the hands whose skill
>   Aimed the light arrow,
>   Strong once to cure or kill,
>   Pierce to the marrow;
>   Gone are the lips whose kiss
>   Held hives of honeyed bliss;
>   Gone too the little feet,
>   Overfond, overfleet.

---

[95] A landscape garden in Rome, the third largest in the city, containing several important buildings and museums, including the Galleria Borghese.

[96] As Sara Lyons has noted, this ekphrasis of a broken sculpture of Cupid that Blind saw in the Villa Mattei in Rome 'seems to allegorize the imaginative work of aestheticism; that is, its attempt to extrapolate a more vital conception of eros from a fragmentary classical heritage'. In keeping with Blind's poetic project of demythologizing Christianity, she provocatively links Cupid's broken body to that of the crucified Christ. Lyons writes that the mixture of 'maternal pity and erotic longing' in the poem 'constructs the ekphrastic encounter as a blasphemous, latter-day pietà, in which a liberated female tourist mourns the fact that modernity or perhaps the ascendancy of Christianity has "maimed" Cupid, or only allowed sexual love to survive in dismembered form' ('"Let Your Life on Earth Be Life Indeed": Aestheticism and Secularism in Mathilde Blind's "The Prophecy of St. Oran" and "On a Torso of Cupid"', in *Writing Women of the Fin de Siècle: Authors of Change*, ed. by Adrienne E. Gavin and Carolyn Oulton (New York and Basingstoke: Palgrave Macmillan, 2012), 55–69 (pp. 66, 67)).

O helpless god of old,
  Maimed mid the tender
Blossoming white and gold
  Of April splendour!
Shall we not make thy grave
Where the long grasses wave;
Hide thee, O headless god,
Deep in the daisied sod?

Here thou mayst rest at last
  After life's fever;
After love's fret is past
  Rest thee for ever.
Nay, broken God of Love,
Still must thou bide above
While, left for woe or weal,
Thou has a heart to feel.

Villa Mattei.[97]

The Mirror of Diana

Popular Name for Lake Nemi[98]

She floats into the quiet skies,
  Where, in the circle of hills,
  Her immemorial mirror fills
With light, as of a Virgin's eyes
When, love a-tremble in their blue,
They glow twin violets dipped in dew.

---

[97] Now known as the Villa Celimontana, Villa Mattei is a villa on the Caelian Hill in Rome, best known for its gardens, covering most of the valley between the Aventine Hill and the Caelian.

[98] Blind's title alludes both to the Roman goddess of the moon and the belief that from the shores of Lake Nemi, south-east of Rome, one might witness a perfect reflection of the moon upon the lake's still waters. The poem can be read as Blind's ars poetica, as she likens the mind, like the moon, to a 'perfect Sphere' that in its search for 'some Ideal set on high' produces 'many a burst of sweet delight'. Writing in her Commonplace Book in the early 1890s, Blind asserted that '[t]he poet only truly lives when he feels the rapture of communion; when his soul mirrored in a sister soul is doubled like the moon glassed in the Lake of Nemi' ('The Commonplace book of Mathilde Blind', p. 36). This poem is also further evidence of the Shelleyan strain in Blind's poetry; it both evokes and derives from Shelley's conception of the epipsyche, 'the soul within the soul', expressed in his long poem 'Epipsychidion' as well as his essays 'On Love' and 'A Defence of Poetry'. Shelley and Blind's metaphors of self-reflection as identity also draw on Plato, including his dialogue Alcibiades I, in which the soul is compared to the mirror of the eye's pupil (see Maxwell, *The Female Sublime from Milton to Swinburne*, pp. 52–54).

Mild as a metaphor of Sleep,
  Immaculately maiden-white,
  The Queen Moon of ancestral night
Beholds her image in the deep:
As if a-gaze she beams above
Lake Nemi's magic glass of love.

White rose, white lily of the vale,
  Perfume the even breath of night;
  In many a burst of sweet delight
The love throb of the nightingale
Swells through lush flowering woods and fills
The circle of the listening hills.

White rose, white lily of the skies,
  The Moon-flower blossoms in the lake;
  The nightingale for her fair sake
With hopeless love's impassioned cries
Seems fain to sing till song must kill
Himself with one tumultuous trill.

And all the songs and all the scents,
  The light of glowworms and the fires
  Of fire-flies in the cypress spires;
And all the wild wind instruments
Of pine and ilex as the breeze
Sweeps out their mystic harmonies; —

All are but Messengers of May
  To that white orb of maiden fire
  Who fills the moth with mad desire
To die enamoured in her ray,
And turns each dewdrop in the grass
Into a fairy looking-glass.

O Beauty, far and far above
  The night moth and the nightingale!
  Far, far above life's narrow pale,
O Unattainable! O Love!
Even as the nightingale we cry
For some Ideal set on high.

Haunting the deep reflective mind,
  You may surprise its perfect Sphere
  Glassed like the Moon within her mere,
Who at a puff of alien wind

Melts in innumerable rings,
Elusive in the flux of things.

On Guido's Aurora[99]

Glorious, in saffron robes and veil unfurled,
  Borne on the wind of her ecstatic flight,
  Aurora floats before the Lord of Light,
And showers her roses on a jubilant world.
Lo, where he beams, ambrosial, yellow curled,
  The God of Day, with unapparent might,
  Checking his fiery steeds, that plunge and bite
As if from heaven his Chariot should be hurled.

And on the Clouds a many-tinted band
  Of Hours dance round their Leader, grave or gay
  As glowing near or in his wake they sway;
While poised above the sun-awakened land
  The Morning Star, fair herald of the day,
Hovers, a Cupid, back-blown torch in hand.

Spring in the Alps

The flowers are at their Bacchanals
  Among the lusty green;
Wild Orchis and Narcissus waltz
  With Marguerite for queen.
Birds join in glees and madrigals
  To little loves unseen;
And unimprisoned Waterfalls
  Flash laughing in between.

The Sunlight, leaping from the Heights,
  Flames o'er the fields of May,
Winged with unnumbered swallow-flights
  Fresh from the long sea way;
And butterflies and insect mites,
  Born with the new-blown day,
Cross fires in shifting opal lights
  From spray to beckoning spray.

---

[99] L'Aurora is a large Baroque ceiling fresco painted in 1614 by Guido Reni for the Casino, or garden house, adjacent to the Palazzo Pallavicini-Rospigliosi in Rome. The work, considered Reni's fresco masterpiece, depicts Aurora (Dawn) in a billowing golden dress with her garlands flying over a dimly lit landscape, leading a blond Apollo in his horse-drawn chariot, surrounded by a chain of female 'Hours', bringing light to the world. Cupid hovers above Apollo's steeds, his eyes fixed on Aurora.

The dandelion puffs her balls,
  Free spinsters of the air,
Who scorn to wait for beetle calls
  Or bees to find them fair;
But breaking through the painted walls
  Their sisters tamely bear,
Fly off in dancing down, which falls
  And sprouts up everywhere.[100]

And far above Earth's flower-filled lap
  And rosy revelry,
The mountain mothers feed her sap
  From herded clouds on high —
Each pinnacle and frozen pap
  Whose life has long gone by,
A bridge which spans the mighty gap
  Between the earth and sky.

St. Gotthardt.[101]

The Agnostic[102]

Not in the hour of peril, thronged with foes,

---

[100] One of Blind's many wryly feminist assertions: because dandelion flowers contain both male and female organs on the same flowers, they can pollinate themselves. By describing them as emancipated spinsters, she is aligning them with women who, like Blind herself, rejected marriage and lived lives of sexual nonconformity. See Barbara Barrow, 'Queer Poetry and Darwin at the *fin de siècle*: Mathilde Blind, Constance Naden, and Laurence Hope', *Victorian Poetry*, 59.1 (2021), 97–118.

[101] St. Gotthard is a mountain pass in the Alps traversing the Saint-Gotthard Massif and connecting northern and southern Switzerland. Blind had traversed the pass in mid-August on her way to Lake Geneva (Lac Léman in French). She wrote to Garnett on 23 August 1891 from the Grand Hotel, Lerritel-Montreux, Switzerland, describing the landscape which inspired this poem, saying that it 'makes you feel as if the human soul had passed into it. The swelling outline of the Alps, the banks and hillsides prodigally clotted with foliage of flowers and the wide spreading lake Léman with its infinite gradations of tenderest blue all have a smiling air as if for centuries past they had been on friendly terms with man. You can't imagine the glory of the sunset on the waters, but remember that Byron must give the exact impression in some of his stanzas on Clarens in Childe Harold' (Mathilde Blind ALS to Richard Garnett, Add. MS 61929, fols 73–74).

[102] As this sonnet demonstrates, Christianity had an emotional appeal for Blind despite her lifelong antitheism. Here, the birth of organic life and beauty in the springtime suggests a kind of transcendence the speaker yearns for even while asserting (in both the octave and sestet) that God is absent from this world. Like the German thinkers she read — Ludwig Feuerbach, David Strauss, and Friedrich Nietzsche — Blind rejected teleology, the idea that there is an end goal or ultimate purpose to things. Yet the sublimity of nature here tempts her away from atheism to agnosticism. Consider this passage from Blind's letter to Garnett (23 August 1893) describing her ascent by funicular to the top of Monte Generoso (a mountain bordering Italy and Switzerland): 'This is a new sensation to be borne up and

Panting to set their heel upon my head, —
Or when alone from many wounds I bled
Unflinching beneath Fortune's random blows;
Not when my shuddering hands were doomed to close
  The unshrinking eyelids of the stony dead; —
Not then I missed my God, not then — but said:
'Let me not burden God with all man's woes!'

But when resurgent from the womb of night
  Spring's Oriflamme[103] of flowers waves from the Sod;
  When peak on flashing Alpine peak is trod
By sunbeams on their missionary flight;
When heaven-kissed Earth laughs, garmented in light; —
  That is the hour in which I miss my God.

A Bridal in the Bois de Boulogne[104]

How the lilacs, the lilacs are glowing and blowing!
  And white through the delicate verdure of May
The blossoming boughs of the hawthorn are showing,
  Like beautiful brides in their bridal array;
    With cobwebs for laces, and dewdrops for pearls,
    Fine as a queen's dowry for workaday girls.

In an aisle of Acacias enlaced and enlacing,
  Where the silvery sunlight tunnels the shade,
Where snowflakes of butterflies airily chasing
  Each other in trios flash down the arcade:
    Arrayed in white muslin the wedded bride
    Looks fresh as a daisy, the groom by her side.

The guests flitted round her with light-hearted laughter;
  They hunted the slipper, they kissed the ring;
Of days gone before and of days coming after
  They thought of no more than the bird on the wing.
    Were the loves and the laughter and lilacs of May,
    With the sunshine above, not enough for the day?

---

up the steep and almost perpendicular incline almost like a sense of flying while wood and valley, hill and river slide away beneath you and you rise higher still and higher "as if you were going up to heaven" like Jesus Christ himself' (Mathilde Blind ALS to Richard Garnett, Add. MS 61929, fols 70–71).

[103] From Latin aurea flamma ('golden flame'), an Oriflamme was the battle standard of the King of France in the Middle Ages. Equally relevant to the implications of the sonnet are the figurative connotations of the word — an inspiring principle or ideal.

[104] The Bois de Boulogne is a large public park located along the western edge of the sixteenth arrondissement of Paris.

And the lilacs, the lilacs are blowing and glowing!
  They pluck them by handfuls and pile them in a mass;
And the sap of the Springtide is rising and flowing
  Through the veins of the greenwood, the blades of the grass;
    Up, up to the last leaf a dance on the tree,
    It leaps like a fountain abundant and free.

The blackbirds are building their nests in the bushes,
  And whistle at work, as the workpeople do;
The trees swing their censers, the wind comes in gushes
  Of delicate scent mixed of honey and dew.
    Now loud and now low through the garrulous trees
    A burst of gay music is blown with the breeze.

And the girls and the boys from the faubourgs of Paris,
  The premature gamins as wise as fourscore;
The vain little Margots and the wide-awake Harrys,
  Surprised into childhood, grew simple once more,
    And vied with the cuckoo as, shouting at play,
    They dashed through the thickets and darted away.

Ah, fair is the forest's green glimmering splendour,
  The leaves of the lime tree a network of light;
And fringing long aisles of acacia, a tender
  And delicate veiling of virginal white,
    Where, framed in the gladdening flowers of May,
    The bride and her bridesmaids beam gladder than they.

They have crowned her brown tresses with hawthorn in blossom,
  They have made her a necklace of daisies for pearls;
They have set the white lily against her white bosom,
  Enthroned on the grass mid a garland of girls;
    With the earth for a footstool, the sky-roof above,
    She is queen of the Springtide and Lady of Love.

Oh, the lilacs, the lilacs are glowing and blowing!
  They pluck them by bushels as blithely they go
Through the green, scented dusk where the hawthorn is showing
  A luminous whiteness of blossoming snow.
    And the Sun ere he goes gives the Moon half his light,
    As a lamp to lead Love on the bridal night.

A White Night[105]

The land lay deluged by the Moon;
  The molten silver of the lake

---

[105] The title is a double entendre: a literal description of the moon-illumined landscape that envelops the two lovers, the phrase also conveys the colloquial meaning of a sleepless night.

Shimmered in many a broad lagoon
   Between grey isles, whose copse and brake
Lay folded on the water's breast
Like halcyons in a floating nest.

And like a child who trusts in God
   When in the dark it lies alone,
Stretched on the aromatic sod
   My heart was laid against your own,
Against your heart, which seemed to be
Mine own to all Eternity.

Lapped in illimitable light,
   The woods and waters seemed to swoon,
And clouds like angels winged the night
   And slipped away into the Moon,
Lost in that radiant flame above
As we were lapped and lost in love.

Achensee.[106]

The Forest Pool

Lost amid gloom and solitude,
A pool lies hidden in the wood,
A pool the autumn rain has made
Where flowers with their fair shadows played.

Bare as a beggar's board, the trees
Stand in the water to their knees;
The birds are mute, but far away
I hear a bloodhound's sullen bay.

Blue-eyed forget-me-nots that shook,
Kissed by a little laughing brook,
Kissed too by you with lips so red,
Float in the water drowned and dead.

And dead and drowned 'mid leaves that rot,
Our angel-eyed Forget-me-not,
The love of unforgotten years,
Floats corpse-like in a pool of tears.

Delamere Forest.[107]

[106] Achensee is a lake north of Jenbach in Tyrol, Austria. Blind's first published short story, 'A Month at the Achensee' (*Dark Blue* (March 1872), pp. 227–38), uses this area as its setting.
[107] Delamere Forest, in the village of Delamere in Cheshire, England, is the largest area of woodland in the county.

Noonday Rest

The willows whisper very, very low
  Unto the listening breeze;
Sometimes they lose a leaf which, flickering slow,
  Faints on the sunburnt leas.[108]

Beneath the whispering boughs and simmering skies,
  On the hot ground at rest,
Still as a stone, a ragged woman lies,
  Her baby at the breast.

Nibbling around her browse monotonous sheep,
  Flies buzz about her head;
Her heavy eyes are shuttered by a sleep
  As of the slumbering dead.

The happy birds that live to love and sing,
  Flitting from bough to bough,
Peer softly at this ghastly human thing
  With grizzled hair and brow.

O'er what strange ways may not these feet have trod
  That match the cracking clay?
Man had no pity on her — no, nor God —
  A nameless castaway!

But Mother Earth now hugs her to her breast,
  Defiled or undefiled;
And willows rock the weary soul to rest,
  As she, even she, her child.

Hampstead Heath.[109]

Cross-Roads

The rain beat in our faces,
  And shrill the wild airs grew;
The long-maned clouds in races
  Coursed o'er heaven's windy blue.

The tortured trees were lashing
  Each other in their wrath,

---

[108] In his review of Birds of Passage for *Woman*, Arnold Bennett had special praise for this poem — and this stanza (see p. 268).
[109] A heath is large area of uncultivated land. Hampstead Heath is a large grassy public space sitting astride a sandy ridge, one of the highest points in London.

Their wet leaves wildly dashing
　　　Across the forest path.

　　We did not heed the sweeping
　　　Of storm-bewildered rain;
　　Our cheeks were wet with weeping,
　　　Our hearts were wrung with pain.

　　For where the cross-roads sever,
　　　Parting to East and West,
　　We bade good-bye for ever,
　　　To what we each loved best.

The Moors.[110]

The Moat

　　Around this lichened home of hoary peace,
　　　Invulnerable in its glassy moat,
　　　A breath of ghostly summers seems to float
　　And murmur mid the immemorial trees.
　　The tender slopes, where cattle browse at ease,
　　　Swell softly, like a pigeon's emerald throat;
　　　And, self-oblivious, Time forgets to note
　　The flight of velvet-footed centuries.

　　The very sunlight hushed within the close,
　　　Sleeps indolently by the Yew's slow shade;
　　　Still as a relic some old Master made
　　The jewelled peacock's rich enamel glows;
　　And on yon mossy wall that youthful rose
　　　Blooms like a rose that never means to fade.

Groombridge.[111]

---

[110] The North York Moors is an upland area in North Yorkshire, England, containing one of the largest expanses of heather moorland in the United Kingdom.

[111] Groombridge, a village of about 1600 people, is best known for Groombridge Place, a seventeenth-century moated manor house. Much of the house, along with the bridges and moat gates, was designed by renowned architect Sir Christopher Wren, who rebuilt London after the Great Fire, including the redesign of St Paul's cathedral. Groombridge is near Royal Tunbridge Wells, whose medicinal baths Blind often visited in the 1880s and early 1890s seeking relief from her chronic bronchitis.

Shakespeare Sonnets[112]

Anne Hathaway's Cottage

Is this the Cottage, ivy-girt and crowned,
  And this the path down which our Shakespeare ran,
  When, in the April of his love, sweet Anne
Made all his mighty pulses throb and bound;
Where, mid coy buds and winking flowers around,
  She blushed a rarer rose than roses can,
  To greet her Will — even Him, fair Avon's Swan —
Whose name has turned this plot to holy ground!

To these dear walls, once dear to Shakespeare's eyes,
  Time's Vandal hand itself has done no wrong;
  This nestling lattice opened to his song,
When, with the lark, he bade his love arise
In words whose strong enchantment never dies —
  Old as these flowers, and, like them, ever young.

Anne Hathaway[113]

His Eve of Women! She, whose mortal lot

---

[112] These poems resulted from a trip to Stratford-upon-Avon in September 1894, six months after Blind's return from her second trip to Egypt. Unlike Shakespearean sonnets, divided into three quatrains and a couplet, Blind adopts the Petrarchan model of an octave and sestet.

[113] Blind sent draft copies of this poem and 'Anne Hathaway's Cottage' to Garnett, and the changes she made to 'Anne Hathaway' at his suggestion are worth noting. Her original octave read as follows:

> His Eve of Women, fresh and ivory fair,
>   In morning glory met him in this spot;
>   Thrilled to her marrow his gelding's trot
> Her heart leaped in her heaving bosom, ere
> She leaped into his arms, with arms all bare,
>   Flung round him in a perfect lover's knot.
>   And, one in passionate concord, both forgot
> The petty world of men and all its care.

While the comic contrast between the virile male lover and his unsexed horse seems apt in a stanza stressing the woman's erotic agency and energy, and in a volume of poetry with decidedly feminist implications, Garnett demurred. He complained that 'gelding' and 'trot' are 'unpoetical' words, and then added that Blind's use of the word 'gelding' 'suggests ideas singularly antipathetic to the passion of love', asserting that 'it is inconceivable that an ardent lover should trot upon a gelding to his mistress. He must gallop upon a courser, all the way at least!' (Richard Garnett ALS to Mathilde Blind, 18 September 1895, Add. MS

Was linked to an Immortal's unaware,
　With Love's lost Eden in her blissful air,
　Perchance would greet him in this blessed spot.
No shadow of the coming days durst blot,
　The flower-like face, so innocently fair,
　As lip met lip, and lily arms, all bare,
Clung round him in a perfect lover's knot.

Was not this Anne the flame-like daffodil
　Of Shakespeare's March, whose maiden beauty took
　His senses captive? Thus the stripling brook
Mirrors a wild flower nodding by the mill,
　Then grows a river in which proud cities look,
And with a land's load widens seaward still.

Cleve Woods

Sweet Avon[114] glides where clinging rushes seem
　To stay his course, and, in his flattering glass,
　Meadows and hills and mellow woodlands pass,
A fairer world as imaged in a dream.
And sometimes, in a visionary gleam,
　From out the secret covert's tangled mass,
　The fisher-bird[115] starts from the rustling grass,
A jewelled shuttle shot along the stream.

Even here, methinks, when moon-lapped shallows smiled
　Round isles no bigger than a baby cot,
Titania found a glowworm-lighted child,
　Led far astray, and, with anointing hand
　Sprinkling clear dew from a forget-me-not,
Hailed him the Laureate of her Fairyland.[116]

61929, fols 120–21). Blind's revisions diminish both the status of Anne and the erotic charge of the poem itself. She is still 'his Eve of Women' but is reduced to his subordinate, her finitude contrasting with his infinite greatness, their love now rendered as loss, Eros nearly subsumed by Agape. Once flinging her arms around him, she now clings to him, and the colloquial energy of the 'gelding's trot' has been replaced by the arid archaism of 'durst blot'.

[114] The Avon is the river that flows through Stratford-upon-Avon, the medieval market town in England's West Midlands and birthplace of William Shakespeare.

[115] A kingfisher. Although there are some eighty species of kingfishers in the world, only the common kingfisher is native to Great Britain.

[116] *A Midsummer Night's Dream* ends with Titania's husband Oberon in possession of the 'Indian boy', but Blind elides this element of the plot (and Oberon himself), focusing instead on Titania's discovery of the boy, here metaphorically transformed into the playwright himself, whose imagination she nurtures and sustains.

Lost Treasure

The autumn day steals, pallid as a ghost,
  Along these fields and man-forsaken ways;
  And o'er the hedgerows bramble-knotted maze
The whitening locks of Old Man's Beard are tost.
Here, shrunk by centuries of fire and frost,
  A crab tree stands where — lingering gossip says —
  In ocean-moated England's golden days,
Great treasure, in a frolic, once was lost.

Here — fresh from fumes of some Falstaffian bout,[117]
  When famous champions, fired by many a bet,
  Had drained huge bumpers[118] while the stars would set —
Beneath its reeling branches by the way,
Till twice twelve hours of April bloom were out —
Locked in oblivion — Shakespeare lost a day.[119]

The Avon[120]

What are the Willows whispering in a row,
  Nodding their old heads o'er the river's edge?
  What does the West wind whisper to the sedge
And to the shame-faced purples drooping low?
Why sobs the water, in its broken flow
  Lapping against the grey weir's ruined ledge?
  And, in the thorny shelter of the hedge,
What bird unloads his heart of woe?

---

[117] Falstaff is the vain, boastful, cowardly knight and would-be friend of Prince Hal in *Henry IV* parts 1 and 2 who spends his time drinking at the Boar's Head Inn with petty criminals, living on stolen or borrowed money.
[118] Cups or glasses filled to overflowing with alcoholic drinks.
[119] This sonnet alludes to a legend regarding Shakespeare's Crab, a crab-apple tree under which Shakespeare and a group of friends supposedly slept after losing a drinking contest (see Sylvia Morris, 'The Legend of Shakespeare's Crabtree', *The Shakespeare blog*, 5 August 2015 <http://theshakespeareblog.com/2015/08/the-legend-of-shakespeares-crabtree/> [accessed 11 January 2021]).
[120] This sonnet may be read as Blind's version of Poussin's famous seventeenth-century painting 'Et in Arcadia ego', meaning 'Even in Arcadia, there am I' — 'I' signifying death. In *As You Like It*, Jacques is a nobleman attending on Duke Senior, living with him in the Forest of Arden. While the Duke proclaims 'sweet are the uses of adversity', and finds 'tongues in trees, books in the running brooks, | Sermons in stones, and good in everything', Jacques constantly reminds the other characters, and the audience, that grief, sorrow, and death shadow all of human life. Here Blind positions Jacques between two of Shakespeare's most tragic heroines — Ophelia from *Hamlet*, a suicide, and Desdemona from *Othello*, strangled by her husband in a jealous rage. The poem also suggests that once we have encountered a poet's representations of specific landscapes, our experience of those landscapes is forever altered.

Green Avon's haunted! Look, from yonder bank
  The willow leans, that hath not ceased to weep,
Whence, hanging garlands, fair Ophelia sank;
Since Jacques moped here the trees have had a tongue;
  And all these streams and whispering willows keep
The moan of Desdemona's dying song.

Evensong

(Holy Trinity Church)[121]

The hectic autumn's dilatory fire
  Has turned this lime tree to a sevenfold brand,
  Which, self consuming, lights the sunless land,
A death to which all poet souls aspire.
Above the graves, where all men's vain desire
  Is hushed at last as by a Mother's hand,
  And, Time confounded, Love's blank records stand,
The Evensong swells from the pulsing choir.

What incommunicable presence clings
  To this grey church and willowy twilight stream?
  Am I the dupe of some delusive dream?
Or, like faint fluid phosphorent rings
  On refluent seas, doth Shakespeare's spirit gleam
Pervasive round these old familiar things?

Shakespeare

Yearning to know herself for all she was,
  Her passionate clash of warring good and ill,
  Her new life ever ground in Death's old mill,
With every delicate detail and *en masse*, —
Blind Nature strove. Lo, then it came to pass,
  That Time, to work out her unconscious Will,[122]
  Once wrought the Mind which she had groped for still,
And she beheld herself as in a glass.

The world of men, unrolled before our sight,
  Showed like a map, where stream and waterfall
And village-cradling vale and cloud-capped height
  Stand faithfully recorded, great and small;
For Shakespeare was, and at his touch, with light
  Impartial as the Sun's, revealed the All.[123]

---

[121] Shakespeare, the 'incommunicable presence' of the octave, worshipped in this church, and is buried in its churchyard.
[122] A pun on the shortened version of Shakespeare's first name.
[123] Blind imagines Shakespeare as the ultimate artist, through whom 'Time' created a

Cedars of Lebanon at Warwick Castle[124]

Cedars of Lebanon! Labyrinths of Shade,
  Making a mystery of open day;
  With layers of gloom keeping the Sun at bay,
And solemn boughs which never bloom or fade.
Contemporaries of that great Crusade,
  When militant Christendom leaped up one day,
  Fired by the Cross, and rushing to the fray,
Poured Eastward as oracular Peter[125] bade.

Borne hither when Christ's Sepulchre was won,
And planted by hoar Warwick's feudal walls,
  You grew, o'ershadowing every rival stem.
When English woods don May's fresh coronals,
  Say, — Mourn ye still lost Jerusalem,
Funeral trees — beloved of Lebanon?

mirror held up to nature. In describing Shakespeare's light as being 'Impartial as the Sun's', Blind may be alluding to the poet John Keats' definition of the 'poetical Character': 'it has no self — it is everything and nothing — It has no character — it enjoys light and shade; it lives in gusto, be it foul or fair, high or low, rich or poor, mean or elevated — It has as much delight in an Iago [the villain of Shakespeare's *Othello*] as an Imogen [Shakespeare's heroine in *Cymbeline*]. What shocks the virtuous philosopher delights the camelion [sic] Poet' (*The Letters of John Keats*, ed. by H. E. Rollins, 2 vols (Cambridge: Cambridge University Press, 1958), I, pp. 386–87).

[124] Warwick Castle, near Stratford-upon-Avon, was originally built by William the Conqueror in 1068. Robert, Duke of Normandy, the eldest son of William, became one of the leaders of the first Crusade, helping capture Jerusalem in 1099. *Cedrus libani*, the Lebanon cedar, is native to the mountains of the Eastern Mediterranean basin and can grow to be over 100 feet tall and eighty feet wide. It has biblical significance — it was used by King Solomon when he built his temple in the forest of Lebanon. It was introduced to England in 1638, and the Warwick Castle grounds boast several of the finest specimens in Great Britain.

[125] A reference to a priest of Amiens, France, a key figure during the First Crusade, popularly known as Peter the Hermit.

Miscellaneous Pieces

Pastiche

I.
Love, oh, Love's a dainty sweeting,
Wooing now, and now retreating;
Brightest joy and blackest care,
Swift as light, and light as air.

II.
Would you seize and fix and capture
All his evanescent rapture?
Bind him fast with golden curls,
Fetter with a chain of pearls?

III.
Would you catch him in a net,
Like a white moth prankt with jet?[126]
Clutch him, and his bloomy wing
Turns a dead, discoloured thing!

IV.
Pluck him like a rosebud red,
And he leaves a thorn instead;
Let him go without a care,
And he follows unaware.

V.
Love, oh Love's a dainty sweeting,
Wooing now, and now retreating;
Lightly come, and lightly gone,
Lost when most securely won!

Marriage

Love springs as lightly from the human heart
    As springs the lovely rose upon the brier,
    Which turns the common hedge to floral fire,
As Love wings Time with rosy-feathered dart.
But marriage is the subtlest work of art
    Of all the arts which lift the spirit higher;
    The incarnation of the heart's desire —
Which masters Time — set on Man's will apart.

---

[126] A colloquial expression meaning 'pleated' or decorated with black. The wings of the white ermine moth are speckled with black spots.

The Many try, but oh! how few are they
   To whom that finest of the arts is given
Which shall teach Love, the rosy runaway,
   To bide from bridal Morn to brooding Even.
Yet this — this only — is the narrow way
   By which, while yet on earth, we enter heaven.

Once We Played

Once we played at love together —
  Played it smartly, if you please;
Lightly, as a windblown feather,
  Did we stake a heart apiece.

Oh, it was delicious fooling!
  In the hottest of the game,
Without thought of future cooling,
  All too quickly burned Life's flame.

In this give-and-take of glances,
  Kisses sweet as honey dews,
When we played with equal chances,
  Did you win, or did I lose?

Was your heart then hurt to bleeding,
  In the ardour of the throw?
Was it then I lost, unheeding,
  Lost my heart so long ago?

Who shall say? The game is over.
  Of us two who loved in fun,
One lies low beneath the clover,
  One lies lonely in the sun.

Affinities

I.

I will take your thoughts to my heart;
  I will keep and garner them there
Locked in a casket apart.
  Far above rubies or rare
Pearls from the prodigal deep,
  Which men stake their lives on to find,
And women their beauty to keep,
  I will treasure the pearls of your mind.

How long has it taken the earth
  To crystallize gems in a mine?

How long was the sea giving birth
  To her pearls, washed in bitterest brine?
What sorrows, what struggles, what fierce
  Endeavour of lives in the past,
Hearts tempered by fire and tears,
  To fashion your manhood at last!

II.

Take me to thy heart, and let me
  Rest my head a little while;
Rest my heart from griefs that fret me
  In the mercy of thy smile.

In a twilight pause of feeling,
  Time to say a moment's grace,
Put thy hands, whose touch is healing,
  Put them gently on my face.

Found too late in Life's wild welter,
  All I ask, for weal and woe,
Friend, a moment's friendly shelter,
  And thy blessing ere I go.

III.

Full many loves and friendships dear
  Have blossomed brightly in my path;
  And some were like the primrose rathe,[127]
And withered with the vernal year.

And some were like the joyous rose,
  Most prodigal with scent and hue,
  That glows while yet the sky is blue,
And falls with every wind that blows —

Mere guests and annuals of the heart;
  But you are that perennial bay,
  Greenest when greener leaves decay,
Whom only death shall bid depart.

To a Friend

With a Volume of Verses

To you who dwell withdrawn, above
  The world's tumultuous strife,

---

[127] Blooming early in the season. This stanza and its simile allude to John Milton's 1637 poem 'Lycidas', an elegy for a close friend who died young, specifically the line 'Bring the rathe Primrose that forsaken dies'.

And, in an atmosphere of love,
  Have triumphed over life;

To you whose heart has kept so young
  Beneath the weight of years,
I give these passion flowers of song,
  Still wet with undried tears.

You too have trod that stony path
  Which steeply winds afar,
And seen, through nights of storm and wrath,
  The bright and Morning Star;

Where, shining o'er the Alps of time
  On valleys full of mist,
It beckons us to peaks sublime,
  Oh, brave Idealist.

As Many Stars

As many stars as are aglow
  Deep in the hollows of the night
As many as the flowers that blow
  Beneath the kindling light;

As many as the birds that fly
  Unpiloted across the deep;
As many as the clouds on high,
  And all the drops they weep;

As many as the leaves that fall
  In autumn, on the withering lea,
When wind to thundering wind doth call,
  And sea calls unto sea;

As many as the multitude
  Of quiet graves, where mutely bide
The wicked people and the good,
  Laid softly side by side; —

So many thoughts, so many tears,
  Such hosts of prayers, are sent on high,
Seeking, through all Man's perished years,
  A love that will not die.

Love's Vision

Transported out of self by Youth's sweet madness,
   Emulous of love, to Love's empyrean height,
   Where I beheld you aureoled in light,
My soul upsprang on wings of angel-gladness.
Far, far below, the earth and all earth's badness —
   A speck of dust — slipped darkling into night,
   As suns of fairer planets flamed in sight,
Pure orbs or bliss unstained by gloom or sadness.

Lo, as I soared etherially on high,
   You vanished, from my swimming eyes aloof,
Alone, alone, within the empty sky,
I reached out giddily, and reeling fell
From starriest heaven, to plunge in lowest hell,
   My proud heart broken on Earth's humblest roof.

A Parable[128]

Between the sandhills and the sea
  A narrow strip of silver sand,
  Whereon a little maid doth stand,
Who picks up shells continually
Between the sandhills and the sea.

Far as her wondering eyes can reach
  A Vastness, heaving grey in grey
  To the frayed edges where the day
Furls his red standard on the breach,
Between the skyline and the beach.

The waters of the flowing tide
  Cast up the seapink shells and weed;
  She toys with shells, and doth not heed
The ocean, which on every side
Is closing round her vast and wide.

It creeps her way as if in play,
  Pink shells at her pink feet to cast;
  But now the wild waves hold her fast,
And bear her off and melt away
A Vastness heaving gray in gray.

---

[128] The opening and closing lines of this poem's first stanza echo the poem 'Between the Sunset and the Sea' in Swinburne's *Chastelard: A Tragedy* (1865).

Between Sleep and Waking

Softly in a dream I heard,
    Ere the day was breaking,
Softly call a cuckoo bird
    Between sleep and waking.

Calling through the rippling rain
    And red orchard blossom;
Calling up old love again,
    Buried in my bosom;

Calling till he brought you too
    From some magic region;
And the whole spring followed you,
    Birds on birds in legion.

Youth was in your beaming glance,
    Love a rainbow round you;
Blushing trees began to dance,
    Wreaths of roses crowned you.

And I called your name, and woke
    To the cuckoo's calling;
And you waned in waning smoke,
    As the rain was falling.

Had the cuckoo called 'Adieu',
    Ere the day was breaking?
All the old wounds bled anew
    Between sleep and waking.

Rest

We are so tired, my heart and I.[129]
Of all things here beneath the sky
One only thing would please us best —
Endless, unfathomable rest.

We are so tired; we ask no more
Than just to slip out by Life's door;
And leave behind the noisy rout
And everlasting turn about.

Once it seemed well to run on too
With her importunate, fevered crew,

---

[129] A near-quotation from the first line of E. B. Browning's poem 'My Heart and I': 'Enough! We're tired, my heart and I'.

And snatch amid the frantic strife
Some morsel from the board of life.

But we are tired. At Life's crude hands
We ask no gift she understands;
But kneel to him she hates to crave
The absolution of the grave.

Mystery of Mysteries

Before the abyss of the unanswering grave
    Each mortal stands at last aloof, alone,
      With his beloved one turned as deaf as stone,
However rebel love may storm and rave.
No will, however strong, avails to save
    The wrecked identity knit to our own;
      We may not hoard one treasured look or tone,
Dissolved in foam on Death's dissolving wave.

Is this the End? This handful of brown earth
    For all releasing elements to take
And free for ever from the bonds of birth?
    Or will true life from Life's disguises break,
Called to that vast confederacy of minds
Which casts all flesh as chaff to all the winds?

Sea-Music[1]

The voices of the whispering woods are still;
  No truant brook runs chattering to the stream;
  Like heaven's own likeness mirrored in a dream.
The sea coils round each jutting rock and hill.
Nay, hark! what faint aerial harpings thrill
  The lonely bay; what choral voices seem
  To float around and melt like rolling steam
On air as quiet as a windless mill.

No holy chant in hushed cathedral naves
  Had ever such unearthly harmony.
  As these mysterious chords ineffable
That peal from organ-pipes of fluted caves,
  Reverberate in hollow mountain shell,
  The music of the everlasting sea.

---

[1] *The Savoy* (January 1896), p. 111; rpt. in *The Poetical Works of Mathilde Blind*, p. 438. In a note appended to the poem as it appeared in *The Savoy*, Blind wrote: 'This sonnet is founded on a singular experience I had at Wooda Bay in North Devon. While leaning over the cliff I was startled by hearing sounds as of harps and violins blending with muffled organ notes, and human voices soaring above the music. The effect was magical, and must have been due to an echo produced by the wave-hollowed rocks'.

SELECTED PROSE AND CRITICAL RESPONSES

Shelley's View of Nature Contrasted with Darwin's[1]

Ladies and Gentlemen, — I venture this evening to offer a few remarks on a very complex and far-reaching subject, and before beginning I must crave your indulgence if you find, as must almost unavoidably be the case, that my treatment of it is more fragmentary than could be wished. Speaking broadly, I think it will be admitted that the poet's attitude toward, and interpretation of, Nature may be said to undergo continual modification in harmony with the development of religious and scientific thought. For although the poet in his happiest intuitions often leaps at truths far in advance of the conclusions reached by the slower processes of methodical research, yet on the whole, the representative poems of the world seem to body forth the view of Nature, which is essentially the product of their age and nation.

In the *Iliad* and the *Odyssey* we find the aspects of the visible universe personified in a thousand and one shapes of plastic beauty. The vivifying power and splendour of the sun radiates through the limbs of Apollo; shaggy-breasted Pan is the expression of lush-teeming forest life, and the fatal allurement of lapping waters murmurs for ever in the sweet-voiced sirens. The manifestations of the inorganic world are regarded, by Homer for example, as synonymous with human nature; and the gods, demi-gods, titans, nereids, dryads, and fauns, which represent sky, clouds, ocean, rivers, and forests, are neither better nor worse than the men and women that people the earth.

With the Christian conception of the world this feeling towards Nature underwent a complete transformation. She was now regarded as something opposed to the divine, something inherently bad given over to the flesh and the devil. There is a stanza in Milton's *Ode on the Morning of Christ's Nativity* which aptly expresses this view: —

> Only with speeches fair
> She woos the gentle air
> To hide her guilty front with innocent snow:
> And on her naked shame,
> Pollute with sinful blame,

---

[1] Mathilde Blind, *Shelley's View of Nature Contrasted with Darwin's*, in *The Shelley Society's Papers*, series 1, no. 1, pt. 1 (London: Reeves and Turner, for the Shelley Society, 1886), pp. 36–46.

> The saintly veil of maiden white to throw;
> Confounded that her Maker's eyes
> Should look so near upon her foul deformities.

Indeed all through the Middle Ages there was a distinct recoil from the material universe, which may be traced more or less clearly in all mediæval poets. They liked snugly hedged-in gardens and sunny closes surrounded by venerable cloisters and 'the waste and solitary places', which Shelley loved, appalled them with thoughts of bogies and hobgoblins. For in their day the vapour-shrouded mountain-top, the wild and desolate moorland, the tumbling stream, were the haunts of the Evil One — as is still attested, indeed, by a thousand significant appellations of bridge and pass; while to their superstitious fancies the exiled gods of Greece and Rome, now changed into demons, were supposed to hold their ungodly revels in moonlit woods and valleys. In fact, the poetic feeling of mediæval times toward the more remote and unfamiliar scenes of Nature, seems to find expression in that weird German ballad where the witch Lorelei warns the belated traveller: —

> Es is schon spät, es ist schon kalt,
> Kommst nimmermehr aus diesem Wald.

> Full late it is, and chill the eve,
> This wood thou nevermore shalt leave.[2]

But as men shook off the gloomy and cruel superstitions engendered by the oldest and most oppressive form of the Christian religion, the idea that Nature was accursed passed away along with the belief in witches, spells, dæmoniacal possessions, and other hideous fancies begotten of ignorance and credulity. The human heart turning thirstily towards a rehabilitated nature, saw that she was fair, and felt a thrill of delight at the beauty of moonlight on still waters, at the radiance of snow-crowned Alps, at the sublimity of seas in storm or calm. This new sensation of wonder and admiration in the splendour of the material Universe found its apostle in Jean Jacques Rousseau.[3] He became the High Priest

---

[2] In 1801, German author Clemens Brentano published his ballad *Zu Bacharach am Rheine*, which introduced the legend of Lorelei. In the ballad, a beautiful woman named Lore Lay, convicted of bewitching men and murdering them, falls to her death from a cliff, leaving an echo of her name behind her. In 1824, Heinrich Heine adapted Brentano's theme in one of his most famous poems, 'Die Lorelei'. It describes Lorelei as a kind of siren who sits on the cliff above the Rhine combing her golden hair and causing shipmen to crash on the rocks.

[3] Rousseau (1712–1778), the Swiss philosopher who had a profound influence on Enlightenment thought, wrote *Discourse on Inequality* (1755) and *The Social Contract* (1762). The former argues that civilization is a corrupting influence on individuals, who should live as close to nature as possible. The latter, one of the defining texts of modern political philosophy, argues that no law or government is legitimate unless it rests directly or indirectly on the consent of the individuals concerned.

of this modern Nature-worship. In his eyes Nature was entirely good, sinless, and beneficent. Man alone, by introducing an artificial kind of civilisation, with its kings and priests, its class distinctions, its arbitrary division of property, its irresponsible power and abject poverty, had brought injustice into the world and all the evils that oppress society. Let him but return to a state of nature, and it would be as well with him as with the fish disporting themselves in the water, or with the birds in the air. Considering these violent transitions from one mode of thought to its opposite, one can't help owning that Luther[4] was not so far out when, with his sledge-hammer wit, he likened mankind to a tipsy boor who has no sooner been lifted into the saddle on one side that he tumbles down on the other. And we must own that the leap from the mental state of St Bernhardt,[5] who, passing along the shore of the lake of Geneva, was so absorbed in his pious meditations as to be quite oblivious of the scenery around him, to that of Jean Jacques, whose whole soul went out in adoration to the beauty of this identical landscape, is quite as whimsical a performance as the boor's toppling from one side of the saddle to the other. But be that as it may, there can be little doubt that Rousseau and the French Encyclopédists,[6] with their rose-coloured view of Nature, powerfully influenced that group of English poets to which Wordsworth, Coleridge, Southey, Byron, Keats, and Shelley may be said to belong. For widely as they differ from each other, they yet have one thing in common — that passionate, that all-absorbing love of Nature which sustained them in all disappointments they were doomed to meet in regard to their social aspirations. Shelley, above all, was profoundly and permanently swayed by this fervid feeling. In his youth, as is testified by *Queen Mab*, and the notes appended to it, he had been vitally influenced by the study of Rousseau's writings, and those of the other philosophical precursors of the French Revolution. From them he had to a great extent imbibed the firm conviction that if you could only rid society of kings and priests we should immediately enter on the Golden Age, and instead of discord, war, and wretchedness, the earth would become the abode of love and harmony. This is the keynote of Shelley's most important poems — of *The Revolt of Islam*, of *Prometheus Unbound*, of *Hellas*. The same ideas, packed in a narrow compass, are expressed in *The Ode to Liberty* — that noble and inspired poem which is

[4] Martin Luther (1483–1586) was a German professor of theology, a composer, a priest, an Augustinian monk, and a key figure in the Protestant Reformation.
[5] The French churchman St Bernard of Clairvaux (1090–1153) was a Cistercian monk and founder and abbot of the monastery of Clairvaux.
[6] The *Encyclopédists* were members of the *Société des gens de lettres*, a French writers' society, who contributed to the massive seventeen-volume *Encyclopédie* from 1751 to 1765, under the editorship of Denis Diderot and Jean le Rond d'Alembert. Most of the well-known writers who wrote for the project, including Diderot, Rousseau, and Voltaire, were also members of the intellectual group known as the *philosophes*, and their project promoted the ideals of the Enlightenment: the advancement of science, secular thought, political reform.

a kind of epitome of the development of man from the beginnings of life to its culmination in the loftiest intellectual achievement. Shelley here seems to us nearly to approach the threshold of the new era, and almost to apprehend that revolution in our conception of Nature which was to take place not so very long afterwards, when the Darwinian theory of the evolution of life gave a new aspect to man's relation to the world around him. Had Shelley only lived longer, he might have succeeded in harmonising his views of Nature with those so luminously developed by Darwin, Alfred Russel Wallace, and other scientific thinkers, and by doing so there can be little doubt that the body of his poetic work would have gained in backbone and solidity. It is just because Shelley was a philosophic poet, because he aimed at grasping the world as a whole, and at embodying sound ideas in his loftiest flights of imagination, that we must regret that his conception of Nature is rather the off-spring of the eighteenth century than of the nineteenth. Two evils, or more properly speaking, one evil with two heads, like the Austrian eagle, is ever present to Shelley's mind — the double yoke of superstition and tyranny. Let but triumphant liberty abolish this, and it seems to him that all the rest must inevitably follow. From hard-hearted oppressors men will become kind, sympathetic, and gentle, while women, no longer required to be hypocrites by Mrs Grundy,[7] will naturally turn into brave, generous, and sincere human beings. There will be a return to a primitive state of innocence, and man, no longer divorced from Nature, will be guided by her benign influences. This idea is enunciated in many of Shelley's works, but perhaps the clearest expression of it is in *Queen Mab*, where he says: —

> Look on yonder earth:
> The golden harvests spring; the unfailing sun
> Sheds light and life; the fruits, the flowers, the trees,
> Arise in due succession; all things speak
> Peace, harmony, and love. The universe
> In nature's silent eloquence, declares
> That all fulfil the works of love and joy, —
> All but the outcast man. He fabricates
> The sword, which stabs his peace; he cherisheth
> The snakes that gnaw his heart: he raiseth up
> The tyrant, whose delight is in his woe,
> Whose sport is in his agony.

Mark here that man the outcast is contrasted with the peace, harmony, and love which otherwise prevail on the earth. I should like to quote still another passage to the same effect: —

> Hath Nature's soul
> That form'd this world so beautiful, that spread

---

[7] The personification of oppressive conventional propriety, Mrs Grundy originated as an off-stage character in Thomas Morton's 1798 play *Speed the Plough*.

> Earth's lap with plenty, and life's smallest chord
> Strung to unchanging unison, that gave
> The happy birds their dwelling in the grove,
> That yielded to the wanderers of the deep
> The lovely silence of the unfathom'd main,
> And fill'd the meanest worm that crawls in dust
> With spirit, thought, and love; on Man alone,
> Partial in causeless malice, wantonly
> Heap'd ruin, vice, and slavery; his soul
> Blasted with withering curses; placed afar
> The meteor-happiness, that shuns his grasp,
> But serving on the frightful gulf to glare,
> Rent wide beneath his footsteps?
> Nature! — no!
> Kings, priests and statesmen, blast the human flower
> Even in its tender bud; their influence darts
> Like subtle poison through the bloodless veins
> Of desolate society. The child
> Ere he can lisp his mother's sacred name,
> Swells with the unnatural pride of crime, and lifts
> His baby-sword even in a hero's mood.

We see here that, according to Shelley, all living creatures, 'from the meanest worm that crawls' to the happy birds in the grove, enjoy peace and happiness, all excepting poor miserable man, who, by some fatality of his constitution, has ever been the prey of some few among his own kind who, by superior force or cunning, have befooled him, despoiled him, enslaved him, and generally rendered his state one of abject fear and wretchedness. If such were the case, society would certainly have to be regarded as an unmixed evil, and the sooner human beings followed Rousseau's advice and returned to the state of primitive nature the better!

But is it true that all things in Nature, where man is not, speak 'peace, harmony, and love'? Why, if we open our Darwin, the very opposite fact meets us at every turn. Yes, in the very vegetable kingdom, amid the gentle race of flowers so dear to Shelley, precisely the same forces are at work, the same incessant strife is raging, the same desires and appetites prevail, which he so abominated in the world of man. For gnawing at the root of life itself seems this power of evil from which the poet's sensitive soul shrank with such horror — lust, hunger, rapine, cruelty. So far from peace being the law of Nature, we learn on the contrary, from our great naturalist, that from the lowest semi-vital organism to the highest and most complex forms of life battle is being waged within battle for the right to breath, to eat, and to multiply on the earth. Look, for example, at the flower-like sea-anemones, with their exquisite forms and delicate rainbow-tints. What a shock it is to one's moral being to see them suddenly close like a tightly-drawn sack on a lot of little living creatures that one sees madly struggling through the semi-diaphanous substance till they are stifled in their living tomb. And this law which bids animal prey upon animal, however revolting to the human conscience, is a necessity of that Nature, which, if not as terribly unjust as the God of Calvinistic theology,[8] seems, at least to our human apprehension, to be callous to the sanguine strife and destruction which is going on in every nook and corner of the earth. Darwin, like Shelley, admits that we see the face of Nature bright with gladness: but he adds, 'we do not see, or we forget, that the birds which are idly singing around us mostly live on insects or seeds, and are thus constantly destroying life; or we forget how largely these songsters, or their eggs, or their nestlings, are destroyed by birds and beasts of prey'.

Inch by inch every available space of air, of earth, and of water is contested, fought for, finally conquered by some living creature or other, the stronger ever devouring the weaker, or at least beating him out of the field and leaving him to perish. So that the reckless competition, the selfishness, the cruelty which to Shelley appeared as essentially the result of bad government, nay, as almost an accident of human society, might have been traced by him feature by feature throughout the animal kingdom, from the slave-making ant to the thievish sparrow. For Dr Watt's admonition to the children that 'birds in their little nests agree',[9] is, unfortunately, one of those amiable delusions which, on closer examination, turn out anything but true. On the contrary, not only does active jealousy exist between the different species of birds, but they are the most omnivorous of creatures, and one is sorry to think that, in spite 'of the spirit, thought, and love which fill the meanest worm that crawls', they swallow the poor innocent with no more compunction than the human biped does his lamb and mint sauce. And then what unchronicled tragedies happen in those leaf-embowered nests, whose form and structure look indeed as if they were presided over by the spirit of love and peace. What, for one thing, should we see if we were to peep into some of them? Perhaps a cuckoo, uninvited, laying her egg in the nest of another kind of bird, whose own brood, when she has hatched the intruder, will be ruthlessly ejected by him. For, according to Darwin, the young cuckoo has not only the instinct, but a back actually adapted for getting rid of his foster-brothers, who thus, poor things, unceremoniously thrown on the ground, perish of cold and hunger.

Then again, if we take the hive-bees, we shall see in that wonderfully-

---

[8] John Calvin (1509–1564), a French theologian, pastor, and reformer, emphasized the moral weakness of humanity and predestination — the idea that an all-powerful God chooses in advance who will be allowed to enter heaven.

[9] The phrase is from a 1715 poem by Isaac Watts in his *Divine Songs Attempted in the Easy Language of Children*: 'Birds in their little nest agree'; and 'tis a shameful sight, when children of one family fall out, and chide, and fight'.

regulated community something not unlike an old-fashioned monarchy with a ruler 'by the grace of God'. For the queen-bee is so absolute in her own domains that she will suffer no second near her, and promptly destroys the young queens her daughters, as soon as they are born, or perishes herself in the combat. Shelley would have had to own here that even 'those royal murderers, whose mean thrones are bought by crimes and treachery and gore', could hardly match the savage instinctive hatred of this little insect fresh from Nature's hand. There is perhaps something even more appalling in the fact that the slave-making instinct should exist among animals. But it seems that certain species of ants are in the habit of carrying off the pupæ of another species to their nests and there rearing them as slaves. These slaves are black and not above half the size of their red masters, so that the contrast in their appearance is striking. With some kinds of ants, the *Formica rufescens*, the tyrants, by never doing any work, have actually lost the power of helping themselves, and are so dependent, that when a migration takes place the slaves have to carry their masters in their jaws!

These, alas! are but a few examples taken at random of the oppression, strife, and cruelty, which seem to pervade all organic beings according to that dread law formulated by Darwin: 'Let the strongest live and the weakest die'.

The fact is, that Shelley, when flying to Nature away from the hard-hearted ways of men, was really leaping from the frying-pan into the fire. For the very thing he abhorred most in human society — the implacable struggle for supremacy of one individual with another — was raging with tenfold force in the world around him, because less tempered by the mitigating influences of conscience and sympathy. It is true that the sensitive organisation of Shelley, shrinking from the rough contact with reality, never quite looked Nature in the face; and in west wind and sunset cloud, in running stream and fragrant flower, he recognised a more benignant manifestation of power than that which he saw in the Social State of Man, because what he saw reflected by these passive phenomena was in reality the shade of his own soul. And his own soul, being one of the loveliest as well as loftiest that ever passed across the stage of the world, transmuted the visible Universe to something after its own likeness.

In *Prometheus Unbound* Shelley grapples with the problem of good and evil, and with the moral regeneration of man; but, as I remarked before, it is to be regretted that in the working out of this magnificent idea the poet was not able to profit by those great generalisations of Darwin which have revolutionised the modern conception of life. I am inclined to call this poem the Passion-Play of Humanity. Instead of the Crucifixion of Christ we have here Man himself, or perhaps, rather the Human Mind, enduring an agony of thousands of years through being held captive by Jupiter. Now Jupiter is in a certain sense the creation of Prometheus, and primarily holds his sway in heaven through him.[10]

---

[10] In Greek mythology Prometheus was one of the immortal Titans, and the creator of

So that all the misery endured by the Titan, and by the world of men and women for whom he suffers, and by the earth herself in sympathetic pity for her offspring, is due in reality to the phantasm of a celestial tyrant whose shadow clouds the universe. But surely the existence of evil is more deeply entwined with the roots of life than seems here admitted; and though the abolition of irresponsible tyrannic power in heaven and on earth would no doubt do much to lessen the ills of life, it can certainly not be regarded as a universal panacea for them. I do not know whether I shall be ignominiously expelled from the Shelley Society, or perhaps even stoned, if I confess that there has always seemed to me to be something crude and undigested in the manner in which the poet tries to solve the problem of good and evil in *Prometheus Unbound*. His leading motive is apparently the same as that which constitutes the vital teaching of all great religions — namely, the redemption of Man. The Titan, by the endurance of woes which hope thinks infinite, by the forgiveness of wrongs darker than death or night, by the defiance of power which seems omnipotent, has wrought out this deliverance. But it is curious how vaguely this great triumph is described. The principle of evil incarnated in Jupiter simply topples down or is hurled down, one hardly knows how, by Demogorgon, his son, and the change which straightway transforms the earth from a scene of toil, famine, war and tyranny, to one of boundless love and harmony, is equally shadowy. The spirit of the hour thus describes the change which has come over things on his proclaiming the glad tidings of the liberation of Prometheus: —

> But soon I look'd,
> And behold thrones were kingless, and men walk'd
> One with the other even as spirits do,
> None fawn'd, none trampled; hate, disdain, or fear,
> Self-love or self-contempt, on human brows
> No more inscribed, as o'er the gate of hell,
> "All hope abandon ye who enter here",
> None frown'd, none trembled, none with eager fear
> Gazed on another's eye of cold command,
> Until the subject of a tyrant's will
> Became, worse fate, the object of his own,
> Which spurr'd him, like an outspent horse to death...
> Thrones, altars, judgment-seats, and prisons; wherein,
> And beside which, by wretched men were borne
> Sceptres, tiaras, swords, and chains, and tomes
> Of reason'd wrong, glozed on by ignorance,
> Were like those monstrous and barbaric shapes,

mankind. He also gave fire to humans, for which Jupiter punished him by chaining him to a cliff and having an eagle come and eat his liver every day. Shelley's *Prometheus Unbound* (1820), a four-act lyrical drama, represents Prometheus as a symbol of what he calls in his preface 'the highest perfection of moral and intellectual nature'.

> The ghost of a no more remember'd fame,
> Which, from their unworn obelisks, look forth
> In triumph o'er the palaces and tombs
> Of those who were their conquerors: mouldering round
> Those imaged to the pride of kings and priests,
> A dark yet mighty faith, a power as wide
> As is the world it wasted, and are now
> But an astonishment; even so the tools
> And emblems of its last captivity,
> Amid the dwellings of the peopled earth,
> Stand not o'erthrown, but unregarded now.

This ultimate triumph of the human mind over the forces of evil by which it is encompassed, and the consequent advent of a Golden Age, has been mystically foreshadowed by all great religious and ethical teachers, and Shelley could not have chosen a finer or more stupendous subject for a great dramatic poem. But I venture to think that if he had worked out this theme with more historic realism — if he had not unfortunately been debarred from casting into a poetic mould the modern scientific conception of evolution and the struggle for existence — that he would have shown the human race as typified in Prometheus, not as physically and morally depraved, owing to its gradual alienation from Nature, but, on the contrary, as emerging from a semi-brutal, barbarous condition, and continually progressing to higher stages of moral and mental development. For the true conflict consists in man's struggle with the irresponsible forces of Nature, and the victory in his conquest over them, both as regards the subjection of his own lower animal instincts and in his continually growing power through knowledge of turning these elemental forces, that filled his savage progenitors with fear and terror, into the nimblest of servants. This, I take it, would have been a conclusion more in harmony with the Darwinian conception of the universe, and also more consoling on the whole. For I suppose most of us would agree with Strauss's view that, just as it is more honourable in a citizen to have raised himself from a lower to a higher station in the social scale instead of having lapsed into degradation from some former proud estate, so Man himself gains in moral value, when one reflects that with infinite pain and struggle he has slowly risen above the thraldom of physical nature, and eating of the fruit of the tree of knowledge has learned, at whatever cost of mere sensuous enjoyment, to distinguish good from evil. Shelley, on the contrary, bitten by the nature worship of Rousseau, was too much inclined to glorify not only the future but also the remote past, at the expense of the present. As, for example, when he says 'that at some distant period man forsook the path of nature, and sacrificed the purity and happiness of his being to unnatural appetites, and that ALL VICE arose from the ruin of healthful innocence'. Here is hardly the place, or it would be easy to prove, from Darwin's *Descent of Man*, that every kind of unnatural appetite and vice has prevailed among men in a state of nature. Thus the murder of infants was practised on the largest scale throughout the world, the robbery of strangers was considered as honourable, women were commonly like slaves, among some savage tribes it was custom to kill their old and decrepit parents, while intemperance, licentiousness, and unnatural crimes were the common practice. Considering that such was the original bias of humanity, we may perhaps apply to it the remark of an American humourist on being told that some one was a self-made man, to wit, that it relieved his Maker of a great responsibility.

In concluding these few remarks, I can only trust that I have not been tiresome by dwelling too exclusively on Shelley's philosophy of Nature, and scarcely at all on the simply artistic value of his work. But as we meet to help each other in a fuller comprehension of his poetry, I hope I shall be forgiven if I have ventured to point out certain imperfections in the work of our beloved poet. 'Swear by no master's words' is a saying of Goethe's[11] that would have been heartily endorsed by Shelley, the iconoclast of authority. But if he failed comparatively in his attempt 'at solving the universe', if I may be permitted to use a favourite expression of my friend, the late W. K. Clifford, Shelley succeeded, perhaps more completely than any other poet, in marrying the most sublime or evanescent appearances of the material universe to human emotion.[12] Indeed, the essence of Shelley's being seems to have become one with the impetuous west wind, his heaven-aspiring song thrills us in the notes of the skylark, and the rapture of his words has added a new radiance to the beauty of flowers.

And though I have hitherto only dwelt on the contrast between the views of Nature held by Shelley and Darwin, I should like before concluding to say a few words as regards the final junction of their views in the glorious vistas they disclose of ever higher types of life replacing those that had gone before. For, judging by analogy, better, wiser, and more beautiful beings will inhabit

---

[11] In 1876 Blind published a selection of English translations, 'Maxims and Reflections, from the German of Goethe' (*Fraser's Magazine* (March 1876), pp. 338–48). Although it does not include this maxim, it is likely that Blind encountered some version of it in her reading of Goethe. In Part 1, scene 4, of Goethe's *Faust*, Mephistopheles calls on a student beginning his studies with Faust to focus on words over meanings, telling him to 'swear by your master's words', advice Goethe assumed his audience would reject, as it came from the devil.

[12] In his short life W. K. Clifford (1845–1879) made major contributions to algebraic theory, but he was best known by Blind and other writers for his philosophical writings and, more specifically, his evolutionary aestheticism (see p. 25). In his 1877 essay 'Cosmic Emotion', Clifford argued that Darwinian theory, in challenging the notion of immutable human nature, would prove a liberating force in human culture, since it demonstrates that 'the nature of man and beast and of all the world is changing, is going somewhere' (*Nineteenth Century* (October 1877), 411–29 (p.422)).

this planet in the ages to come, according to the laws of evolution, than we can now have any conception of. And I hope that we are all agreed that in Shelley himself we have already a certain foreshadowing of something better — for with his exquisitely sensitive organisation, of which he might well say, 'I am but as a nerve o'er which do creep the else unfelt oppressions of the earth', with his scorn for vulgar aims ending in self-aggrandisement, with his impatience of the conventional, continually hampering standards of morality, and with his passion for reforming the world, he seems lifted, not only above the needs and greeds of sensual desires, but also above fierce competition, the corroding jealousy, and malignant rivalries from which intellectual workers are so rarely exempt: failing, where he did fail, because he could not help investing the imperfect natures of transitory individuals with an ideal beauty which, fading on a closer view, induced in him a shuddering recoil of dismay and disillusion. Outsoaring the limits of the actual world, Shelley's mind foreshadowed loftier types than any yet in existence, his purpose being, as he says, 'to familiarise the highly-refined imagination of the more select classes of poetical readers with beautiful idealisms of moral excellence; aware that, until the mind can love, and admire, and trust, and hope, and endure, reasoned principles of moral conduct are seeds cast upon the highway of life, which the unconscious passenger tramples into dust, although they would bear the harvest of his happiness'. In the noble-hearted Laon, the liberator of his country, who only suffers defeat because he is fain to overcome his enemies by generosity; in Cythna, the high-souled woman, who rouses her sex in harem and seraglio from the inanition of a weak dependence to an ardent participation in the noble war of liberation; and, above all, in Prometheus himself, the heroic martyr who vanquishes hell by pitying his torturers, the Furies: in these and similar types Shelley has incorporated nearly all of goodness, love, and wisdom that it is at present possible to conceive. But his creations have been accused of being vague and unsubstantial shadows that take no more hold of us than the visionary shapes seen in a sunset sky. And we cannot deny that the accusation contains more truth. For poets have unfortunately always been more successful in depicting scenes of passion, crime, and agony than in their descriptions of divine love and beatitude. Take only as an example the *Inferno* of Dante as compared to his *Paradiso*, or Milton's Satan contrasted with the angelic hosts; and to come to more mundane subjects, the most tragic themes have always taken the strongest hold of men, as witness the murder of Agamemnon, the doom of Œdipus, the madness of King Lear, the ambition of Macbeth, the imprisonment of Margaret, the ordeal of Fantine.[13]

---

[13] Margaret of Anjou was Queen of England and nominally Queen of France by marriage to King Henry VI from 1445 to 1461 and again from 1470 to 1471. After the Lancastrian defeat at Tewkesbury during the Wars of the Roses she was imprisoned in England for five years. In

And it must be confessed that though, as a rule, we know very little of heaven, our experience of hell is pretty considerable. Now, as the substance of all poetry has to be extracted mostly from experience, Shelley, when he tried to embody his beautiful idealisms of moral excellence, and found that reality yielded him a rather meagre crop of impressions, had to weave his aërial webs too much from his own inner consciousness. But his glowing anticipation of a better future in store for humanity is, in a certain sense, the warrant of its own fulfilment, and his poetry will become a factor in helping to bring it about; for in the continual process of selection there is no reason why the moral ideals of one generation should not become the stepping-stones toward their realisation in another. And in this process of evolution the final triumph of the human mind over the brute forces of nature may be achieved, and Shelley's magnificent prophecy at the close of the fourth act of the *Prometheus* turn to simple truth, the prophecy that

> The man remains, —
> Sceptreless, free, uncircumscribed, but man:
> Equal, unclassed, tribeless, and nationless,
> Exempt from awe, worship, degree, the king
> Over himself; just, gentle, wise: but man.
> Passionless? no: — yet free from guilt or pain, —
> Which were, for his will made or suffered them;
> Nor yet exempt, though ruling them like slaves,
> From chance, and death, and mutability, —
> The clogs of that which else might oversoar
> The loftiest star of unascended heaven
> Pinnacled dim in the intense inane.

1476, the king of France paid a ransom to England for her, and she returned to France, where she lived in poverty until her death in 1482. Fantine, a fictional character in Victor Hugo's 1862 novel *Les Misérables*, is a young working-class woman in Paris who becomes pregnant by a rich student. After he abandons her, she is forced to look after their child, Cosette, on her own.

SELECTED REVIEWS OF POETRY BY MATHILDE BLIND

An excerpt from the review of *Love is Enough; or, the Freeing of Pharamond: A Morality*, by William Morris[14]

Mr Morris may be said to have, in point of form, enlarged the limits of English verse in his new poem. Its metrical construction, although fundamentally, perhaps, the only purely national one, had fallen into such total disuse, that its reviver might be fairly entitled to the claim of invention. It is the more singular that this species of rhythmical expression should have been ignored, as it clearly adapts itself with admirable pliability to the peculiar genius of our language. No stronger proof of this could be adduced than the latest production of the poet.

'Love is Enough' is, for the greater part, written in alliterative measure. This style of versification was habitual with Northern nations. It was rhymeless, like the poetry of the Greeks; but possessed no system of foot measure, depending on accent instead. The finest examples of this kind of verse are to be met with in the Icelandic songs of the Elder Edda, and in the Middle English poem of the fourteenth century, 'Piers Ploughman'. Some of the choicest of Eddaic pieces were translated with remarkable felicity in Mr Morris's version of the Volsunga Saga; but the structure of his verse in the present work has a greater affinity with English than Norse models.

Let us briefly examine what was the general law which regulated all alliterative metres. Syllables of identical sound and following each other at regular intervals invariably bring about the harmonious unison of a couplet. The Icelandic language possessed a much stricter rule of alliteration than the Anglo-Saxon. In the former it was absolutely requisite that the first line of a couplet should possess two alliterative syllables; the second line being rigorously enchained to it from the necessity that its initial letter should reiterate the preceding alliteration. The only modification of this latter rule was, that occasionally a short syllable was allowed to precede it. To make this sort of structure clear, we

---

[14] [Unsigned], Mathilde Blind, Review of *Love is Enough; or, the Freeing of Pharamond: A Morality*, *Athenæum* (23 November 1872), 657–58. The middle section of this review, featuring a full summary of the narrative and extended quotations from the poem, has been omitted so as to focus on Blind's analysis of Morris's versification and her assertion that the aesthetes' revival of earlier modes of representation served their quest for new forms of poetic truth. Her argument here reflects her reading of and agreement with Walter Pater's influential 1868 *Westminster Review* essay 'Poems by William Morris'. For more on the influence of Pater on Blind's aestheticism, see Diedrick, *Mathilde Blind*, pp. 88–89, 120–21.

will quote two lines from a fourteenth-century Icelandic poem:

> *Sk*apan ok fœðing, *sk*írn ok pryði
> *Sk*ysend full, at betre er gulli.

The chief distinction between this metre and that in use amongst the Anglo-Saxons was that here we find a strict regulation as to the number of times the alliteration may be employed. Not only was it forbidden to exceed or fall short of the three alliterative accents, but these must also succeed each other at stated periods.

The Anglo-Saxons allowed themselves more latitude. They sometimes only employed two alliterative syllables in couplets of four, five, and even six accents, while, on the other hand, they would not scruple to exceed the number of three. The opening lines of 'Piers Ploughman' may, however, be cited as the more regular specimen of alliteration: —

> In a somer seson
> When softe was the sonne,
> I shoop me into shroudes
> As I a sheep weere,
> In habit as a heremite,
> Unholy of werkes,
> Wente wide in this world
> Wondres to here.

It is manifest that Mr Morris has greatly improved on this measure. Under his hands it has assumed statelier proportions. The rise and fall of its sound-waves have acquired a more majestic sweep. The fusion of the two short lines of a couplet, as formerly used, into one, thus obtaining four accents in a single line, at once gives more scope to narrative, and allows of more freedom in the employment of the alliteration.

It would be impossible here to enter into the minutiæ of Mr Morris's treatment of alliteration, and of his deviation from the old writers in the respect. A few points that have struck us most may, however, be briefly enumerated here. Mr Morris does not confine himself to the three customary alliterative syllables in a couplet. An exquisite specimen of this kind may, however, stand here: —

> It shall change, we shall change, as through rain and through sunshine
> The green rod of the rose-bough to blossoming changeth.

A slighter alliteration, as here in '*b*ough' and '*bl*ossoming', is so repeatedly to be met with in the track of the principal one, that it cannot be imputed to accident, and often enhances the melodious beauty of the verse. The alliteration is not always confined to a couplet, but is sometimes arranged in metrical clauses, from one and a half to two or three lines, apparently in harmony with the spirit of the narrative. For example: —

> Thou hast followed my banner amidst of the battle,
> And seen my face change to the man that they fear,
> Yet found me not fearful nor turned from beholding.

Occasionally, we find a double alliteration of double consonants, which has a very fine effect, as thus: —

> There is a place in the world, a great valley,
> That seems a green plain from the brow of the mountains.

And again: —

> By the fair wife, long dead, and thy sword-smitten children,
> By thy life without blame, and thy love without blemish.

Sometimes a single line will contain a complete alliterative verse, as thus: —

> O woe, woe is me that I may not awaken!

As a splendid example of the general character of the metre, we will quote the following lines: —

> Who shall ever forget it? the dead face of thy father,
> And thou in thy fight-battered armour above it,
> Mid the passion of tears long held back by the battle;
> And thy rent banner o'er thee, and the ring of men mail clad,
> Victorious to-day, since their ruin not a spear-length
> Was thrust away from them. — Son, think of thy glory,
> And e'en in such wise break the throng of these devils!

Here, it appears to us, we detect an admirable innovation on the old system. This consists in the rise of a new alliterative wave before the preceding one has completely subsided, and produces an inexpressibly rich and far-reaching echo of sounds. By such means the sense is thrown into vivid relief. We not merely realize a scene, or an image, by means of a mental effort, but are brought into an immediate sensuous contact with it. Triumphs of this kind are of the essence of poetry. The least sensitive ear must, in the verses above cited, become conscious of the strong forcible colouring which the use of alliteration imparts to the description.

A metre which possesses such remarkable rhythmical capacities, while at the same time it allows the poet almost the latitude of prose, might have been chosen as the appropriate form for an English Iliad, had we any such. It certainly seems to possess, to a greater extent than blank verse, the quality of minutely assimilating its modulating to every graduation of the thought which it clothes.

We must not forget here to point out the crowning beauty of this poem — its songs. They are based on the same metrical arrangement as the other portions, excepting that rhyme is superadded. This at once transforms narrative into lyrical poetry. The melodiousness of their liquid numbers makes them unique of their kind. We select the shortest, that it may answer for the rest: —

> *Love is Enough*: though the World be a-waning,
> And the woods have no voice but the voice of complaining,
> Though the sky be too dark for dim eyes to discover
> The gold-cups and daisies fair blooming thereunder,
> Though the hills be held shadows, and the sea a dark wonder,
> And this day draw a veil over all deeds passed over,
> Yet their hands shall not tremble, their feet shall not falter;
> The void shall not weary, the fear shall not alter
> These lips and these eyes of the loved and the lover.

Turn we now to the story. In celebration of the marriage of an emperor and empress a Morality is performed. A pair equally happy, although they be but humble peasant-folk, Giles and Joan, look on wonder-eyed from amidst the throng of people. The bride is held up in the crowd by the goodman, and their *naïve* remarks form a charming introduction, as likewise the couple charmingly conclude the poem, by settling that they will invite the player-king and player-maiden, who are also a newly-wedded pair, to their homestead, and treat them there to the best cheer.

In the Morality itself, in harmony with the character of that species of mediæval play, we find one allegorical personage introduced. It is Love, who appears under various disguises, — as a king, as a pilgrim, as a maker of pictured cloths, — and who might be regarded as the real hero of the play, considering how completely he triumphs over its ostensible one, King Pharamond.

[...]

On considering this story, this dream within a dream rather, we are conscious of a strangely-mingled sensation, in which exquisite enjoyment is yet tinged by a shade of regret. The rare mastery with which Mr Morris handles an unusual and truly magnificent form of versification, — a form the full scope of which reveals itself in passages where the grandeur of conception requires to be vigorously embodied, — is father to the wish that the subject thus presented had been possessed of the loftier proportions.

In this metre we may repeat Homer would, for the first time, become truly naturalized on English soil. In this metre some of the grand but fragmentary Norse tales might, for the first time, unfold their eagle plumage to the full, or the Arthurian legends at last attain to complete development. Mr Morris has already, in his earliest work, selected some incidents from the latter for poetical presentation, and he was singularly successful. Why should he not once again select this subject for more exhaustive treatment? — for it seems to be the only really national tradition which contains inherent epic and narrative capacities.

And the mysticism, the weird sweetness, of these Celtic legends, their strange, dreamy fascination, would marvellously harmonize with some of the most distinctive characteristics of Mr Morris's genius.

Surely the fact of Mr Tennyson having, in a manner, for the first time selected this theme, could not and ought not to act as a deterrent motive. As it is, his Idyls,[15] beautiful as they are for the greater part, do not pretend to any faithful rendering of the spirit of the old tale, but aim at a perfectly modern and individual treatment. So far from precluding, this method of dealing with the subject would rather seem to challenge a fresh attempt, starting from an entirely different conception. There would be a double charm in this: that of the work itself in the first instance; in the second, the pleasure which is always experienced in instituting a comparison of the dissimilarity of treatment between similar subjects. For in this treatment, of course, reside the Alpha and the Omega of the poet's power; and we are inclined to think that, on the whole, it is rather a gain than a loss to Art that the same theme should be handled over and over again. If we had as many 'King Arthurs' as the Greeks possessed tragedies concerning the woes of the house of Agamemnon, or the Italians representations of the Madonna, we should probably find that in this way we could not fail to attain some culminating achievement. And one inestimable result would certainly be arrived at, the poet would at once have a type, a firm substratum, which, like the block of marble under the sculptor's hands, he could mould, elaborate, and fashion forth into perfect loveliness, while, nevertheless, he in some senses would be bound down by the necessary conditions of his material. This, it appears to us, is an immense advantage to the poet, and it will be a subject of regret if he does not avail himself of it. That King Pharamond is no such type, it is unnecessary to add. He is, in fact, but a vague shadowy king, whose deeds impress us with a sense of unreality akin to his dreams. Who can deny, however, that those possess an exquisite enchantment, which transports us for the time into a land of mingled romance and færie, or resist the undefinable sweet glamour they cast over him? In fact, this kind of poetry always produces on our imagination an effect somewhat resembling the impression received on looking at a familiar landscape through the mellow emblazonry of a painted casement. We cannot say that objects we see thus are idealized; for to idealize is not to lose sight of reality, but to sever what is impure and transient from the lofty and imperishable. Here, however, if the comparison be permissible, we see reality, not enhanced, but transformed. We behold her through an unfamiliar medium of strange and deceptive splendour; and it is in this splendour, glowing as well as soft, that the present poem is steeped.

---

[15] Tennyson composed what he called his 'English Idyls' in the 1830s; they were an attempt to adapt the poetic form of Theocritus to English verse. Revised versions of several of these poems became part of his Arthurian cycle *Idylls of the King* (1859–1885), including 'Morte d'Arthur', incorporated into the *Idylls of the King* as 'The Passing of Arthur'.

Review of *Music and Moonlight*, by Arthur O'Shaughnessy[16]

There is a beautiful old legend, narrating how the child Jesus used to form sparrows of the mud, by the wayside, which flew away singing as he clapped his hands. This feat is not unlike the lyrical poet's, should he succeed in winging his words by breathing into them the soul of music. Nothing, at first sight, appears more eminently natural, indeed, than the song proper, the lyrical cry as it has been called. Yet owing to the complete spontaneity of inspiration requisite for its production, we not only find that few poets, comparatively speaking, have been absolute masters in that species of composition, but also that even those who were masters have only occasionally succeeded in producing lyrics of consummate excellence. The very simplicity of the song, whose themes essentially consist of what is primal and universal in the fate and feelings of man, renders complete success in it so difficult of achievement. Of course it may again be subdivided into many varieties, whose character always consists, however, in the fact that they form a sort of simple musical accompaniment to the vicissitudes of human life, its range thus extending from the lullaby over the cradle, of which Tennyson's 'Sweet and low, sweet and low', is probably the most perfect specimen in English, to the last pathetic wail of the dirge which but implores the 'quiet consummation' of the grave. Thus it is but natural that we shall find a certain similarity of tone and manner in the most perfect models of lyrical poetry, a similarity considerably modified, however, on the one side by individual diversities of character, on the other by the periodic growth of new schools of poetry.

If we have dwelt for a moment on the peculiar nature of the difficulties and excellences proper to the genuine song, it is because Mr O'Shaughnessy appears to us particularly happy in this species of composition; his shorter lyrics being eminently distinguished by spontaneity of feeling, grace of diction, and an aerial delicacy of rhythm. In proof of the exquisite musicalness of the poet's endowment let us quote the following beautiful verses: —

> Has summer come without the rose,
>   Or left the bird behind?
> Is the blue changed above thee,
>   O world! Or am I blind?
> Will you change every flower that grows,
>   Or only change this spot,
> Where she who said, I love thee,
>   Now says, I love thee not?

---

[16] *Examiner* (28 March 1874), 320–21. Blind saw O'Shaughnessy, whose verse reflects French as well as American influences, as a fellow cosmopolitan aesthete, and as someone who, along with Swinburne, shared her belief in a poetry of ethical engagement. This review is one of Blind's most sustained discussions of lyric poetry, a form she would repeatedly turn to during her own poetic career. For more on O'Shaughnessy, see Jordan Kistler's *Arthur O'Shaughnessy, A Pre-Raphaelite Poet in the British Museum* (London: Routledge, 2016).

> The sky seemed true above thee,
>   The rose true on the tree;
> The bird seemed true the summer through,
>   But all proved false to me:
> World, is there one good thing in you,
>   Life, love, or death — or what?
> Since lips that sang, I love thee,
>   Have said I love thee not?
>
> I think the sun's kiss will scarce fall
>   Into one flower's gold cup;
> I think the bird will miss me,
>   And give the summer up.
> O sweet place! desolate in tall,
>   Wild grass, have you forgot
> How her lips loved to kiss me,
>   Now that they kiss me not?
>
> Be false or fair above me,
>   Come back with any face,
> Summer! — do I care what you do?
>   You cannot change one place —
> The grass, the leaves, the earth, the dew,
>   The grave I make the spot —
> Here, where she used to love me,
>   Here, where she loves me not.

This is but one of several songs equally noticeable for their sweet ease of rhythm and subtle grace of sentiment. As particularly fine in this respect we would call the reader's attention to the lyrics beginning: — 'I made another garden yes', 'She has gone wandering, wandering away', 'Now I am on the earth', 'I went to her who loveth me no more', &c. Charmingly quaint is the poem entitled 'Prophetic Birds', in which the latter are imagined singing on a May morning in a wood which two lovers have made their trysting-place. We cannot refrain from quoting the two following stanzas: —

> 'Sure', said the thrush, 'we'll wed them soon',
> 'Yea', said the turtle-dove, 'in June';
> 'They'll make fine sport ere the year is out',
> Said the magpie between a laugh and a shout.
> And heedlessly the lovers heard
> The senseless babble of bird with bird.
> 'Sure', croaked the jackdaw, 'in July
> They'll quarrel, or no daw am I —
> Why let them, since they are but men',
> 'They can make it up though', quoth the wren.
> And heedlessly the lovers heard
> A senseless babble of bird with bird.

Even from a few specimens like the above the reader will be able to judge of the exquisite finish of the workmanship. In many senses Mr O'Shaughnessy is indeed a master of the formal art of poetry; there is a peculiar flavour of individuality about the ring and flow of his verses, which are original without being far-fetched, and seem to set themselves to a music of their own as one peruses them; a music too that is full of a subtle play and transition of sound very rare and consequently eminently precious where it exists.

The leading phrase of Mr O'Shaughnessy's poems, so to speak, is scarcely to be expressed adequately by any word but that significant German one of '*Sehnsucht*'; the passionate aspiration to something afar and above, which finds its symbol in nature in the receding azure of hills in spring, or the tremulous haze of fading horizons. That plaintive minor which is so expressive of the discrepancy, the profound incongruity, between life and the ideal, forms the key-note of all Mr O'Shaughnessy's work. It is, perhaps, strange that we should nowhere be able to trace an attempt at the solution of the problem, except it be in the poems entitled 'Europe' and 'Ode to a New Age', which bear, however, too evident traces of a Swinburnian influence. Peculiarly inspired, on the other hand, by this sense of loss, this home-sickness in a bleak materialistic world, this brooding glow of mystic passion, are the poems 'The Song of Betrothal', 'Outcry', 'Nostalgia des Cieux', 'Azure Islands', and 'Music and Moonlight'. The conception of this latter poem, which gives its name to the book, is extremely poetical; Music, as personified from the point of view of a spiritual force, liberating and redeeming us from this sense of want, this superincumbent weight of custom; the rapture of a gifted musician transported out of herself by the entrancing creation of a Chopin; the keen, tense-strung fervour of ideal passion; the final snapping of a string in the instrument, and of a string, too, in that other instrument, the beautiful Lady Eucharis, who has sat playing alone in the moonlight chamber of her stately house, and is found there in the morning as one having fallen asleep — dead. All this is profoundly felt and full of fine imaginative qualities. It is deficient, on the other hand, in a certain massing of effects; the result being too often a confused brilliancy and sense of satiety, partly due to indefiniteness of outline, partly to a glut of such expressions as 'amber water', glittering opal', 'soft illumination', 'gleaming amethyst', &c.

We must still advert to the hymn-like poem, 'The Earth', which in form resembles the unrhymed verse of the Bible; a poetical style resuscitated by Walt Whitman, and destined, we believe, to have a magnificent future. As regards the spirit, however, it proceeds from the profoundest springs of the poet's individuality, and we should pronounce it the most powerful, touching, and eminently sincere of his productions. The following extract, however inadequate, may serve as a specimen of its style: —

It is wonderful that I never preferred the thought of you before, O still, mysterious, unalterable earth!

It is wonderful that I never longed to know you, to feel you, to become one with you; that I never had strange revelations of you in dreams; that I never stopped loving, or thinking, or speaking, or singing, to consider about and understand you;

It is most wonderful that I never stopped suffering to think how undisturbed, and changeless, and full of rest is the earth out of which I came, and to which I shall one day return.

In conclusion, we will only remark that the present volume is sure to add Mr O'Shaughnessy's reputation, and that, by its many beauties of versification, style, and genuine poetic feeling, it cannot fail to charm a wide circle of admirers.

Review of *Yu-Pe-Ya's Lute. A Chinese Tale, in English Verse.* By Augusta Webster[17]

Nothing certainly so attunes the mind to a vivid sympathy with races and nations removed from us by the intervening distances of space or time, renders us so conscious, even while sharply attenuating the lines of demarcation in manners and customs, of that touch of nature which 'makes the whole world kin', as the songs and stories of a people, revealing as they do these profounder human emotions, which, like bright eyes through a mask, startle us by shining with a clear light through the customary wraps and trappings of nationality. In this sense, we are daily realising a more vital imaginative unity with peoples alien from ours, the fancy becoming naturalised, so to speak, in Russia and Norway, India and Japan, by means of fables, stories, and poems, rendered more and more accessible by careful translations, or paraphrastic versions. Mrs Webster has, therefore, earned our best thanks for introducing this delicious story of 'Yu-Pe-Ya's Lute' to the English public, and for preserving, to a great extent, in her freehand rendering of the original, its quaint and foreign flavour,

---

[17] *Examiner* (6 June 1874), p. 600. Blind met Webster in the early 1870s at several of the salons they both attended, and she admired Webster's efforts on behalf of women's rights (Webster worked for the London branch of the National Committee for Women's Suffrage). With the publication of *A Woman Sold and Other Poems* in 1867 (the same year Blind published her first volume of poetry), Webster announced herself as a politically engaged poet. During their careers, both writers made distinctive contributions to the dramatic monologue, the lyric, and the sonnet, and both wrote hybrid poems that drew on both lyric and narrative traditions. Yu-Pe-Ya's Lute is one of these, a narrative poem in heroic couplets interrupted by the songs of its title character. For an extended analysis of *Yu-Pe-Ya's Lute*, see Emily Harrington, 'Augusta Webster: Time and the Lyrical Ideal', in *The Oxford Handbook of Victorian Poetry*, ed. by Matthew Bevis (Oxford: Oxford University Press, 2013), pp. 507–20.

combined, as this is, with touches of the simplest natural pathos.

The story, indeed, as here rendered in an English dress is by no means a translation or even a paraphrase, as the authoress, although faithfully adhering to the leading incidents of the Chinese narrative, has made its mode of presentation entirely her own. Mrs Webster has been particularly successful in conveying to us by a few descriptive touches certain characteristic features in the landscape and habits of China. The tale in brief outline is this. Yu-Pe-Ya, the Emperor's favourite, returning from an embassy to his native principality, is overtaken while journeying down the river by a terrific storm, so that the crew are fain to anchor the ships in a little quiet cove till the tempest be over. Yu-Pe-Ya seeks to wile away the time by playing on his lute —

>   That second heart
> Which seemed to share his pulse and be a part
> Of the great heart within him, and expound
> In living rhythms and sweet articulate sound,
> Its mute, dim longings, and to himself reveal,
> Some secret of himself he could not feel
> Until the music spoke it.

But the instrument, so far from responding to his touch, emits only a few sighing sounds. From this the minstrel infers the presence either of some skilled musician thirstily drinking in the sounds, or else of thieves of a more practical sort. Search being made along the banks, however, no one is found save a woodman, who confesses to having lingered by the wayside in order to enjoy the exquisite harmony. Now ensues an interview between prince and peasant rich in suggestions of a peculiarly high-wrought poetic mood. The former, who in the midst of boundless wealth and fortune has yet gone lonely-hearted on his way through life, is greeted for the first time by accents that thrill him as of some long-lost kinsman's voice. Eagerly he questions Tse-Ky, listens to his description of the origin of the lute, plays him subtle and intricate airs the hidden meaning of which he unravels with unerring skill, and at last, when the latter has interpreted to him the tenderest emotions but half expressed in his music, he clasps him in his arms in an ecstasy of delight, adopts him as his brother, and would fain take him to the capital. The woodman refuses to leave his aged parents. However, Yu-Pe-Ya promises to return to the same spot within the year, 'when this ripe month of leaves and gold is here'. He comes, indeed, but Tse-Ky is not there to meet him and when —

>   Unfolded from its broidered shrouds,
> The lute was wooed to speak, the strings denied
> Their vibrant resonance, and but replied
> With muffled whispers, save when one long wail
> Rung from the chord of Wen-Wang.

Tse-Ky has kept the tryst, indeed, even in death; for he lies buried by the hillside which looks down the river, and thither Yu-Pe-Ya, escorted by his friend's father, resorts, and taking his lute, wakes shrill sounds of grief on its resonant strings.

Mrs Webster, in her metrical adaptation of this quaintly beautiful tale, has evinced much delicacy and grace of handling; her versification, if lacking the inmost living pulse of rhythm, is yet smooth and well-sustained throughout. It would be ungracious to cavil at the minor blemishes of a poem that has afforded us true pleasure, both on account of the really charming story and beauty of workmanship; we hope, therefore, it may deservedly find an audience thoroughly fitted to appreciate and enjoy both the one and the other.

SELECTED REVIEWS OF MATHILDE BLIND'S POETRY

Review of *The Ascent of Man: and other Poems*, by H. F. Wilson[18]

The accomplished author of 'The Prophecy of St. Oran' and 'The Heather on Fire' has produced perhaps the earliest embodiment in verse (on any considerable scale) of the theories of Charles Darwin and his followers that has appeared in England. German bards have already essayed the thing, but then in modern Germany the boundary line between poetry and prose is not particularly distinct. It takes some time for a creed so startling in its novelty to become a part of the general consciousness of the race, and even now, in the thirtieth year of its existence, there are still whole tracts of human opinion which the theory of evolution has hitherto failed to conquer. Yet there have not been wanting signs that the consummation is fast approaching. The voice of the Extension lecturer (our modern English equivalent for the young man of intemperate habits, our modern English equivalent for the unjustly abused Sophist of ancient Greece) is heard in the land. Popular primers are issued by enterprising publishers. Daring sermons are preached by eminent divines, for, to use Clough's expressive words,

> not by eastern windows only
> When daylight comes, comes in the light;
> Eastward the sun climbs slow, how slowly!
> But westward, look, the land is bright![19]

'The Ascent of Man', as its author would be ready to admit, and as her critic must be careful to observe, does not bear toward evolution a relation in any way comparable to that which exists between the 'De Rerum Natura' of Lucretius and Epicureanism. Its style is far more sketchy, and its exposition of the facts with which it has to deal is infinitely less complete. We find in it none of the scientific *minutiae* in which the soul of the great Roman poet delighted, and but scanty traces of the sublime, if sombre eloquence that illumines the pages

---

[18] [Unsigned], H. F. Wilson, Review of *The Ascent of Man*, Athenæum (20 July 1889), 87–88. Along with Augusta Webster, A. Mary F. Robinson, Arthur Symons, and poetry editor Theodore Watts-Dunton, Wilson was one of the regular poetry reviewers for the *Athenæum* in the late 1880s. Wilson was for a time a Fellow at Trinity College, Cambridge, where he studied classical languages and literature.

[19] From 'The Struggle' (1855), by Arthur Hugh Clough.

of his masterpiece. Yet with these reservations the effort which Miss Blind has made is one deserving of high praise. From Chaos to Kosmos, from the 'indefinite incoherent homogeneity' to the 'definite coherent heterogeneity', she hurries her reader along, breathless and perspiring perhaps, but never anxious to stop. We have known her book to be read in the Underground Railway, and the reader to be so absorbed in its contents as to be carried unawares several stations past his destination.

After a stirring prelude addressed to the soul, in which she urges it to take an upward flight, in the spirit of Virgil's

> Sicelides musae, paullo majora canamus,[20]

Miss Blind in 'Chants of Life' [sic] describes the salient facts (as science in the person of Mr Herbert Spencer marshals them for us) to make 'the round world and all that therein is': —

> Struck out of dim fluctuant forces and shock of electrical vapour,
> Repelled and attracted the atoms flashed mingling in union primeval,

and of the gradual emergence of land and water and the lower forms of vegetable life. Next comes an able epitome the continuous evolution of higher types from which we may quote the following stanzas: [see p. 57]. The stanzas which follow, depicting the fierce and cruel work of 'Nature red in tooth and claw', or, as Miss Blind puts it,

> ... the long portentous strife,
>   Where types are tried even as by fire,
> Where life is whetted upon life
> And step by panting step mounts higher,

are full of vigour. At last we reach the 'new strange creature' Man,

> Wild — stammering — nameless — shameless — nude;

and the next division of the poem, written in heroic couplets, treats of his mental and moral development, with a glance at the 'ghost theory' of the origin of religion and the anthropomorphism of early theologies, in which the following lines have something of the stately movement of Lucretius: —

> ... behold beside him in the night, —
> Softly beside him, like the noiseless light
> Of moonbeams moving o'er the glimmering floor
> That come unbidden through the bolted door, —
> The lonely sleeper sees the lost one stand
> Like one returned from some dim, distant land, ...

From man's appearance on the earth to the fall of the Roman Empire is a

---

[20] 'Ye Sicilian muses, let us sing rather grander strains'.

sufficiently long period, but Miss Blind vaults across the interval — if she will pardon us for the expression — with ease and grace, in some twenty stanzas. From the lines describing the kaleidoscopic fortunes of the huge kingdoms of the East we select those in which she felicitously touches on the stupendous antiquity of Egypt: —

> Hers are imperial halls
> With strangely scriptured walls
> And long perspectives of memorial places,
> Where the hushed daylight glows
> On mute colossal rows
> Of clawed wild beasts featured with female faces,
> And realmless kings inane whose stony eyes
> Have watched the hour-glass of the centuries.

We have now indicated what is the style and scope of these 'Chants of Life', which form, in our opinion, the best portion of 'The Ascent of Man', and we need not follow Miss Blind through her further references to the growth of Christianity, the rise of the Papal power, the Reformation, the Revolution in France, and the birth of Democracy, all of which topics are to be met with by the astonished reader in the next few pages. Nor do we purpose to dwell at length upon the remaining sections of the poem, entitled respectively 'The Pilgrim Soul' and 'The Leading of Sorrow'. The former is a mystical parable of the human soul wandering in search of Love, and finding him in the shape of a neglected child, as Plato pictures *erôs* in the Symposium, 'sleeping without covering before the doors, and in the unsheltered streets, | spurned and despised by the licentious, who have enthroned Lust in his place'. It contains some fine descriptive passages, but is too diffuse in treatment, and is disfigured by excessive alliteration and other imitations of Mr Swinburne's manner, to which we need not more particularly allude. The same defects are observable in 'The Leading of Sorrow', and the eight-line metre in which it is written, though on the whole skilfully handled, tends to become monotonous. As a specimen of its quality we may extract the following stanzas, in which the great cosmic processes are nobly pictured: [see p. 101]. This high level is, however, by no means always attained. The long episode treating of the condition of the poor is weakened by over-violent denunciation, and contains several false and jarring notes. Miss Blind's rhymes too, like those of Mrs Browning, are often mere assonances, such as 'follow' and 'yellow', 'planets' and 'minutes', 'shadows' and 'widows', 'ranges' and 'avalanches', while her luxuriant periods would now and then be the better for judicious pruning. Her gift of song is genuine, and her imagination powerful, but she lacks, or so it seems to us, the sense of restraint which imparts finish and distinction to verse no less than to pictures and statuary. Yet when all is said and done 'The Ascent of Man' remains a remarkable poem, and cannot fail to increase its author's reputation as a brilliant and original writer.

Half the remainder of the volume is occupied with some twenty lyrics and sonnets grouped together as 'Poems of the Open Air', in which Miss Blind's delicate susceptibility to the influence of nature is continually displayed. The longest poem is 'The Teamster', and this, like 'The Leading of Sorrow', is marred by certain faults of taste, its style at times perilously approaching bathos, as in the following verse: —

> Unrecognized Sam took his glass of beer,
>   And picked up gossip which the men let fall:
> How Farmer Clow had failed, and one named Steer
>   Had taken on the land, repairs and all;
> And how the Kimber girl was to be wed
>   To Betsy's Ned.

Village talk of this kind needs the touch of a Tennyson to make it endurable. In Miss Blind's hands it is bald to the verge of banality. Far pleasanter is the 'Highland Village' — a dainty picture of some Speyside townlet like Kingussie or Aviemore. The effect of a windless August afternoon is well given in 'Reapers' with its odd metre and vivid word-painting: [see p. 114].

The poems entitled 'Love in Exile', with which the book concludes, remind us a good deal of Mrs Browning in the intensity of their expression of personal passion. Many of them would, we think, go admirably to music, as, for example, No. vii., 'Why will you haunt me unawares?' and No. xv., 'Dear, when I look into your eyes'. We commend them to the favourable notice of Miss Maude Valérie White.[21]

Review of *The Ascent of Man*, by Louise Chandler Moulton[22]

A volume of poems has just been published here by Messrs Chatto & Windus which deserves your attention. It is entitled 'The Ascent of Man', and it deals with the progress of the world from chaos until the present time, with a grasp and a power of continuous thought we are hardly accustomed to expect from a woman. It is the work of Miss Mathilde Blind, already well known to the reading public as the author of two previous volumes of poems (not yet, I

---

[21] Maude Valérie White (1855–1937), a French-born English composer who became one of the most successful Victorian songwriters.

[22] *The Sunday Herald* (Boston; 14 July 1889), p. 20. Moulton, an American poet, fiction writer, and critic, wrote a weekly literary letter from London for the Sunday issue of the *Boston Herald* from 1886 to 1892, which is where her review of *The Ascent of Man* appeared. She spent many of her summers in London, where she met Blind and established friendships with many members of London's literary community.

believe, republished in America), a brilliant novel entitled 'Tarantella', and the biographies of George Eliot and of Mm Roland, contributed to the 'Famous Women Series'.

In the 'Ascent of Man' Miss Blind has chosen a theme both lofty and difficult. She contemplates the world in its successive stages — the limitless deserts and the wilderness of tropic growth evolved by the Will of Love from primeval chaos — the virgin forest, the sparkling sea, the beasts that fought for their loves, and the birds that sing for them — the animal existence that was war — and then the strange, new creature, man, 'most unprotected of earth's kin', until thought stirs in him and he becomes aware of something in himself that is stronger than the strength of the beasts he fears. He shapes his flints and carves his horn, and begins thus gropingly that progressive civilization which today flashes tidings with the speed of lightning from shore to shore, crosses the sea in gigantic steamers and the land in cars like palaces. To quote Miss Blind, about that far beginning:

> And from the clash of warring Nature's strife
> Man day by day wins his imperilled life;
> For goaded on by want, he hunts the roe,
> Chases the deer, and lays the wild boar low.
> In his rude boat made of the hollow trees
> He drifts adventurous on the unoared seas. [*sic*; comma in original]

Having thus provided for life, man begins to perceive and to consider death. He bends above those whom great death has silenced — 'the beautiful, the brave', who have 'vanished like bubbles on a breaking wave'. He begins to see visions in the moonlight, which convince him that his dead live still; his longing is father to his faith; and so is born, in the savage mind, belief in immortality. Then comes the thought that these surviving and triumphant spirits must have more than mortal power; and gradually he grows to fear the Daemon rulers of the destinies of men. But as man becomes less cruel himself, his gods improve with him; and he sees some vague realms of hope, toward which he turns his face. He gains, with every generation, in strength and wisdom, until, instead of building huts, he builds cities. And then come great nations (still with the instinct for prey) and great wars. And then at last, into the midst of the world's tumult, comes the new note of 'Peace on earth and good will toward man' — the Christ is born. But, out of the very gospel of love, the spirit of persecution is presently evolved; for:

> Better rack them here,
> Mutilate and sear,
> Than their souls should go
> To the place of everlasting woe.

So the necessity for law and the orderly arrangement of affairs begets monarchies, and the tyranny of monarchs begets revolution: and always the story of the struggle and progress goes on. The second part of 'The Ascent of Man' deals with 'The Pilgrim Soul'. The life of the city, where are 'The men that are marred and the maids that are sold', to the bare desert end of the town, against which white waters break, in the white moonlight. And there he finds Great Love, in the semblance of a little half-starved, half-naked boy, with eyes flashing through tears, 'Like eyes that from heaven have looked upon hell'. And when the soul clasped him, he grew strong and lofty of stature, until he towered above all the soul's lost gods, and became king and saviour.

Part third is devoted to 'The Leading of Sorrow'; and sorrow teaches that, though men die, man endures, and that

> From man's martyrdom in slow convulsion
> Will be born the infinite goodness — God.

Does it really comfort most people, I wonder, to feel that, through their own suffering and watered by their tears, the growth of the race goes on toward some far-off perfection? It ought to cheer us, no doubt, according to the highest code of altruism; but — does it?

I greatly like some of Miss Blind's 'Poems of the Open Air'. 'The Teamster' is a realistic and touching idyl; and the lines 'On a Forsaken Lark's Nest', with their lament for the 'poor, pathetic brown eggs' that will never open, are genuinely charming. Read for yourself this briefer lyric: ['The Songs of Summer'; see p. 115].

And here is a bit of autumnal suggestion which I must give you: ['Green Leaves and Sere'; see p. 116].

The last section of the book contains 24 poems under the general title of 'Love in Exile', and this is certainly the most moving portion of the volume, though not the most uncommon; since there have been plenty of women to utter the lyric cry of longing love, and comparatively few to treat such themes as 'The Ascent of Man'. Nothing can be more absurd than to consider love poems as the direct result of personal experience. We are not wont, we rhymers, to confide our intimate joys and sorrows to the world, yet what one writes is the result, no doubt, of what one has felt; and a woman must have clasped hands with both love and pain before she could write such poems as the last 24 in Miss Blind's volume. Read, for instance, the following: ['Love in Exile' II; see p. 122].

To turn from this picture of love, complete and happy, to some of the subsequent numbers, is to find the minor chord in the music — the pathos of humanity which mocks our fleeting joys. Hear the questioning of the woman's bereft and lonesome heart in this other song: ['Love in Exile' VI; see p. 124].

To read the work of Mathilde Blind, whether in prose or verse, is to come in contact with a strong and fine nature — to make the acquaintance of a woman who has not only thought and read, but who has felt and lived.

Review of *Dramas in Miniature*, by Arthur Symons[23]

The 'Dramas in Miniature' which Miss Blind presents to her readers are all, with one exception, tragedies, and they are tragedies of the kind which many people are apt to sum up, and, as they imagine, to condemn, in the one word 'painful'. It is a little difficult, in this ready-made condemnation, to distinguish the proportion borne by conventional morality to merely distressed sensation. The liberty of the subject in art — which is something different from the liberty of the subject in the more temporary sphere of actual life — is a question which will probably always remain in the flexible state of discussion. How, indeed, can there ever be more than a compromise, an armed and alert truce, between the artist, of whatever age, and his casual contemporaries, the people who buy his books in order not to appear ignorant, who talk of him in parlours, and discuss his morality with their spiritual advisers for the time being? To the artist the question is one of art — a question to be seriously considered, with a full comprehension of the invaluable services which morality confers upon art. But with the general reader, even with the cultivated general reader, there is nothing to consider. It is admitted that the Greeks are to be excused for choosing horrible subjects, and the Romans for treating ordinary themes in an offensive manner. Shakespeare's audacity in the confusion of virtue is to be forgiven him, and we are even to read Ford,[24] so long as we refrain from mentioning his plays by name. But when it comes to the present every one is to avoid reminding us that there are commandments to be broken, except, indeed, in French, where all the novels are founded on the splintered fragments of a single commandment. No artist, of course, holds this view of art, but it is not in the nature of every artist — fortunately for the variety of literature and the happiness of the greatest number — to feel any attraction to the darker side of things. With Miss Blind there has always been a certain adventurous spirit of discovery, passionately interested in the sorrows of those who have perhaps, in the charitable phrase, 'deserved' their sorrows — the outcasts of the earth, the disinherited of society. It was particularly noticeable in the section of 'The Ascent of Man' called 'The Leading of Sorrow', certainly one of her most vigorous and eloquently sympathetic pieces of work. It is yet more marked in the present volume, where four of the longer poems deal with aspects of life which are usually conspicuous only by their absence from such of our art as professes to be realistic.

But, it may be added, Miss Blind's art does not profess to be realistic, and here there is both something to be thankful for and something to regret. Her

---

[23] [Unsigned], Arthur Symons, Review of *Dramas in Miniature*, *Athenæum* (21 May 1892), 659–60.

[24] John Ford, the English playwright whose 1633 play *'Tis Pity She's a Whore* deals with incest. When produced in the nineteenth century it was retitled *The Brother and Sister*.

studies of sordid, unholy life are, after all, the impressions at second hand which a woman must, almost of necessity, have of

> — the rose shut in a book
> In which pure women may not look.[25]

They thrill with a compassionate emotion which gives them a certain poetic exaltation; and so far both they and we are the gainers. But they do not always convince us of their reality as pictures of life. In Rossetti's 'Jenny' we have the one almost flawless poem of its kind; it satisfies our artistic sense and it satisfies our sense of reality. The picture is precisely right in tone. With Miss Blind there is a sort of brutal vividness which is decidedly striking, and there is that deep compassion which only a woman could feel for a woman. But at times the tone of her picture is too crude — at times her sufferers seem in fact to adjust an aureole which appears a little out of place. The poem called 'The Message' tells the story of a half-delirious death in hospital — tells it vigorously, impressively, in perhaps somewhat too intentionally prosaic language. 'The Russian Student's Tale' is much the finest of these studies, and here the language, not being put into the mouth of the girl of whom it tells, is sustained at an equal elevation, and is, indeed, full of lyric passion. The episode has the interest of a scene from a novel and it lends itself admirably to poetic treatment. A remarkable effect is produced by a sort of refrain — some fervid lines describing the song of the nightingale heard without — which comes, as it were casually, at the pauses of the narrative. The story is practically that of Jules and Phéné in 'Pippa Passes',[26] but with another ending. It ends thus: [see p. 141].

'The Battle of Flowers', another miniature drama, is a sort of companion picture, by way of contrast, to the sordid interior of 'The Message'. In 'A Carnival Episode' we have a passionate love-scene, with the strangest ending that fact or fancy could suggest. It has that glowing fervour which Miss Blind's verse rarely lacks, and which in 'The Mystic's Vision' — oddly inserted among these 'Flowers of Evil' — rises to the point of spiritual ecstasy.

> Ah! I shall kill myself with dreams!

— the cry of many souls, not only from behind convent walls — comes with poignant effect as the first line of a piece which can only be compared with Mr George Meredith's 'Song of Theodolinda'.[27]

The last of the 'Dramas in Miniature', 'Scherzo', seems to belong more appropriately to the lyrical section of the book. It has the gay measure which suits its name, and, melody and picture in one, it calls up a charming vision of gracious youth: [see p. 172].

[25] Dante Gabriel Rossetti, 'Jenny' (1848; 1869).
[26] Verse drama by Robert Browning.
[27] In *Ballads and Poems of Tragic Life* (1887).

A beautiful little poem 'On a Viola d'Amore' has the same dainty charm; and in some of the short lyrics — 'Love's Somnambulist', 'Lassitude', 'Seeking', and 'Only a Smile', for instance — there is a note of genuine feeling which is perhaps the rarest quality to find in contemporary verse. How poignantly such lines as these express the particular sensation which they essay to render! —

> I feed my love on smiles, and yet
>   Sometimes I ask, with tears of woe,
> How had it been if we had met,
>   If you had met me long ago,
> Before the fast, defacing years
>   Had made all ill that once was well?
> Ah, then your smiling breeds such tears
>   As Tantalus may weep in hell.

In these lyrics, as well as in the longer poems, there are dramas in miniature, and the emotion is at times more convincing. For indeed Miss Blind is pre-eminently successful as a writer of lyrics. In her lyrics she is 'simple, sensuous, and passionate';[28] she catches at times the heart's own rhythm in its troubled exquisite moments. Her best work gives one the impression of having been lived: it has the impromptu of nature. And for this it should be prized by those who value the simpler, deeper, qualities of an art which must needs be so close to nature.

Review of *Birds of Passage*, by Arnold Bennett[29]

Closing Miss Mathilde Blind's new book, *Birds of Passage, songs of the Orient and Occident* (Chatto and Windus), I try to define for myself and for you the general impression with which her verses have left me. But I cannot. Miss Blind sings in many modes — she is probably more various than any other woman-poet in English literature — and in all her songs there is an original, intimately personal accent which one can catch, but not imprison within a paragraph. This volume emphasizes a known fact, namely, that its author excels in lyric verse. 'Prelude' and 'A Fantasy', especially the former, are distinguished achievements, and they show, I think, a more complete technique than anything even in *Dramas in Miniature*. The first part of Miss Blind's book is devoted to Egypt,

---

[28] From John Milton's *Of Education* (1644).
[29] Signed 'Barbara', *Woman* (22 May 1895), p. 7. Bennett (1867–1931), who went on to become a distinguished novelist, was assistant editor of the penny weekly *Woman* from 1894 to 1896 and editor from 1896 to 1900. He disguised the fact that he was the editor of the magazine by adopting a series of female pseudonyms, including 'Sal Volatile', 'Lady Betty', and 'Barbara'. Anita Miller identified Bennett as the author of this review in her *Arnold Bennett: An Annotated Bibliography, 1887–1932* (New York: Garland, 1975), p. 35.

and it is clear that this wonderful old land has cast a powerful spell upon a mind anxious to be enthralled; but though she writes with distinction and dignity of the Arab and the desert, the sphinx and the blindfold oxen, I doubt if she has said anything strikingly new; and for myself I would rather have her sing of England. Take the fine poem 'Noonday Rest', written on Hampstead Heath under the willows —

> Sometimes they lose a leaf which, flickering slow,
> *Faints* on the sunburnt leas.

How wonderfully the one word which I have italicized suggests the intolerable heat of a scorching noon! This poem is perhaps the best in the book, a book that contains nothing trivial, nothing shallow, nothing that is not poetry.

Review of *Birds of Passage: Songs of the Orient and Occident*, by Arthur Symons[30]

The poetry of Mis Blind, careless and unfinished as it not infrequently is, possesses the unusual merit of being sincerely felt, of being the almost unconscious outcome of an eager poetic nature. It is unusual, too, in being at once thoughtful, concerned with large issues, and passionate, concerned with individual experience. Few women who have attempted the art of verse have brought with them to the undertaking so wide a culture, so varied an experience, so many keen interests, or have had so rich and exceptional a nature to express. More than most women Miss Blind has lived her own life, has followed the dictates of her own individuality; now singing of the 'Ascent of Man', now of the crofters, becoming a biographer for the sake of Madame Roland, a translator for the sake of Marie Bashkirtseff, a novelist in order to invent a new form for experiences and emotions which could scarcely have been rendered in any other way. Now, in her present book, she has endeavoured to combine the ecstasy of the poet with the enthusiasm of the traveller, and to bring before English readers, for the first time in English verse, the mystery, the charm, the colour of the East. The twenty poems about Egypt, the 'Songs of the Orient', only fill, it is true, the first half of the book, and among the 'Songs of the Occident' there are several delightful lyrics; but it is certainly for the Eastern poems that most readers will turn to these pages. And they will find, not, indeed, a study or a picture, not a delicate series of impressions, but a vision, intensely personal and intensely sympathetic, of an entirely poetic East. The gods and kings of Egypt are almost more acutely realized, with a more present and intimate interest, than the 'dying dragoman' or the 'beautiful Beeshareen boy'. From one of the

---

[30] [Unsigned], Arthur Symons, Review of *Birds of Passage: Songs of the Orient and Occident*, Athenæum (27 July 1895), 121–22.

finest of these poems (fine in a sort of impassioned poetic rhetoric), 'The Tombs of the Kings', we may quote some lines typical of an attitude of mind which is not exactly that of Fromentin[31] or of M. Pierre Loti[32]: [see p. 189].

But the Egypt of to-day also, if so strange a survival may in any due sense be called contemporary, finds eloquent expression throughout these poems. 'The Moon of Ramadan' is perhaps the most entirely successful, the most impressive, of a series of singularly impressive pieces. It is written entirely in that chanting measure in which Miss Blind is at her best, without such attempts at a kind of realism as those which she is fond of making, not always with success. In 'The Beautiful Beeshareen Boy', for instance, we read: —

> Ah! just like other ware,
>   For a lump sum or so
> Shipped to the World's great Fair —
>   The big Chicago Show!
> With mythic beasts and things,
> Beetles and bulls with wings,
> And imitation Sphinx,
>   Ranged row on curious row!

This sort of momentary modernism, in the midst of a poem mainly written in a more elevated tone, has rarely, if ever, been quite successfully done. Rossetti has perhaps come nearest to success, in, however, what is scarcely one of his finest poems, 'The Burden of Nineveh'; but even there the lines about the 'school-foundations' and the 'zealous tract' are amusing rather than anything else. At times Miss Blind falls into the opposite error of overstrained rhetoric; her exuberant fancy hurries her into all kinds of extravagances; and her verse is marred by frequent blemishes of form, so that she will rhyme 'oases' with 'roses', and tolerate a word like 'instantaneously' in a passage of really poetic eloquence. But, coming refreshingly into the midst of a mass of verse-writing which is accomplished, elegant, full of excellent negations, here, for once, is verse which is at all events alive. It has the genuine poetic impulse, it has the genuine note of personal sincerity. And at times, in addition to those qualities of fervour, speed, and largeness which we have noted, it has a brief and pathetic simplicity, as in the touching poem called 'Rest', which comes at the end of a volume containing so much that is fine, in so different an order of fineness: [see p. 234].

---

[31] Eugène Fromentin (1820–1876), French painter and writer. He earned early fame for his pictorial interpretations of Algeria.
[32] Pseudonym of Louis Marie-Julien Viaud (1850–1923), French naval officer and writer who travelled widely and became known for his exotic novels and short stories, including *Fleurs d'ennui* (*Flowers of Boredom*) (1882).

Review of *Birds of Passage: Songs of the Orient and Occident*, by George Cotterell[33]

Miss Blind has attained a high and definite position among English poets. What her precise rank is, one hesitates to ask or to suggest; and there is the less reason for doing either because merit in a poet is not necessarily an affair of rank. She has the distinction also of being one of the very few women poets, whether of our own time or of any other, who have made any mark in English literature. It is not pertinent to my present object to inquire why this number is so few; but it is remarkable that, while in other branches of imaginative literature women in great numbers are the successful rivals of men, in poetry, which has so much to do with the emotions, the men vastly preponderate. But the fewness of the women is a good reason for paying all proper tribute to those we have. In Miss Blind's case the tribute should be large, for her work in verse is considerable as well as excellent. It is of almost all kinds, from the idyllic to the dramatic, and from simple narrative to the elucidation of subtle problems of life. Perhaps she touched her highest point in 'The Ascent of Man', a poem in which the intuitions of genius are unmistakable. The poems in the present volume are less ambitious; but, in their place, they are not less striking or less genuine. They are nearly all short, and for the most part, as the title of the book implies, they are suggested by incidents of travel. The first note one discovers in them is that of picturesque eloquence, which is struck in the 'Prelude', and particularly in these stanzas: [see p. 185].

Miss Blind is fond of this measure, which she repeats in a powerful poem on the tombs of these same kings. She describes the greatness in life, the magnificence in death, of monarchs who conceived themselves to be 'the living incarnation of imperishable gods'. They proposed to put a bridle on Time, to cheat death and corruption; and they did it. 'Pale and passive in their prisons, they have conquered.' But the very assertion of their victory brings a question as to its worth, as to its reality: [see p. 191].

The East has more than its common charms for Miss Blind. She has penetrated some of its remoter secrets. Its forgotten gods and temples, its glorious dreams, the types of men and things that breathe the spirit of the Orient — of all of them she gives us vivid suggestions, now compressed into a

---

[33] *The Academy* (12 October 1895), 288–89. This is one of the few notices of any of her books that Blind commented on in her correspondence. She wrote to Garnett to thank him for sending it to her: 'the notice came just at the moment when I wanted it most badly. [...] so striking is the reaction of mind on the body at times that after reading that extremely sympathetic notice by Mr. Cottrell [...] I felt as if I had taken a powerful stimulant. [...] My mind needs it as much as my body does food and I think without it existence is often only a living death' (Mathilde Blind ALS to Richard Garnett, 15 October 1885, Add. MS 61929 fols 145–47).

line or two, as in this picture of the desert:

> Uncircumscribed, unmeasured, vast,
>   Eternal as the sea;
> The present here becomes the past,
>   For all futurity;

now expanded in language visibly and audibly made to express images of beauty and freedom, as in 'The Beautiful Beeshareen Boy': [see p. 197].

The poems that derive their inspiration from the west have nothing of the querulousness of modern thought. The sadness of a long-dead time in the East seems always to be irradiated by perpetual sun. It is only the West that has gloom which no sun penetrates. But it has its loftier aspirations also, its more spiritual realisation of the joy and beauty of life; and Miss Blind is only concerned with this side of things. She gives us the very air and essence of it in a little poem called 'Soul-Drift', which is short enough to be quoted whole: [see p. 213].

The lyrics in this section of the book are bright and full of music. 'A Bridal in the Bois de Boulogne', with its bell-like refrain,

> How the lilacs, the lilacs are glowing and blowing,

is alive with festal colour and bridal merriment. 'Spring in the Alps' pleasantly recalls that impetuous season in the lines:

> The dandelion puffs her balls,
>   Free spinsters of the air,
> Who scorn to wait for beetle calls,
>   Or bees to find them fair.

Even the mood of the Agnostic is exalted into an avowal of helplessness that amounts to faith,

> By sunbeams on their missionary flight.

A few 'Shakespeare Sonnets' and some miscellaneous pieces complete the volume. They are all full of the atmosphere and aglow with the charm only to be found in poetry of the higher sort. As an example of their quality, I must be content to quote a happy fancy from 'Cleve Woods', one of the Shakespeare Sonnets: [see p. 225].

Review of *A Selection from the Poems of Mathilde Blind*, edited by Arthur Symons, by Edith Nesbit[34]

Mr Arthur Symons has done good service in making from the poems of

---

[34] [Unsigned], Edith Nesbit, Review of *A Selection from the Poems of Mathilde Blind*,

Mathilde Blind a selection which will be welcome to those who are familiar with her work, and which offers to those who have not hitherto made acquaintance with it an excellent taste of its quality. Mr Symons has exercised singular discretion, and shows that sympathy with the verse he edits which is too often lacking in critics introducing the work of others.

The reading of these selections serves to reproduce sharply the old impression wrought in past days by Mathilde Blind's poems — the impression of breadth and variety of inspiration, resulting rather in weakness than strength. There can be no doubt that the wider and more varied the inspiration of a great poet the better for all who love great poetry; yet for any but the very great — alas! also the very few — it is certain that the more limited inspiration gives birth to the better poetry.

Mathilde Blind's also was no serene or tranquil mind to reflect accurately a number of different moods or scenes. Hers was a passionate soul, deeply touched by a multitude of emotions; and while a number of thoughts strengthen the mind, a number of emotions personally experienced weaken each other, and in time weaken the possible expression of any one of them. Her poetry covers an astonishingly wide range; the subjects with which she deals — transcendental religion, love, nature, history, modern life — show the scope of her mind. Christina Rossetti was dominated by one or two perfectly simple ideas, and her poetry has left a mark on the English language. It may be questioned whether that of Mathilde Blind will ever do this. She had intellect, Christina Rossetti temperament; both were poets, but the difference in their poetry which will send one down to posterity and may relegate the other to the shelves of the collector is mainly this of inspiration.

Let us not be thought to belittle in any least particular the beautiful and passionate work of our author. We are ourselves among her most fervent admirers.[35] But it were idle to deny that her verse is not likely to appeal, with the intimate and personal appeal of Miss Rossetti's poems, to the great body of the English poet-loving public.

In looking through Mr Symons's excellent selection one is confounded by the *embarrass de richesses* — the jewels shining on every page. 'The Tombs of the Kings' is a remarkable poem, and has many memorable lines.

Athenæum (3 December 1898), 783–84. Nesbit, best known today as the author of many children's books under the name E. Nesbit, was a prolific author of novels and poetry, and among the many New Woman writers active at the *fin de siècle*. Like Blind she was a political radical: she co-founded the socialist Fabian Society in 1884.

[35] One possible clue to Nesbit's estimation of Blind's stature comes in her review of Rosamund Marriott Watson's *Vespertilia and Other Poems* two years earlier. 'Now that Christina Rossetti has left us, there remain to us but three women poets, and of these Mrs. Marriott-Watson is one' (Edith Nesbit, 'Recent Verse', *Athenæum* (4 April 1896), p. 442). Since August Webster had died in 1894, it is possible that Nesbit's unnamed other two are Blind and Alice Meynell.

> We, the living incarnation of imperishable gods,

Has a fine swing; and

> Night, that was before Creation, watches sphinx-like, starred with eyes,

Is peculiarly happy in a poem dealing with ancient Egypt.

In 'The Pilgrim Soul' the reader is carried away on a flood tide of pity and sympathy and deep human tenderness. Whatever the occasional faults of workmanship, the poem leaves him with the lump in his throat and the pricking in his eyes, and the conviction that so intense an inspiration fired the singer as to lift her, for good or ill, above the possibility of sandpaper or the harmless, necessary shears. 'Love in Exile' contains extremely beautiful renderings of the subtler phases of passion. The following charming lyric commends itself, not by supremacy of achievement, but by convenience of length, for quotation: [see p. 125].

This moves us, despite the 'wildest moan' and the 'coldly glares'.

The 'Poems of the Open Air' are all perfumed with the scent of memory and delight. 'The Sleeping Beauty', and especially the eighth line of it, rings in our ears and clamours for quotation: [see p. 106]. A delightful little poem — but alas for the last line!

'The Moat'[36] — but for an over-imitative line — is a highly pleasing piece of work: [see p. 223].

Throughout the workmanship, though good, is loose. It is not good in the one, the only, the inevitable and perfect way. Yet the book holds in it the promise of deep pleasure, and it is one which none who loves contemporary poetry should willingly allow to be absent from his shelf.

We have only one cause of quarrel with Mr Symons. Why has he omitted the wonderful wild 'Song of the Willi'?

---

[36] Republished in *The Eclectic Magazine*, 2 (July 1899), p. 146.

SELECT BIBLIOGRAPHY

Works by Mathilde Blind

This list includes books written or edited by Blind, as well as editions of her works published after her death.

Poems, as Claude Lake (London: Alfred W. Bennett, 1867)
A Selection from the Poems of Percy Bysshe Shelley, ed. with a memoir by Mathilde Blind (Leipzig: Bernhard Tauchnitz, 1872)
The Old Faith and the New, a Confession, by David Friedrich Strauss, trans. by Mathilde Blind, 2 vols (London: Asher and Co., 1873; New York: Henry Holt, 1873)
The Old Faith and the New, a Confession, by David Friedrich Strauss, trans. (with final preface) and an original memoir of the author by Mathilde Blind, 2 vols (London: Asher and Co., 1874; New York: Henry Holt, 1874)
The Prophecy of St. Oran and Other Poems (London: Newman and Company, 1881)
George Eliot (London: W. H. Allen & Company, 1883; Boston: Roberts Brothers, 1883)
Tarantella, a Romance, 2 vols (London: T. Fisher Unwin, 1885; Boston: Roberts Brothers, 1885)
The Heather on Fire: A Tale of the Highland Clearances (London: Walter Scott, 1886)
Madame Roland (London: W. H. Allen & Company, 1886; Boston: Roberts Brothers, 1886)
The Poetical Works of Lord Byron: Childe Harold's Pilgrimage, Don Juan (abridged), ed. by Mathilde Blind (London: Walter Scott, 1886)
The Poetical Works of Lord Byron: Miscellaneous Poems, ed. by Mathilde Blind (London: Walter Scott, 1886)
The Letters of Lord Byron, ed. with introduction by Mathilde Blind (London: Walter Scott, 1887)
The Ascent of Man (London: Chatto & Windus, 1889)
The Journal of Marie Bashkirtseff, trans. with an introduction by Mathilde Blind, 2 vols (London: Cassell & Company, 1890)
Dramas in Miniature (London: Chatto & Windus, 1891)
Songs and Sonnets (London: Chatto & Windus, 1893)
Birds of Passage: Songs of the Orient and Occident (London: Chatto & Windus, 1895)
A Selection from the Poems of Mathilde Blind, ed. by Arthur Symons (London: T. Fisher Unwin, 1897)
The Ascent of Man, New Edition, with introduction by Alfred Russel Wallace (London: T. Fisher Unwin, 1899)
The Poetical Works of Mathilde Blind, ed. by Arthur Symons, with a memoir by Richard Garnett (London: T. Fisher Unwin, 1900)
Shakespeare Sonnets (London: The Delamore Press, 1902)

Biographical and Critical Studies

ARMSTRONG, ISOBEL, *Victorian Poetry: Poetry, Poetics, and Politics* (New York: Routledge, 1993)

AVERY, SIMON, '"Tantalising Glimpses": The Intersecting Lives of Eleanor Marx and Mathilde Blind', in *Eleanor Marx (1855–1898): Life, Work, Contacts*, ed. by John Stokes (Aldershot: Ashgate, 2000), pp. 173–87

BARROW, BARBARA, 'Deep Time and Epic Time in Alfred Tennyson's *In Memoriam* (1850), Matthew Arnold's *Empedocles on Etna* (1852), and Mathilde Blind's *The Ascent of Man* (1889)', *Nineteenth-Century Contexts*, 40 (2018), 115–31

BIRCH, KATY, '"Carrying Her Coyness to a Dangerous Pitch": Mathilde Blind and Darwinian Sexual Selection', *Women*, 24 (2013), 71–89

DIEDRICK, JAMES, *Mathilde Blind: Late-Victorian Culture and the Woman of Letters* (Charlottesville: University of Virginia Press, 2016)

—— '"My Love is a Force That Will Force You to Care": Subversive Sexuality in Mathilde Blind's Dramatic Monologues', *Victorian Poetry*, 40.4 (2002), 359–86

—— 'A Pioneering Female Aesthete: Mathilde Blind in *The Dark Blue*', *The Victorian Periodicals Review*, 36.6 (2003), 210–41

—— '"The Hectic Beauty of Decay": Positivist Decadence in Mathilde Blind's Late Poetry', *Victorian Literature and Culture*, 34 (2006), 631–48

—— 'Mathilde Blind's (Proto-) New Women', in *Latchkey: Journal of New Woman Studies*, 9 (2017/18) <http://www.thelatchkey.org/Latchkey9/essay/Diedrick.htm> [accessed 11 January 2021]

DOWLING, LINDA, 'The Decadent and the New Woman in the 1890s', *Nineteenth-Century Fiction*, 33 (1979), 431–49

EVANGELISTA, STEFANO, 'Transnational Decadence', in *Decadence and Literature*, ed. by Jane Desmarais and David Weir (Cambridge: Cambridge University Press, 2019), pp. 316–31

FLETCHER, ROBERT, '"Heir of all the Universe": Evolutionary Epistemology in Mathilde Blind's *Birds of Passage: Songs of the Orient and Occident*', *Victorian Poetry*, 43 (2005), 435–53

GAGNIER, REGINIA, *Individualism, Decadence and Globalization: On the Relationship of Part to Whole, 1859–1920* (New York and Basingstoke: Palgrave Macmillan, 2010)

GARNETT, RICHARD, 'Memoir', in *The Poetical Works of Mathilde Blind*, ed. by Arthur Symons (London: T. Fisher Unwin, 1900), pp. 1–46

—— INTRODUCTION TO 'Mathilde Blind, 1841–1896', in *The Poets and Poetry of the Century*, vol. 7, ed. by Alfred H. Miles (London: Hutchinson, 1898), pp. 609–10

HUGHES, LINDA K., 'A Club of Their Own: The "Literary Ladies", New Women Writers, and *Fin-de-Siècle* Authorship', *Victorian Literature and Culture*, 35 (2007), 233–60

—— 'Introduction', in *New Woman Poets: An Anthology*, ed. by Linda Hughes (London: The 1890s Society, 2001), pp. 1–11

LAPORTE, CHARLES, 'Atheist Prophecy: Mathilde Blind, Constance Naden, and the Victorian Poetess', *Victorian Literature and Culture*, 34 (2006), 427–41

LOUIS, MARGOT K., *Persephone Rises, 1860–1927: Mythography, Gender, and the Creation of a New Spirituality* (Burlington, VT: Ashgate, 2009)

Lyons, Sara, 'Secularism and Secularisation at the *Fin de siècle*', in *The Edinburgh Companion to Fin de siècle Literature, Culture, and the Arts*, ed. by Josephine M. Guy (Edinburgh: Edinburgh University Press, 2017), 24–145

—— '"Let Your Life on Earth Be Life Indeed": Aestheticism and Secularism in Mathilde Blind's *The Prophecy of St. Oran* and "On a Torso of Cupid"', in *Writing Women of the Fin de Siècle: Authors of Change*, ed. by Adrienne E. Gavin and Carolyn Oulton (New York and Basingstoke: Palgrave Macmillan, 2012), pp. 55–69

Maxwell, Catherine, 'Swinburne's Friendship with Women Writers', in *A. C. Swinburne and the Singing Word*, ed. by Yisrael Levin (Farnham: Ashgate, 2010), pp. 127–48

—— *The Female Sublime from Milton to Swinburne: Bearing Blindness* (Manchester: Manchester University Press, 2001)

Morgan, Monique, 'Genres', in *The Cambridge Companion to Victorian Women's Poetry*, ed. by Linda K. Hughes (Cambridge: Cambridge University Press, 2019), pp. 13–27

Ostdiek, Katherine E., 'Mathilde Blind, the Highland Clearances, and the "Trappings of Nationality" in the British Isles', *The Journal of the Midwest Modern Language Association*, 51 (2018), 137–68

Reed, John R., *Decadent Style* (Athens: Ohio University Press, 1985)

Rudy, Jason, 'Rapturous Forms: Mathilde Blind's Darwinian Poetics', *Victorian Literature and Culture*, 34 (2006), 443–59

Sznaider, Nathan, *Jewish Memory and the Cosmopolitan Order* (Cambridge: Polity Press, 2011)

Tate, Gregory, 'Mathilde Blind: Rhythm, Energy, and Revolution', in *Nineteenth-Century Poetry and the Physical Sciences: Poetical Matter* (New York and Basingstoke: Palgrave Macmillan, 2020), pp. 185–222

Vadillo, Ana Parejo, *Women Poets and Urban Aestheticism: Passengers of Modernity* (New York and Basingstoke: Palgrave Macmillan, 2005)

—— 'Poetries of Asceticism and Excess', in *The Cambridge Companion to Victorian Women's Poetry*, ed. by Linda K. Hughes (Cambridge: Cambridge University Press, 2019), pp. 230–46

Weir, David, *Decadence and the Making of Modernism* (Amherst: University of Massachusetts Press, 1995)

Wilhelm, Lindsay, 'The Utopian Evolutionary Aestheticism of W. K. Clifford, Walter Pater, and Mathilde Blind', *Victorian Studies*, 59 (2016), 9–34

www.ingramcontent.com/pod-product-compliance
Lightning Source LLC
Chambersburg PA
CBHW071424150426
43191CB00008B/1030